Also by Mitsuru Kodama

BOUNDARY MANAGEMENT
Developing Business Architectures for Innovation

INTERACTIVE BUSINESS COMMUNITIES
Accelerating Corporate Innovation through Boundary Networks

INNOVATION NETWORKS IN KNOWLEDGE-BASED FIRMS
Developing ICT-based Integrative Competences

KNOWLEDGE INTEGRATION DYNAMICS
Developing Strategic Innovation Capability

KNOWLEDGE INNOVATION
Strategic Management as Practice

PROJECT-BASED ORGANIZATION IN THE KNOWLEDGE-BASED SOCIETY
(SERIES ON TECHNOLOGY MANAGEMENT)

THE STRATEGIC COMMUNITY-BASED FIRM

Competing through ICT Capability

Innovation in Image Communication

Mitsuru Kodama
Nihon University, Japan

palgrave
macmillan

First published 2013 by
PALGRAVE MACMILLAN

Palgrave Macmillan in the UK is an imprint of Macmillan Publishers Limited, registered in England, company number 785998, of Houndmills, Basingstoke, Hampshire RG21 6XS.

Palgrave Macmillan in the US is a division of St Martin's Press LLC, 175 Fifth Avenue, New York, NY 10010.

Palgrave Macmillan is the global academic imprint of the above companies and has companies and representatives throughout the world.

Palgrave® and Macmillan® are registered trademarks in the United States, the United Kingdom, Europe and other countries.

ISBN 978–0–230–30138–2

This book is printed on paper suitable for recycling and made from fully managed and sustained forest sources. Logging, pulping and manufacturing processes are expected to conform to the environmental regulations of the country of origin.

A catalogue record for this book is available from the British Library.

A catalog record for this book is available from the Library of Congress.

10 9 8 7 6 5 4 3 2 1
22 21 20 19 18 17 16 15 14 13

Printed and bound in Great Britain by
CPI Antony Rowe, Chippenham and Eastbourne

Contents

Preface and Acknowledgments

On March 11, 2011, Japan was rocked by a magnitude 9 earthquake, now known as the Great East Japan Earthquake. The Japanese media reported that nobody thought of connecting the videoconferencing system in the Prime Minister's official residence when the accompanying nuclear accident happened.[1] In the situation right after the earthquake, there was a greatly elevated level of uncertainty and risk associated with taking new actions, as well as increased urgency due to the speed of change in external circumstances.

As described by this book, people and organizations consciously (or unconsciously) use different types of ICT tools depending on how circumstances change. Particularly when levels of uncertainty, risk and urgency all rise at the same time, content and context dynamically change, and new knowledge emerges that transcends the knowledge domains of individuals and organizations.

This is why ICT tools with higher levels of media richness that give individuals and organizations greater information-processing capabilities are selected and used to overcome the differences between existing knowledge and emergent knowledge, and for these reasons videoconferencing systems, with their superior real-time functionality, are used in situations where there is a need to solve difficult problems and issues and take swift actions.

So what was really going through the minds of those charged with safety and security at the Prime Minister's residence, and those information systems supervisors who were faced with that unprecedented emergency?

The Chief Cabinet Secretary commented: "Safety officers were crammed into the official residence working the phones and fax machines, and I don't really know why the videoconferencing system wasn't used—whether it was because it wasn't needed or because there wasn't time."

These results highlight the fact that it isn't possible to use ICT tools effectively in an emergency situation if the capabilities to network different people and organizations while sharing and transferring dynamically changing contexts do not exist. Just simply supplying people or organizations with the physical ICT resources themselves is not enough—the significance and meaning must be sufficiently understood, and regular learning through dialogue must be pursued, and experience accumulated.

As the title of this book suggests, ICT capability can be seen as having an intrinsic relationship with the intangible assets of practical knowledge that stems from the experiences of people and organizations. This book analyzes and examines the components of ICT capabilities based on the results of surveys of ICT usage taken at the global level.

Currently, I am developing new theories about observations and discoveries of new business phenomena (both at the macro and micro levels) emerging in corporate workplaces. Although general principles such as those found in the natural sciences do not describe the mechanisms of business success or failure in corporations or organizations, there is a uniform logic that can be applied.

However, strategic activity in business is extremely complicated and diverse, and also changes dynamically with changing circumstances. This means that attempting a strategy that has been shown to be successful on one occasion does not necessarily lead to success the second time around, because in formulating and executing strategies, practice at the micro level is highly dependent on dynamic contexts between business people, and their customers—and questions about who is going to do what, why, when, how and with whom must be answered, regardless of the apparent degree of rational or analytical superiority of a strategic plan.

For this reason, people in business need to have a dynamic and overarching view of strategy while simultaneously focusing on the specific and minute aspects of thinking and actions that need to be coordinated to formulate and execute strategies. In other words, "God is in the details."

Research into practical human processes is extremely important. The concept of ICT capability I describe in this book not only illustrates the interactive processes between humans at the micro level, but also offers an analytical framework for the formation of strategy and the knowledge-integration process. There remains much expectation for deeper theoretical and practical future research in this field of study.

I would like to express my sincerest gratitude for the guidance and support I have received in writing this book.

Firstly, I would like to thank all the people who gave their time in interviews and the materials I received to present the case studies described in this book.

I would also like to express my deepest gratitude to Dr. Ikujiro Nonaka, Professor Emeritus at Hitotsubashi University, for the intellectual stimulus he provided me on many occasions. As I have specialized in the fields of science and engineering (electronics and communications),

Chapter 1, "ICT and Boundary Innovation," looks at the developments in corporate management in recent years against the backdrop of the advance of broadband in the ICT field, and presents the progress of ICT and its transcendence of individual corporate boundaries, and the resulting formation of global knowledge communities based on a diverse range of *Ba* (Japanese for "place"). As organizational platforms, these knowledge communities produce "ICT capability," and act as the driving force behind the creation of new boundary innovations.

Chapter 2, "The Advancement of ICT Tools and Knowledge, and Innovation Management," looks at the relationship between corporate knowledge-management activities at the foundations of these global knowledge communities, and the ICT tools that support those activities. In particular, the chapter describes the ICT tools that support communications and collaborations both inside and outside of companies, and with their customers who are used to integrate the knowledge dispersed inside and outside of companies, and further the creation process.

Chapter 3, "The Innovation and Market Expansion of Video Communications," discusses the technological innovations that have led to video communication, a key ICT tool in forming global knowledge networks, and describes how these technologies have become powerful enablers for technological adaptation by people and in organizations, and have lead to corporate transformation and innovation.

Chapter 4, "Collaborative ICT Tools and Organization Development," describes how collaborative ICT tools, typical of video communication technology, encourage communications and collaboration between members in real time and non-real time, and their growing importance as tools for new organizational development and managerial transformation. The chapter also provides new insights into the learning processes in knowledge communities, and organizational characteristics gained from empirical studies of the interactions between people and in organizations, using video communications tools over the last ten years.

Chapters 5 to 7 present case studies.

Chapter 5, "Product Development and Collaborative ICT Tools," describes and analyzes the collaborative ICT-tool usage patterns that are relied upon in product development and innovation processes in high-tech corporations in America, Europe and Asia, based on multi-case studies of product and corporate innovation. This chapter presents a new theoretical model, and describes empirical evidence of the ways in which the use of a variety of functionalities (video, audio, text, etc.) lend their support to knowledge-sharing activities within organizations and decision-making processes, and also discusses the range of collaborative

ICT tool systems in corporate exploratory and exploitative activities, and how these systems foster business processes and innovation.

Chapter 6, "Workplace and Collaborative ICT Tools," discusses new implications drawn from case analyses of Sony and IBM, and illustrates the powerful trigger effect that knowledge sharing and learning with collaborative ICT tools has on the synergies of tacit and explicit knowledge within companies.

Chapter 7, "ICT Innovations in Health care and Welfare," presents in-depth case studies on the introduction of information technology into communities. Actual examples given include remote treatment and nursing schemes in Japan. The chapter presents changes in product innovation in the medical ICT solutions field, and developments that have encouraged "user innovation" and "customers as innovators," and driven advances in user "ICT capability."

Chapter 8, "ICT Capability and Knowledge Integration," presents new insights gained through empirical studies. This chapter describes the four ICT capabilities (ICT application capability, dialectical dialogue capability, context architect capability and boundaries consolidation capability), and the importance of embedding these in an organization to promote its knowledge-integration activities.

Chapter 9 presents the academic and managerial implications gained through this research, and offers conclusions.

1
ICT and Boundary Innovation

1.1 The advance of ICT innovation

The advancements in recent years of communication functions available over broadband networks typical of ICT (information and communication technology) have spawned a range of new businesses. ICT not only provides the high-performance computer-based information processing of conventional IT (information technology), but also enables interactive networking among people all over the world, and is a technological platform that lets people publish, share and create a diverse range of valuable information, data and knowledge.

Both wired and wireless broadband networks now feature bandwidths that have enabled 'always-on' connections to become much more common and thus dramatically improved user convenience. In particular, these developments offer high operational response speed across the board, shorter download time, widespread permanently online connection capability, and a diverse range of services and functions, including cloud computing and SNS (social networking sites—Twitter, Facebook, etc.) platforms that enable the formation of online communities and act as effective corporate marketing tools. As well as this diverse range of web applications, bidirectional video communications have made it into the mainstream with the advent of video posting sites such as YouTube, and video mail, video chat, video phone, video conferencing and movie streaming functions. Broadband-based video and web conferencing systems, and videophone applications aimed at consumers such as Skype or Apple's FaceTime have emerged as a result of the remarkable technological advances of recent years. These ICT tools have not only brought more efficiency to business management, but have also revolutionized existing supply chains ahead of consumer adoption.

ICT, with its huge leaps in computer-processing performance and communications technologies, has made a massive contribution toward more efficient business processes within companies, between companies and with their customers (e.g. Venkatraman, 1990, 1994, 1997; Hammer and Champy, 1993; Ross, Beath and Goodfue, 1996). For example, product development that focuses on customer needs is promoted by concurrent engineering and frontloading (e.g. Khurana and Rosenthal, 1998) and through project management (e.g. Kodama, 2007c) in the development and manufacturing process. Leading corporations all over the world are proactive in their use of a wide range of computer-aided design (CAD) and simulation applications integrated with ICT tools, which streamline and optimize everything across the supply chain from design, development, manufacturing techniques and assembly, through to distribution, marketing, sales and after-sales service (e.g. Kodama, 2007c). The growth of ICT has not only brought with it much greater efficiency in business processes and supply chain management for individual businesses operating in specific business areas, but has also contributed toward the creation of new types of businesses across a diverse range of business fields.

In addition to all the applications for music, e-book, game and video distribution for instance, the advanced developments of tablet PCs and smartphone technologies found in devices such as iPhone, iPad and Android have greatly expanded the number of usage patterns and contents in wide-ranging areas like remote health care and e-learning. Thus, the consumer market of today is an environment that offers not only entertainment but also education, health services and a variety of consulting services that can be accessed virtually. Moreover, the spread of mobile phones, including smartphones, in major countries around the world has already reached 90%.

As these new mobile-based consumer services and businesses continue to expand, most notably in Japan and Korea, these kinds of mobile applications have become infused into almost every aspect of people's daily lives, including their business activities. Smartphones and mobile phones are no longer just communication tools. While these devices enable users to perform web searches and access content services for games and music and video and so on, just like using a PC connected to broadband, they also give users access to the rapidly expanding mobile e-commerce electronic money market, and ubiquitous services that use IC tags (RF tags). There is also an expanding range of mobile phone applications that use infrared communications, QR codes and so forth.

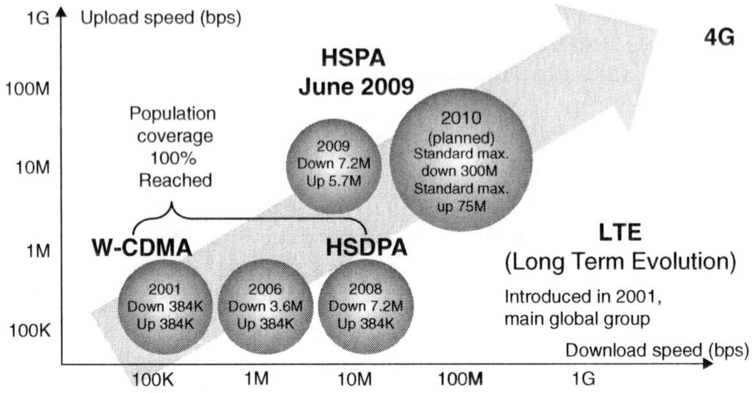

Figure 1.1 Advancements of mobile communications networks

As the gateways to broadband, the development of mobile communication networks has seen the 3G systems (W-CDMA → HSDPA → HSPA) evolve through countries in Europe and Asia, including Japan where the 3.9G systems (LTE: Long Term Evolution) commenced service in December 2010. Moreover, global communications carriers have been developing the 4G mobile communication systems that promise to deliver fiber-optic speeds from 2015 (see Figure 1.1).

This broadband-based service infrastructure, designed to support a diverse range of communications with Web 2.0 and SNS, and the variety of terminals including mobile phones, smartphones and tablet PCs coupled with the high-speed, high-capacity cloud computing information systems and so forth, are accelerating the expansion of business opportunities and speeding up the pace of business transformation while significantly impacting both corporate activity and individual lifestyles, and are thus becoming core platforms for a socio-economic movement.

ICT brings efficiencies to corporate business activities, enables strengthened competitiveness in expanding global markets and even addresses environmental issues by reducing the amount that people have to physically commute by encouraging "smart work" (e.g. working at home), thereby revolutionizing traditional work styles.

On the other hand, corporations need to give increasingly serious consideration to creating new business models and reforms as they incorporate these ICT innovations into their corporate strategy. For example, the most influential products in the global ICT industry—Apple's iPod, iPhone and iPad, and Google's Android—bring with them new markets for a diverse range of new information devices all the way from smartphones and tablet PCs through to smart TVs and software, and at the same time are giving birth to new business models for music, e-book and movie distribution all over the world. As well is that, SNS sites like Twitter and Facebook are becoming powerful tools for new marketing and product development through the formation of customer communities. For these reasons, innovation through ICT is not just a simple matter of dealing with technical aspects (product innovation), but also requires development of service innovations through a new kind of marketing that even involves the creation of markets themselves.

However, the corporate capabilities that are needed to bring forth these new business models and transformations through the use of ICT are also highly dependent on the knowledge that exists in individuals and in groups, and not only on the technical functioning of the hardware and software used with ICT.

In other words for many companies, ICT by itself is not the most important tool used to sustain competitiveness, for it is also the ideas, know-how and skills required to develop new ICT and combine ICT—high levels of condensed intelligence that are otherwise known as "knowledge."

Knowledge is a fundamental organizational capability that provides for continual creativity and dynamic innovation (Nonaka and Takeuchi, 1995; Kodama, 2009b), while ICT itself is a means to acquire new knowledge and achieve innovation.

As described later, the capability of individuals and organizations to maximize ICT use and bring forth new knowledge through ICT interactions is the driving force behind new business innovation and reform. This book defines "the capability of individuals and organizations to bring forth new knowledge through interaction with ICT" as "ICT capabilities".

The aim of this book is to analyze and consider the organizational systems and dynamism in corporations needed to acquire these ICT capabilities, as well as the actual processes adopted by the individuals and groups involved.

The following section describes the ICT business innovation developments behind the paradigm shifts of the changing markets and economies of recent years, the responses to these changes by business organizations, and the way business strategies ought to be.

1.2 Paradigm shifts in business management

As mentioned earlier, a wide variety of twenty-first-century industries have been influenced by innovations made through ICT, which have radically transformed the anatomy of business in these industries. Nowadays, the best core technologies of leading businesses are developed and dispersed in various places around the globe. Individual cutting-edge technologies in top companies in ICT, e-business, green energy, digital contents, and the automotive, electronics and biotech industries are spread out across the world and continually developed in their separate business areas. In addition, there is a great deal of crossing over between industries at the global level, and the resulting convergence between different technologies and services has seen the arrival of a variety of new products, services and business models. Examples of this can be seen with the new products, services and business models that have arisen out of the transcendence of the corporate boundaries between varied and different industries, and the convergence and integration of different knowledge in industries such as the smartphone, tablet PC, game, digital appliance, eco-car and environmental technology industries.[1] Modern innovation is now achieved upon these new strategic technological platforms.

Put simply, we can say that the era of globalized convergence has arrived in earnest (Kodama, 2011b). This means that it is no longer possible for many companies to gain as much control of their innovations as they might like, which stands in contrast to the traditional hierarchies and closed independent systems of the twentieth-century-style mass-production business model.

Under the paradigm of mass production and sales, twentieth-century businesses pursued economics of scale and scope by concentrating their business resources on the company's core competences to offer off-the-shelf products and services. Corporations were also closed organizations with fixed hierarchies, which were able to enact their corporate strategies with a fair degree of predictability in the gently changing business environments of the time. However, the shifts brought about by the multiplicities of technological innovations typical of ICT have been massive.

Nowadays, ICT is built into the core of company strategy in every kind of industry and business, not only for effecting innovation in individual corporations but also because corporations are operating in an era where the ability to delivery speedily in networked businesses make or break a company (successful companies provide customer value by taking advantage of ICT to cross and merge conventional product and service boundaries). In short, appropriately converged and executed real and network business has become a key business model for a great many companies.

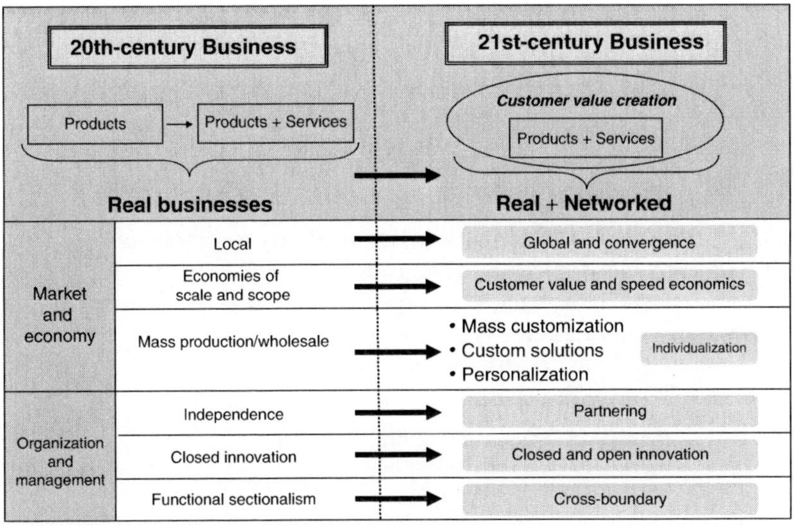

Figure 1.2 Paradigm shifts in corporate management

Furthermore, all kinds of companies need ICT to develop individualization and mass-customization businesses so that they can offer personalized and diverse business solutions that meet customer demands and expectations of the future. Put a different way, all companies will become ICT companies operating in an environment characterized by concurrent demands for speed and customer value coupled with even more pressure to achieve innovation and forge ahead of competitors (see Figure 1.2).

For companies to produce a competitive advantage in this economy of speed and customer value, management that can integrate dispersed and multifaceted knowledge though the formation of diverse and open knowledge networks (Kodama, 2007a, 2007b) both company-wide and intercompany, and include customers, will become more and more important. In other words, in addition to the increased sophistication and diversity of knowledge, aggregation and knowledge convergence across different industries is also a major consideration. Now and into the future, the high-quality knowledge needed to achieve innovation will be dispersed in knowledge networks (Kodama, 2005, 2009b) and spread across businesses and industries, which will mean that for many companies the knowledge-integration process that conquers and transcends the boundaries between companies, and between companies and their customers, will become a crucial element of business activity

(Kodama, 2009b, 2011a). This means that we are entering an era in which "co-evolution management"—the capability to coordinate and collaborate with external partners and customers—will become more and more of an issue for many companies.[2]

Leading businesses, while continuing to pursue profit from their existing businesses, seriously consider the risks that accompany these new and uncertain circumstances, and forge a dynamic view of strategy that enables the company to intentionally and unceasingly form new markets (i.e. products, services and business models) through the merging of different knowledge, by transcending the company's own organizational capabilities (see Chakravarty, 1997; Markides, 1997, 1999; Eisenhardt and Sull, 2001; Kodama, 2007a, 2007b).

This dynamic view of strategy operates to further encourage the formation of cross-boundary partnering through coordination and collaboration with external partners and customers. Therefore, companies need to learn the open innovation processes that are explicitly reliant on external knowledge in order to acquire the speed and applied capabilities needed to respond to disruptive technologies (e.g. Christensen, 1997) and emerging markets. For these reasons, both the advancement of core competencies in traditional closed innovation, and the new knowledge-integration processes used with open innovation are required (see Figure 1.2). In other words, this means management that can hybridize the closed and open innovation processes (also called "hybrid innovation"). For example, P&G having enjoyed success with a well-operated knowledge-integration process as part of its "Connect & Development" strategy is a case in point (e.g. Sakkab, 2002).

Companies that want to propel their businesses through the rest of the twenty-first century will need to foster these closed and open "hybrid innovation" processes through cross-boundary partnering networks in the market economy of global convergence. At the core of this approach lies the formation of knowledge communities for co-evolution management through coordination and collaboration with partners all over the world. In particular, the formation of knowledge communities across a range of different businesses raises the potential to trigger the emergence of new business ecosystems.[3] Since ICT use is the key to the formation of these knowledge communities, its inclusion as the centerpiece of business strategy to absorb the best knowledge from around the world into the company is also a major consideration.

For companies to demonstrate the leadership required to achieve new business innovation by conquering and transcending diverse boundaries with ICT to reinvigorate business, and moreover respond to convergence between different technologies and industries, business people need the ICT capabilities (as they are called in this book) to gain new insights from complex and diverse boundaries and put these to work. The following section describes the importance of the concept of ICT capabilities.

1.3 ICT capabilities

Through extensive business experience and field research,[4] the author has identified fundamental elements of real-life business processes in which business people are involved; ICT developments that spring from people and organizations and the ideas and mechanisms behind their use; and the personal knowledge, patterns of teamwork and leadership in top and middle management that drive productivity and performance in companies that use ICT. The complex interactions of ICT development, ICT use, knowledge, teamwork, leadership and real-life processes enable companies to effect dynamic strategies and respond to changing business environments (and even enable companies to create these environments themselves).

Moreover, this research offers the new view that leading companies use the knowledge born through the frictions and conflicts that arise from interactions along the diverse range of boundaries between people, between teams, and between organizations and companies, and cleverly use ICT along these boundaries to create, use and share new knowledge to achieve business and business model innovation. Clearly then, the "human interactions with ICT" on these boundaries are a crucial factor in the acquisition of ICT capabilities, due to the characteristics of the multilayered boundaries that exist in and out of companies and between companies and customers, and the entrenched interdependence inherent to ICT. Thus, by applying this "ICT and people-interactive model" to boundaries, new knowledge is generated that not only serves to transform companies but also acts as a wellspring of business innovations for new product, service and business-model creation.

For instance, in the highly competitive mobile phone, game, electronics, communications equipment, automotive, industrial machine, environmental technology, high-tech goods, biotech and medical supply industries, companies cut across corporate boundaries by developing their ICT capabilities and drive coordination and collaboration with the seamless integration and use of a multitude of ICT tools to achieve business innovation. These companies not only use ICT to enhance their practical knowledge and accumulated experience base, but also use it as a sophisticated and dynamic way to integrate the diverse range of knowledge in and out of companies. ICT is thus indispensable as companies endeavor to produce new business models and sustainable business reforms. In this book, business entities that produce this type of new knowledge-integration model, enabling them to bring together knowledge both inside and outside of themselves, are referred to as "knowledge-integration firms."

Additionally, most notable in Europe, America, Taiwan and China, the recent digitalization, inclusion of ICT and modularization in development (at the business-process and product-architecture levels) has enabled companies to lower costs within and between themselves, and has allowed companies to separate different business activities (e.g. R&D, manufacturing, sales, etc.) to form horizontally integrated businesses and industrial structures. These various industries use the idea of "selection and concentration" to specialize in, and develop a particular business area (Hegel and Singer, 1999). This idea of a decentralized corporation with its emphasis on business efficiency is a reasonable strategic approach under certain conditions. On the other hand, however, the creative and productive frictions that exist along the various boundaries within companies and between companies raise the likelihood of acquiring new competences that transcend existing core competences, and are thus full of hidden potential for new innovation (Hagel III and Brown, 2005). Accordingly, it is important that many companies consider the proactive use of ICT as a source of new knowledge and innovation, rather than simply branding coordination within or between companies as an expense.

Corporations that have succeeded with a viable horizontally integrated business model (e.g. American corporations such as Dell and Apple, the fabless Qualcomm, or foundry companies like the semiconductor giant TSMC) still require close-knit coordination and collaboration with other companies across varying layers of expertise, and therefore these companies form their value chain models through virtual integration with a kind of a pseudo vertical integration (semiconductor businesses are often called virtual IDMs or Integrated Device Manufacturing). In other words, to achieve a high-performance, high-quality business model (like Dell's supply chain model, or the new content and application businesses associated with Apple's iPod, iPhone and iPad), or to create business solutions that respond to specialized customer needs, companies must have unique ICT capabilities to use ICT within and between themselves to facilitate the close-knit integration and substantive coordination between partners and customers that is required.

In contrast, leading electronics corporations such as Panasonic, Sharp, Canon, Samsung and LG, or companies such as Fanuc or Komatsu involved in tool and heavy machinery engineering, remain oriented toward overall optimization of their value chains through vertical integration, coupled with smooth coordination and collaboration between their different organizations to accumulate and regularly update know-how for their marketing, R&D, production technology, sales and support operations.

Former director and honorary chairman (currently advisory) of the Japanese company Maekawa Mfg, Mr. Masao Maekawa, stressed the significance of the fact that the strength of manufacturing, especially Japanese manufacturing, lies in the overlapping of wisdom and experience among people and between teams, companies and customers, which creates knowledge for a unified approach to manufacturing, sales and technologies (Maekawa, 2009). Furthermore, Panasonic President Kunio Nakamura, and Canon Chairman Fujio Mitarai both point out that "integrated development and manufacturing" is intrinsic to bringing forth technological blackboxing (Kodama, 2009b), and moreover serves to build up manufacturing know-how. Canon's precision device R&D and production technologies for its lenses and digital cameras are borne of assembly technologies combining blackboxed component and seamless cell production techniques created by concentrating the brain power that emerges over cross-organizational teams (Kodama, 2007c). Behind these transformative developmental and manufacturing approaches lies not only friction along a variety of knowledge boundaries between people and teams in real space, but also ICT capabilities that spurn the formation of new knowledge through the proactive use of ICT in virtual-space activities.

These corporate models are the ones used by the "knowledge-integration firms" described in this book—corporations that purposefully use ICT to encourage and promote creative and productive friction, integrate the array of core knowledge that exists inside and outside the company, not only to upgrade existing business processes, but also to achieve innovative new products and services and new business models. These are the processes that strategically use ICT to obtain new knowledge and achieve business innovation—critical outcomes dependent on the acquisition of dynamic ICT capabilities that enable companies to speedily establish their market position in new markets, and with new technologies.

Now and into the future, an increasingly important thing for business people to consider is seizing the *Ba* (Nonaka and Takeuchi, 1995) needed for new knowledge integration through the synergies that arise among people and along various boundaries, regardless of whether these are between individuals in real or virtual ICT space, and acquiring and reinforcing ICT capabilities, and then applying those capabilities diligently in daily business to perpetuate the creation of new knowledge. Twenty-first-century innovation firms do not just simply seek to use ICT to reduce regulatory costs and achieve more efficient operations, but they also place great emphasis on acquiring ICT capabilities in order to unceasingly create the new knowledge that is essential to maintain modern business competitiveness.

Now, let's take a look at the types of processes that bring about these ICT capabilities, from the point of view of ICT environments, interactions between people, and the creation of *Ba*.

1.4 The relationship between ICT environments and *Ba*

What are the impacts of ICT on team formation between organizations, and on human behavior in companies? Patterns of communication and collaboration within organizations are not only affected by organizational structure and office-space factors (Allen and Henn, 2006) but are also heavily influenced by the ICT environment and its use (Kodama, 1999a, 1999b, 1999c). The leading role in an ITC environment is played by human interactions (dialogue and practice), and thus ICT use has a profound effect on the nature of communication and collaboration among people in the virtual space of the Internet. The reason these human interactions with ICT are important is because the questions of where and how people communicate and collaborate with each other in dynamically changing contexts, what types of information and knowledge is being shared, and whether these factors lead to business performance are key considerations for organizational and corporate strategic action.

In the innovation process, creating new ideas and closely linking businesses and organizations is highly dependent on the quality and quantity of communication and collaboration, which is in turn dependent on the shared dynamic contexts among people. Accordingly, ICT environments that can be deployed for real-time communication and collaboration to induce new ideas and trigger inspiration, and the design of their usage patterns, are crucial factors for stimulating innovation activities in companies. The actors who interact with each other in these ICT virtual spaces on a daily basis are individuals, or groups of people. Human beings create this shared space–time called *Ba* by creating constantly changing dynamic contexts and meaning through their interactions via the ICT resources provided to them.

Ba is a concept used to describe an organizational or social phenomenon, and is a "context platform" universally perceived and recognized within the confines of its member interactions and under certain physical or organizational conditions. In particular, *Ba* also provides a framework in which human beings can participate to observe each other either consciously or unconsciously, communicate and collaborate, reach mutual understanding, and share experiences and perceptions and the circumstances behind them. This means that *Ba* is not an official organization within a company or some kind of office environment, nor is *Ba* an organization or office designed by people. Instead, it is formed by people both actively and circumstantially from new contexts and meanings, through their interactions in virtual ICT spaces.

However, *Ba* is also dependent on contexts such as individual circumstances surrounding the company, its strategy, its organizational and corporate culture, and so on. Therefore, even in the same ICT environment the existing individual business contexts differ from one another, and so the *Ba* that are created are specific to individual organizations and companies. Thus, since people are influenced by the ICT environments (or they influence them), *Ba* as "context platforms" are created through human interaction either purposefully or in an improvised manner.

The "situated perspective" given to us by the cognitive sciences provides a lot of insight regarding differences and relationships in ICT environments themselves, and into the human behaviors therein. According to the concept of "situated action" proposed by Suchman (1987), she stresses the view that "situated actions" are actions that have an inherent dependency on physical and social circumstances in the course of all behaviors. Therefore, according to the situated perspective, human behaviors are embedded in circumstances and thus plans people make are like resources for situated actions, although no matter how strong the intent, plans do not ultimately determine human action. Plans then, are not programs that instruct human activity, because individual human activities are responses to the circumstantial conditions that individuals face. In other words, behaviors (situated actions) are embedded in the circumstances, and plans are nothing but abstractions that attempt to represent actual human behavior. Suchman had the following to say about relationships between plans and situated actions:

> So, for example, in planning to run a series of rapids in a canoe, one is very likely to sit for a while above the falls and plan one's descent.

> The plan might go something like "I'll get as far over to the left as possible, try to make to it between those two large rocks, then back-ferry hard to the right to make it around that next bunch." A great deal of deliberation, discussion, simulation, and reconstruction may go into such a plan. But, however detailed, the plan stops short of the actual business of getting your canoe through the falls. When it really comes down to the details of responding to currents and handling a canoe, you effectively abandon the plan and fall back on whatever embodied skills are available to you. The purpose of the plan in this case is not to get your canoe through the rapids, but rather to orient you in such a way that you can obtain the best possible position from which to use those embodied skills on which, in the final analysis, your success depends.
>
> Even in the case of more deliberative, less highly skilled activities, we generally do not anticipate alternative courses of action, or their consequences, until some course of action is already under way. It is frequently only on acting in a present situation that its possibilities become clear, and we often do not know ahead of time, or at least not with any specificity, what future state we desire to bring about.
>
> Suchman (1987, p. 52)

Put simply, the foundations of actions are not plans, rather situated actions based on interactions with the local environment. For corporations designing ICT environments, this could also mean preparing the right resources as part of their *Ba*-creation planning. This is because people use the resources available to them (the ICT environment) in response to changing circumstances, and through these situated actions, and not plans, create *Ba*.

"Situated actions" means, for instance, that people working on a new project might come up with ideas about how to organize themselves or flexibly change organizational structures if needed, or create geographically dispersed project teams while maintaining their ICT systems, which at the same time could induce business collaboration ideas to develop unique ICT environments and usage patterns and achieve specific business activities and goals within the scope of the project. Then, as people become more deeply involved in the ICT environment and its uses, they create *Ba* as shared dynamically changing contexts through the interaction and collaboration of human dialogue and practice. The *Ba* is created from the new meanings that emerge either actively or circumstantially from the synergies in the ICT environment—a resource designed by human beings.

Thus, ICT resources tend to influence the formation of the best *Ba* for the situation. In this way, the ICT environment, optimized for particular business circumstances, spurns the further creation of a more diverse range of *Ba*, or "a chain of *Ba*," and by advancing the interactions between people, therefore, as a resource that encourages the formation of *Ba*, ICT systems are an important "workplace platform."

Moreover, the *Ba* are fundamental to the formation of knowledge community networks that arise along the varied boundaries that exist between business people in and out of companies and among their customers. With the interactions using ICT resources, and through the agency of these human interactions, *Ba* arise from the new contexts that emerge from the transcendence and convergence of boundaries between organizations and knowledge, as responses to circumstances in order to create knowledge communities as new networked organizational systems (or networked knowledge communities arising from "a chain of *Ba*"). The comings and goings of business people in real space and in ICT virtual space in these knowledge communities and networked knowledge communities creates *Ba*, which in turn gives rise to the ICT capabilities needed to integrate wide-ranging knowledge.

Nonaka and Takeuchi (1995) understood that *Ba* is a driving force behind knowledge creation. The spring of new knowledge does not just simply exist in individuals. Rather it is born through the contextualized circumstances of *Ba*, with its interactions among individuals, and between individuals and their circumstances. In other words, the relationships in *Ba* and its shared contexts bring together individuals, which leads to the creation of new knowledge through the sharing of knowledge that those individuals possess.

In contrast to the "stable community of practice" (Wenger, 1998) relationships that enable steady knowledge sharing (described further in Chapter 2), *Ba* not only provide for stability and knowledge sharing but also include co-creation as participants improvise new scenarios as people from different backgrounds bump into each other across their diverse boundaries. *Ba* are physical, virtual and perceptual (mental) spaces in which knowledge is shared, inspired, created and accumulated through the individual, group and organizational relationships that emerge in them. Knowledge communities and networked knowledge communities—the engines for new knowledge integration, which integrate diverse boundaries—arise from the formation of the best *Ba*.

Founded in *Ba*, these knowledge communities and networked knowledge communities are in turn organizational platforms that give rise to the ICT capabilities needed to integrate new knowledge. Then companies

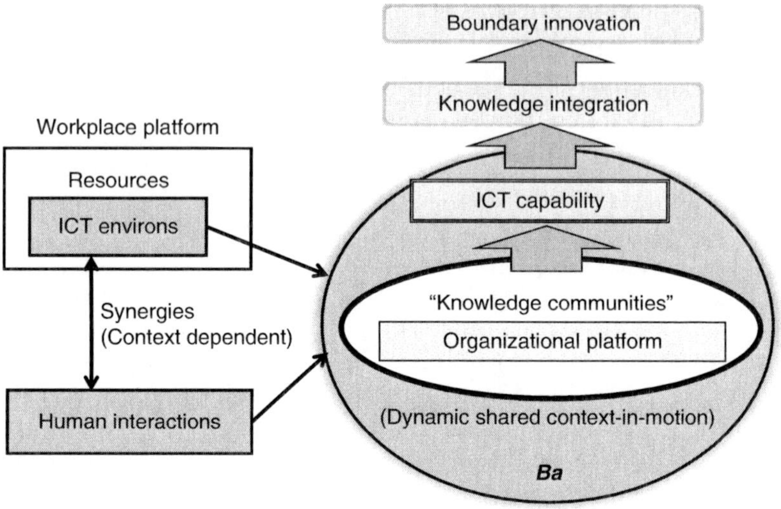

Figure 1.3 Resources, people, *Ba*, knowledge communities, ICT capability

integrate the knowledge that exists inside and outside of themselves and their customers, and bring forth new "boundary innovation" through these ICT capabilities (see Figure 1.3). Boundary innovation means innovation that is achieved as a result of bringing together all kinds of alien knowledge across wide-ranging boundaries. Boundary innovation is an innovation model that enables the strategic and sustainable creation of new products, services and business models through the transcendence of the wide-ranging boundaries that exist between companies and manufacturing businesses, and includes creative business models that transform existing business rules or radically reinvent traditional products and services, and in so doing give corporations a sustainable competitive edge over the long term.

1.5 ICT capability and boundary innovation

In the modern world, "knowledge" has become the most critical factor for companies to maintain an enduring competitiveness, and the key to acquiring knowledge is the formation of *Ba* and their knowledge communities (and networked knowledge communities) as new organizational platforms. This is the essential organizational capability companies need to respond to the paradigm shifts described earlier—the capabilities for the creation of new knowledge and dynamic innovation activities that springs from the "power of execution" gained by acquiring ICT capabilities through the formation of knowledge communities among individuals, groups and organizations in and out of companies to integrate dispersed and wide-ranging knowledge. This is the knowledge-integration process.

Modern companies face a range of challenges—the wildly fluctuating global market, diversifying and upgrading technologies, the breakneck pace of ICT developments, competition between different lines of business that overlap across different industries and the rapid shortening of product life cycles and early obsolescence. For companies to succeed in these tough circumstances, they must use their ICT capabilities to transcend multiple boundaries, persevere in the creation of new knowledge and infuse it deeply within their organizations to speedily actualize boundary innovation to bring forth new technologies and products, and new business models.

The essence of corporate strategic management lies in the dynamic activities that take place through the formation of *Ba* by the interactions among people, organizations and ICT (Kodama, 2007b), which is also the essence of innovations that spring from trial and error among business people using their high-quality practical knowledge in ICT to form strategies and apply them. Knowledge itself is also a dynamic process, and is embedded as tacit knowledge gained through business practitioners' personal experience of conceiving and enacting strategy, and accumulated in individuals and organizations through applied introspective processes.

The starting point for the research questions and issues raised in this book is to answer the question, "What are the ICT capabilities needed to achieve boundary innovation with ICT and maintain a corporate competitive edge?" Fundamental to the framework illustrating these innovation strategies and dynamic ICT capabilities is the dynamic and creative knowledge-integration process needed to bring forth new knowledge through the interactions of individuals and organizations with ICT, both inside and outside of corporations. The creation of these organizational platforms called knowledge communities, formed from the diverse boundaries between business people in and out of companies and their customers, is a key requirement for achieving the knowledge-integration process and hence boundary innovation.

Looking through a lens to more fully understand ICT capabilities—the invisible processes of knowledge-assets creation in corporate activity—gives us a valuable insight into how corporations use ICT to create new knowledge as the strategy, and achieve boundary innovation as the goal.

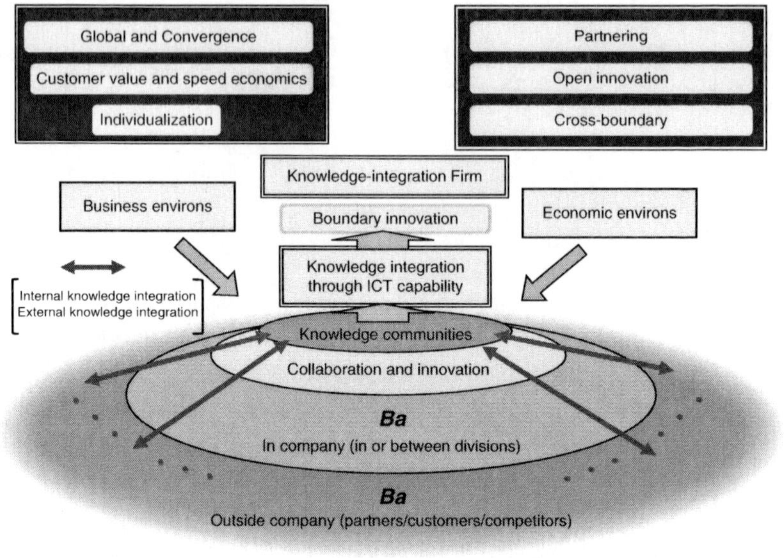

Figure 1.4 Knowledge communities, ICT capability and knowledge-integration firms

In the knowledge-integration firms mentioned earlier, ICT capabilities arise from the formation of *Ba* by people and organizations interacting to form multilayered knowledge communities, and establishing knowledge networks company-wide and intercompany that include customers. These diverse processes that integrate company internal and external knowledge through ICT capabilities drive the business transformations needed to achieve boundary innovation and bring its new products, services and business models to fruition (see Figure 1.4).

Chapter 2 describes the concept of these knowledge communities that drive boundary innovation and the knowledge-integration process, and how these knowledge communities develop in response to changing business and ICT environments. The chapter also considers the importance of the "innovation communities" that have become the central organizational platforms needed to adapt to the paradigm shifts of twenty-first-century business.

2
The Advancement of ICT Tools and Knowledge, and Innovation Management

2.1 ICT in the grand design of business

Now and into the future, proactive ICT use will become even more necessary as a competitive business tool to bring more efficiency, improve production and management, and invigorate organizations in the fierce business environments of modern times. The e-businesses using broadband capabilities and the more efficient business processes and operations within and between companies of recent years are representative of this proactive ICT use, and investing in development or implementation and application of ICT to gain more efficiency and create new network businesses is a major issue that many modern companies face, while ICT continues to bring benefits and advantages to companies. For example, according to existing research, ICT may increase product quality (Thatcher and Pingry, 2004), improve workflow (Buhler and Vidal, 2005), enhance a company's flexibility to respond to customer needs (Gunasekaran and Ngai, 2004) and improve communication between a company and its customers and suppliers (Fiala, 2005). However, it should be noted here that the ICT hardware does not in itself give a company a competitive advantage (e.g. Clemons and Row, 1991; Porter, 1991, 2001; Mata, Fuerst and Barney, 1995; Barney, Wright and Ketchen Jr., 2001; Carr, 2003, 2004). This is because ICT has an intrinsic relationship with corporate strategy and organizational mechanisms. Crucially then business leaders must focus on the importance of understanding how ICT can be put to use as a strategic tool as well as recognize the importance of ICT hardware (Kodama, 1999a, 1999b, 1999c).

Now let's cast our eyes over the past, present and the future of management in business organizations to get a general idea about the huge impact that ICT has had on the grand design of business (see Figure 2.1).

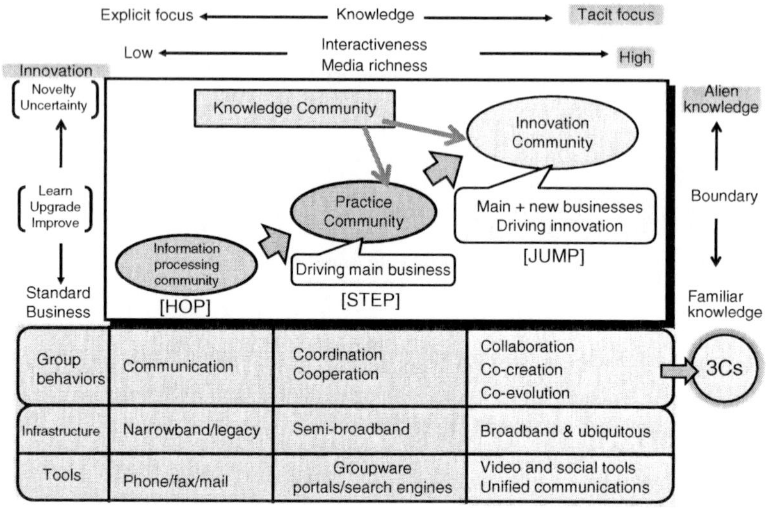

Figure 2.1 Knowledge communities and the 3C era

2.1.1 The Hop phase (the 1950s to 1980s)

In the period before the establishment of the international broadband digital network, the majority of business organizations routinely used telephones and faxes to communicate interdepartmentally, with other businesses, and with clients and customers in their daily operations. Business processes carried out by computers were mostly calculation-type intensive routine processes performed with large, general-purpose host computers and so on. This phase has been called the "Hop" phase on the ICT evolution time line.

In the Hop phase, as this period in ICT development is defined, most communications were voice communications, fax and e-mail sent via phone lines, and corporate data transmissions using the analog and low-speed narrowband digital networks of the time. Organizations were bureaucratic in nature, and characteristically had pyramid-type, administration-centered hierarchical management. Most operations were vertically integrated line operations, so information in companies flowed from the upper organizations down through to the lower ones (or information from the shop floor or work site followed the reverse path), with the company organizations configured in what is known as the "information processing community" model. Business models were by and large mass-production types, and the most pressing issues that management faced were ensuring that information was accurately processed and communicated, and that operating efficiencies and production outputs were improved.

2.1.2 The Step phase (the 1980s to 1990s)

As computer systems became radically more compact, businesses became more decentralized and integrated, and semi-broadband, intranet and Internet network technologies began to advance and become more widespread. Likewise, the number of companies promoting and taking advantage of digital technologies to build intracompany and intercompany networks were also on the rise. Compared to the Hop phase, this communication-centered environment arose through the availability of electronic mail, groupware, and search engine and portal site services that operate across the Internet, while ICT tools became much more interactive, and a substantially richer array of media became available. Consequently, ICT use advanced business transformation to a deeper level than in the Hop phase, and enabled business systems involve more coordination and cooperation with external partners.

Organizations in the Step phase also started becoming flatter than those in the Hop phase, and looser hierarchies enabled faster decision-making and delegation of power. The era of applying the business process management techniques of knowledge management using ICT (e.g. Skyrrme, 2001), business process re-engineering (Hammer and Champy, 1993) and Enterprise Resource Planning (ERP) had arrived.

With these developments, the importance of ICT management also began to gradually permeate companies. This period also saw a growing awareness of new organizational concepts emerging in academia to describe networked organizations (Nohria, 1997), virtual corporations (Davidow and Malone, 1992), virtual teams (Lipnack and Stamps, 1997) and the workplace-centered knowledge community concept called "community of practice" (Wenger, 1998). In particular, the "community of practice" idea involves knowledge sharing among all participants through coordination and cooperation in an organization, which began to gain recognition as an important organizational strategy that served to drive the learning processes needed to upgrade and improve a company's main business. As well as reinforcing the learning processes within an organization, the coordination and cooperation between related divisions or between organizations through the formation of knowledge communities also became an important factor in absorbing and acquiring new knowledge (see Figure 2.1).

However, it also became apparent that it was not always best practice or even possible to apply knowledge management using ICT to a company or to all of the organizations therein (e.g. Davenport and Prusak, 2000), mainly because successful deployment of ICT depends on its compatibility with the nature of the organizations and organizational contexts involved. While ICT is a driver that enables organizational structures to change, it also became clear that the way in which an organization is transformed by ICT deployment is ultimately decided by the purpose of the organization or its context. Therefore, many companies became aware of the significance of the simultaneous transformations in people, organizations and corporate culture that occur when reforming business processes with ICT (Davenport, 1993). Nevertheless, companies also recognized the promise of ICT as infrastructure to invigorate individuals and organizations by enabling actors in and out of companies to disseminate and share information dispersed across the ICT environment, even though many organizational challenges remained.

Even now modern companies commonly use e-mail and a range of groupware applications among others to improve communications between organizations and information sharing, and many companies aim to further corporate transformation by further promoting the use of knowledge and information possessed by individual people. However, it was during the Step period that a problem began to surface—companies that were already changing their organizational culture were not able to improve their internal and external communications or speed up their decision-making processes by the introduction of these new ICT tools and the sole implementation e-mail and groupware.

Company staff use e-mail and groupware ICT tools on a daily basis, and thus encourage the sharing and transmission of data as explicit knowledge (Nonaka and Takeuchi, 1995), and it is certainly possible to achieve some higher degree of business process efficiency through the sharing of explicit knowledge. Robert H. Buckman, former CEO of Buckman Laboratories, a US company known around the world for its promotion of knowledge management through ICT use, made the following comment about the knowledge required by organizations (Buckman, 2003, p. 20):

> This does help, at least initially, by causing knowledge that has been written down to be organized and made available to the organization. Useful as that step is, however, we've found that it is not sufficient to achieve success. It can deal with no more than a small fraction of knowledge in the company – perhaps about 10% of the total. The dynamics of a company don't change when it organizes its

> explicit knowledge.... We found that the vast bulk of the knowledge in Buckman Labs was in the heads of our people – and it was changing every minute of every day. It was not written down. Therefore, if we wanted to achieve success in the fast-changing environment confronting us, we had to learn how to engage people and arouse their interest and trust, making them willing to move their knowledge across the organization to where it was needed, when it was needed.

Using ICT, staffers at Buckman Laboratories submit current problems and issues to their forum in virtual space, and exchange opinions in real-time with other participating staff members who have an interest in, or relationship with those problems and issues. Through this process, the Buckman Labs forum promotes the sharing of knowledge and its inspiration. Importantly, ICT lends itself to be adapted for human thought and behaviors, because knowledge has a dynamic quality unlike the static nature of information in a database.

Human knowledge lies at the foundations of individual practice, corporate business processes and even ICT itself. In general, there are two types of knowledge—tacit knowledge and explicit knowledge (e.g. Polanyi, 1966; Nonaka and Takeuchi, 1995). Characteristically, tacit knowledge is personal, subjective and often difficult to communicate or convey, and includes beliefs, mental images, intuition, skills and know-how. Putting it another way, such things as know-how and skills are the invisible accumulated resources and technical and business capabilities in a company that cannot be easily clarified or formulated. In contrast to tacit knowledge, explicit knowledge includes the formal information found in manuals and documents so forth, the products and services that companies provide to their customers, the manuals and databases that a company has built up over time, or patents and theses available in the public sphere.

In this way it can be seen that there are two different aspects to knowledge, both of which are of importance. In particular, it is tacit knowledge is ultimately the origin of explicit knowledge, and is therefore essential for the creation of any new knowledge (or products and services). Individuals involved in business activities must be able to understand things and communicate them to other people, and they must also be able to put tacit knowledge into words and objectify it. This means that tacit knowledge and explicit knowledge are in no way independent of each other, and in groundbreaking companies, they are mutually complimentary and in constant dynamic and circulatory interaction (Nonaka and Takeuchi, 1995). Knowledge creation (or knowledge integration) means creating new knowledge in individuals, in groups and in entire organizations at all levels, that is over and above what can be known from a business environment.

While it goes without saying that the advances of ICT have bolstered economic activity in human societies and achieved incredible transformations, its greatest accomplishments are the processes human beings use to run their business activities and the superior production "efficiency" that ICT has brought. Captured in the dimensions of human knowledge, the concept of "efficiency" is a relative of explicit knowledge, and in turn, ICT is used to pursue more efficient business processes to communicate and share this explicit knowledge. The ICT tool kit with its e-mail, web-based bulletins, search engines, groupware, databases and so forth have raised the level of efficiency with which human beings can communicate and share their explicit knowledge, and thus has come to provide substantial support to the interpersonal processes of job routines and business activities.

However, the idea that the main thrust of knowledge sharing with ICT should fundamentally involve explicit knowledge rather than the tacit knowledge hidden in people's heads or embedded in human behavior is actually incorrect. In fact, the creation and sharing of tacit knowledge in the pursuit of creativity through ICT can raise the potential for favorable outcomes in human practice (Kodama, 2009a). This cannot be achieved by using ICT to communicate and share existing and complete explicit knowledge; rather, it is attained through the perpetual emergence of new business concepts born through dynamic ICT usage. The new market businesses and social structures that have emerged from sustained human practice using ICT have made the creation and sharing of tacit knowledge possible, and creativity achievable. Although ICT makes it possible to communicate, share and manage explicit knowledge, the creation and sharing of tacit knowledge cannot be achieved only through those processes. The potential for ideas, inspiration and human creativity is raised through the recursive practice of individuals (doing things over and over) and trial and error in organizational learning.

Buckman, as mentioned earlier, points out the importance of the dynamically changing tacit knowledge that exists in people's heads. Therefore, to inspire tacit knowledge in actors, furnishing an environment in which actors use ICT tools hands-on is crucial. Therefore, compared to the information processing communities of the Hop period, the "communities of practice" of the Step period became more important

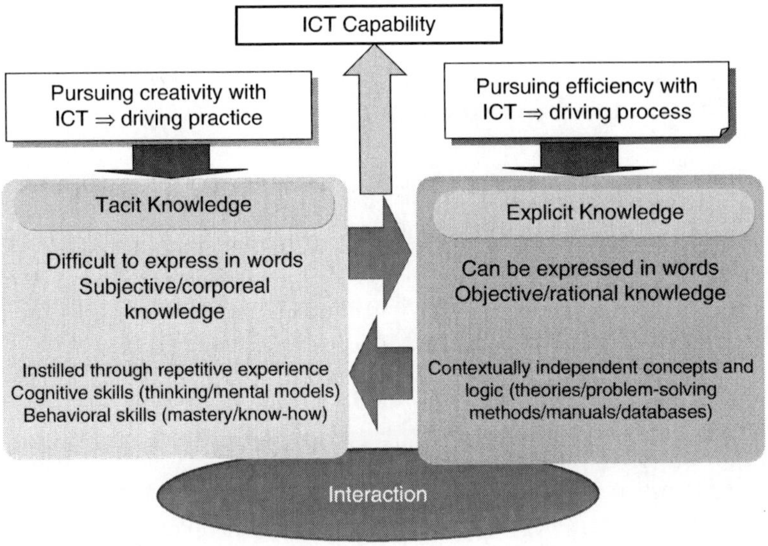

Figure 2.2 Organizational capability using ICT
Source: Based on Nonaka and Takeuchi (1995).

as drivers of ICT-based knowledge management that included greater amounts of tacit knowledge.

As exemplified by the Buckman laboratories example, knowledge management using ICT characteristically gives rise to new tacit knowledge through the real-time dialogue and behavior enacted in virtual space, and originates from the practice of business people who bring about circulatory and mutual interactions between tacit and explicit knowledge. Thus, human interaction itself (through the ICT medium) is the source of this knowledge creation—that is to say, the actual physical nature of ICT that is not dependent on human interaction, and operating and administrative procedures themselves are merely static forms of explicit knowledge. Taking this idea to its destination, as ICT "unifies human thoughts and behaviors," it brings cross-circulation of tacit and implicit knowledge, makes it possible to balance practice with process, and as a result in turn gives rise to ICT capabilities, which are crucial as organizational capabilities (see Figure 2.2).

Winner of the Nobel Prize in Chemistry, Professor Ryoji Noyori, said the following about the acquisition of knowledge and information:

> In actual fact, it is knowledge, not information, that is power. Teachers teach information. Then when students take that information and

> make it their own it becomes [useful knowledge]. Information belongs to all people, but we should bear in mind that knowledge is personal. Therefore, people cannot make knowledge their own without active familiarization, practice and review. This is an immutable fact.

Researchers in the experimental sciences are required to practice creative trial and error to invent new technologies or discover new phenomena. It is not an overstatement to say that whether Lady Luck smiles on a venture really depends on how deeply the researchers delve into their tacit knowledge to achieve creativity.

For example, regarding his invention of the blue light-emitting diode, Professor Shuji Nakamura of the University of California at Santa Barbara stated that the experimental process was a significant factor in the success of the invention (e.g. Nakamura, 2001). Prof. Nakamura designed the experimental apparatus himself, organized the materials needed for it, assembled it and improved and upgraded it by experimentation. With such deep involvement, Prof. Nakamura's experimental equipment came to be as if it were an extension of his own body, and thus he was able to understand its strengths and shortcomings in great detail, and in every nook and cranny. It was through this experience that Prof. Nakamura was able to achieve the thin-film gallium nitride element of a suitable quality and create the blue light-emitting diode.

During the same period, however, researchers in the R&D department of a large corporation were also attempting to develop a blue light-emitting diode. These experimenters did not design and assemble their own apparatus, but had it custom-made by a semiconductor equipment specialist instead. In contrast to Prof. Nakamura, who fine-tuned his equipment himself (adjusting experimental parameters such as base temperature, gas flow rates, spray angles and chamber configurations needed to produce the thin-film), these lax, big-business researchers' approach to fine-tuning was decidedly different (they entrusted this to the equipment maker, probably so they wouldn't get their hands dirty). If we think about this in terms of the previous comments made by Prof. Noyori, the experimental apparatus corresponds to static explicit information, and is accessible to any specialist researcher in the same field, anywhere in the world. However, Prof. Nakamura's example of "becoming one with his experimental apparatus" illustrates the richness of his tacit knowledge, and how it was this that enabled him to make the gallium nitride thin-film a reality, as new explicit knowledge. This example is similar in meaning to "Humans becoming one with ICT."

It is the degree of depth with which humans explore their tacit knowledge and delve into their creativity, through their interactions with physical resources like experimental apparatus or ICT systems, that triggers the formation of new knowledge (both tacit and explicit) and ultimately, innovation. As discussed in the last chapter, ICT resources are planned resources just like an organizational structure or office space, but it is through human interactions with these resources that the more superior *Ba* are created, through which the spiraling circulation of tacit and implicit knowledge can occur. It is these synergies that achieve creativity and efficiency, and balance practice with process, and bring "ICT capabilities" to an organization (see Figure 2.2).

With the non-real-time unidirectional communications and consultation methods of e-mail and groupware and so forth in this Step phase, however, a barrier confronting the advancement of high-quality knowledge management was the sluggishness of the decision-making process and resulting difficulties in making serious judgments or decisions. This is mainly because face-to-face communications in which individuals can share their affinities and express solidarity with each other has always been a preferred method of communications in organizations. It is in the Jump phase that follows when the need eventually arises for communication tools that enable people to overcome the sense of being cloistered and closed off due to the fact that e-mail and groupware do not sufficiently convey an individual's thoughts and intentions. It is these tools that lead to the modern-day business revolutions in companies.

2.1.3 The Jump phase (the 1990s to the present)

As mentioned, an increasing number of future business systems will most likely develop through the merging of a range of resources and alien knowledge in a variety of open knowledge communities both inside and outside of companies that include their customers (e.g. Chesbrough, 2003; Kodama, 2007a). Compared to the Step phase, this phase will be dominated by flatter, more flexible organizational frameworks and more open management protocols.

Moreover, more importance in the Jump phase will be placed on strategic community management (Kodama, 2007a), in which leadership in top and middle management propels dynamic business strategies among and within knowledge communities that include customers. Particularly important will be the formation of "innovation communities" (also knowledge communities) that are able to respond to the uncertainty and unfamiliarity of modern business (see Figure 2.1). The processes of triggering and sharing tacit knowledge through human interaction in these innovation communities will have to be even more seriously considered as mechanisms for achieving innovation (new product, service and business models) through the fusion and assimilation of similar and alien knowledge. Innovation communities must not only advance a company's main businesses, but must also push outward into business territories surrounding the company and pioneer new businesses themselves. For this reason, the prominent organizational activities that innovation communities will involve themselves in will be the processes of collaboration, co-creation, co-evolution among all stakeholders (see Figure 2.1), while business leaders in the Jump phase will need network strategy support tools—more interactive and richer media tools (compared to the Step phase) to support them in their strategic community management endeavors.

In particular, these integrative, broadband and ubiquitous ICT tools enable to focus on the collaboration, co-creation and co-evolution (the 3Cs) that spring from the high-quality interactions between individuals to support knowledge and competence sharing and creation, and provide leaders with assistance in their decision-making and business activities. In the Jump phase, already well underway all over the world, leading global corporations dynamically transform personal culture and entire organizational climates with hands-on videos, unified communications and social tools based on multimedia, communications and networking to develop their corporate activities (for more about tools see Chapter 3). Thus, a major challenge is to drive dynamic innovation in business, with open organizational and managerial structures that operate through various knowledge communities (innovation communities and communities of practice), both in and out of the company.

2.2 Collaboration and knowledge-integration firms

Figure 2.1 describes the evolution of ICT and business. Businesses are often seriously affected by changes in circumstances. There are many factors that cause circumstantial change, and as stated at the beginning of Chapter 1, there is an increasing need for business strategies that can deal with the "convergence" taking place in recent years—the fusing of different technologies and services, and the product development business models that span across different industries. Strategies to adapt to the changing (or self-created) environment of convergence depend on the merging of the wide-ranging knowledge that exists companywide and intercompany. For example, the arrival of e-businesses and content

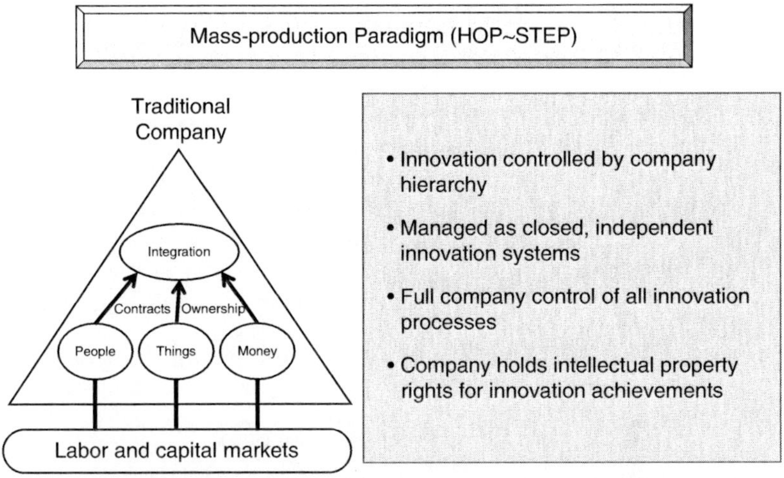

Figure 2.3 Old-school innovation management

industries like Google and Apple is also the result of the integration of knowledge held by diverse players.

In the Hop and Step phases illustrated in Figure 2.1, innovation activities are mainly controlled according to hierarchical systems, because in older-style companies, managing innovation in closed and independent systems was also of great strategic importance, and as these companies controlled the entire innovation process, they also retained the intellectual property rights for their innovations (see Figure 2.3).

However, in the Jump era, closed innovation processes have gradually become more open (see Figure 2.4). One reason is because in recent years, new business models must be brought into being that are based on the new rules of merging technologies, including ICT, to bring forth new product and technological developments from a variety of different industries.

The following describes cases of technological convergence in Japan. In a break from established principles, and to further their internationally dispersed business interests, Japanese manufacturing businesses in recent years have been actively pursuing mergers and acquisitions of businesses internationally, and have been accelerating the pace of international R&D&P (production) deployment as strategies to create innovative technologies overseas. One such company, Toray, has teamed up to develop carbon fiber materials for commercial airliner applications with Boeing in the US, and with AEC and Daimler in Germany

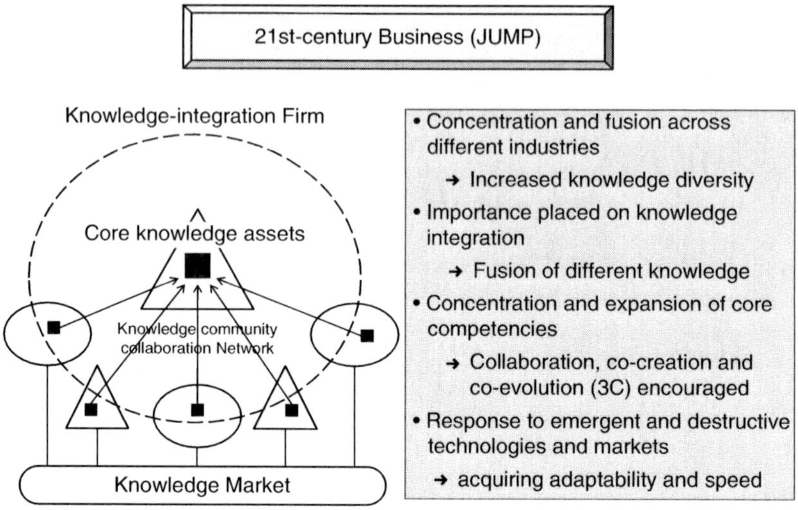

Figure 2.4 New innovation management: The knowledge-integration firm

to develop and mass produce carbon fiber components for electric vehicles. Toray's R&D strategy includes a basic policy of engaging in development activities close to major customers and growing markets,[1] while Canon has said "while the diversification of technologies on a global scale continues, it is impossible to expand business capacity with R&D centers only in Japan"—which is why the company is forging ahead with its global R&D operations by setting up centers in Europe and America, bundling its research and technology businesses, and actively seeking out mergers and acquisitions in Europe and America to use as fertile "culture mediums" for innovation, with American research facilities focusing on health care, and European research facilities focusing on office machinery. Canon CEO Fujio Mitarai has been cited as describing the ability to trigger technical innovation by merging a number of different technologies as "editing capability," which reiterates the importance of the knowledge-integration processes needed to deal with integrating and fusing different technologies.[2]

NEC CEO Kaoru Yano also spoke of the importance of this technical fusion called convergence by saying, "We have two link ups with different industries and make something they can't make in China or Korea!" It became something of a slogan for his company. For instance, these associations make it possible to gather together and access information such as data for electric cars and related charging equipment in grand computing schemes, and develop technologies that enable mass connection of sensors such as RFID (wireless automated identification) and infrared sensors to the Internet. Additionally, in the area of developing environment-friendly cities through the linking of different industries, IT, appliance and automobile makers are joining forces under the grand concept of "smart innovation" to form new industries and create something that just can't be done in China or Korea, which is a vital mission for Japan.[3] Winner of the Nobel Prize in Chemistry, Dr. Koichi Tanaka, also pointed to the importance of fortifying the fusing of different fields of expertise and raising the level of dialogue among people to give birth to new ideas and creativity upon embarking on a manufacturing venture (Tanaka, 2011). He also emphasized the importance of accepting people from outside one's own specialist area, of improving the abilities of people to hold dialogues across different fields of expertise, and of people from diverse backgrounds pooling together their wisdom to raise the level of teamwork capabilities while overcoming their fear of failure.

This is how the phenomenon of convergence is making existing corporate competitiveness even more complicated. Convergence has dramatically accelerated the pace of mergers and acquisitions and strategic partnerships between companies and their customers, and has triggered massive changes along existing corporate boundaries. This means that as cross-industry partnerships transcend the older and simpler competitive axes between businesses, the knowledge-integration process (Kodama, 2011a) is becoming an increasingly important factor as a core driver of corporate strategy. In other words, there is pressure on modern businesses to switch away from focusing on competition between businesses within an industry, or competition between industries, to "collaboration strategies" that span diverse industries and include customers. Therefore, knowledge expanded through convergence and concentration between different industries, and merging and integrating knowledge are important challenges confronting many companies, which in turn leads to the necessity for new innovation management that can foster the 3Cs (see Figure 2.1) with customers and other companies.

Compared to the Hop and Step phases, in the Jump phase companies need to push for even more intensification and expansion of core competencies to acquire the speed and adaptive capability needed to respond to emerging and destructive technologies and to pioneer new markets—the independent production methods of the past are no longer sufficient, so businesses must understand the importance of acquiring skills and creativity through interactions with best partners and special customers to achieve knowledge creation across the boundaries between different businesses (and industries). This dispersed innovation management needs to form collaboration networks as knowledge communities in a new governance approach. This is also the way of the "knowledge-integration firms" described in Chapter 1 (see Figure 2.4).

As described, conventional closed innovation systems are no longer enough. Nor is it enough to just combine various specialized knowledge across different organizations within a company. The greatest challenge facing knowledge-integration firms of the Jump phase is to create global networks with best partners and combine the best knowledge from around the world with the knowledge inside the company. Collaboration strategies are a key component of knowledge management in these organizations, and they can only be enacted through the formation of collaboration networks as knowledge communities consisting of all stakeholders both inside and outside the company (see Figure 2.5).

The convergence phenomenon has also brought with it new market opportunities through the evolution of net businesses and technological integration, and companies need to formulate strategies to forge ahead in these new markets. Companies need to push ahead with collaboration strategies through the formation of knowledge communities

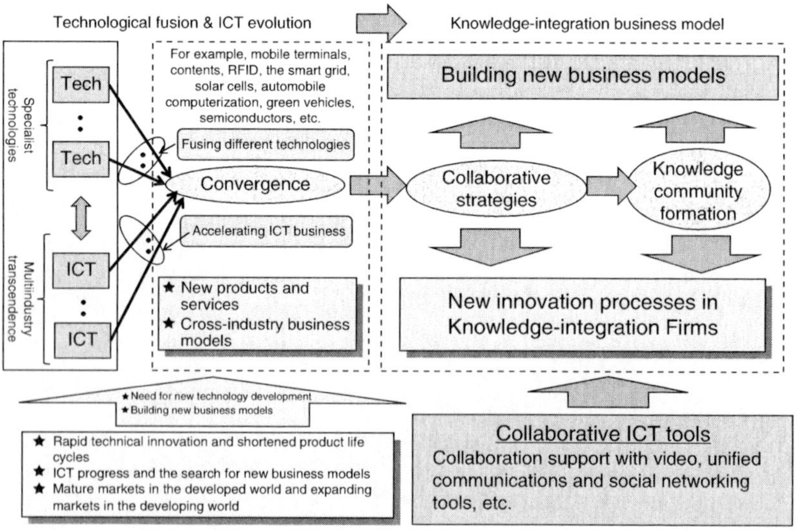

Figure 2.5 Convergence and collaboration

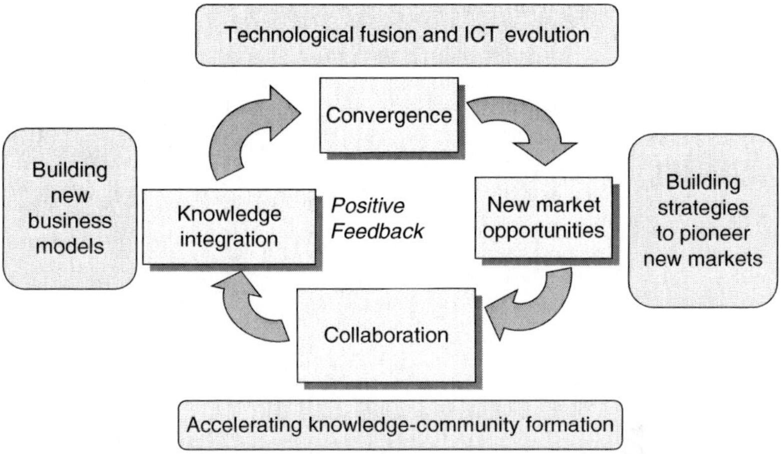

Figure 2.6 Positive feedback through convergence and collaboration

that span all areas inside and outside of their businesses to create new innovations (new products, services and business models) through the global knowledge-integration process, the trigger of all this convergence, and then through this innovation process create mutually beneficial effects further down the track (see Figure 2.6).

ICT use is also indispensable in promoting collaboration between various centers around the world, because ICT use encourages innovation through the knowledge-integration process. The tools that support collaboration within a company and between companies are the video, unified communications and social networking tools already mentioned, and are referred to as "collaborative ICT tools" in this book.

As important platforms for creating wide-ranging social networks, collaborative ICT tools do not only provide corporate and organizational benefits, but are also strategic tools that offer a high level of potential for innovation. Collaborative ICT tools don't just bring more efficiency and speed to business processes, but they also have hidden potential for innovation and even enable the actual creation of new businesses.

Chapter 3 briefly describes the business environments of recent times, and illustrates why the evolution of technical and market innovations of collaborative ICT tools (especially video communication technology) have been an especially important ICT platform for developing knowledge communities within and between companies that include their customers.

3
The Innovation and Market Expansion of Video Communications

3.1 Broadband innovation through collaborative ICT tools

With the developments in ICT of recent years, collaborative ICT tools, including television and web conferencing systems, videophone and chat applications, are spreading in popularity all over the world, thanks to the development of the two core video communications and broadband network technologies as the platform. Video communications functions are included with the Apple FaceTime app, and in social networking services such as Facebook and Google+. No longer limited to the business-to-business and business-to-customer spheres, these tools are now also widely used by customers (C2C—customer to customer) to communicate with each other. Business, education, health care and welfare services are especially becoming more readily available and more widely used through broadband services that offer these new and interactive video communication systems. Not only do these broadband videos systems faithfully transmit video data, but are also a means for individual self-expression, and thus hold the promise of applications in education, health care and social services, and even convergence with art forms. They have long been in focus in the domain of developing technologies for their high potential as communications for companies, in families and between individuals, and are widely expected to enable new virtual businesses to emerge in the future.

On the market side, video communications are encouraging global businesses, accelerating the growth of projects operating across dispersed locations, promoting information sharing and speedier decision-making processes within and between companies, and are advantageous as personnel training tools for instructing and passing on particular skills and know-how, as well as popularizing telework and providing benefits as disaster relief measures and so forth.[1] While on the technical side, video communications have become more widespread thanks to technological developments, including high-speed broadband and Voice over IP or VoIP (and multimedia over IP), lower costs (the emergence of simpler videoconferencing systems and software), the dramatic increases in picture quality and functionality (HD, telepresence, etc.) and the adoption of these technologies into a variety of wireless portable terminals (smartphones, tablet PCs and so on), as well as 'unified communications' (described later).

This book describes how the evolution of technical and market innovations in video communications technology have given rise to these collaborative ICT tools (referred to as video communication tools further), which have become an important ICT platform for developing 'knowledge communities' within and between companies, which include their customers.

3.2 The spread of high-quality, low-cost video communication tools

Video communication tools (VCTs) are classified into six main types: room type, desktop type (includes laptops), simple videophone, mobile and smartphone videophone type, web conferencing with PC, and video chat using Skype and social networking services.

Notably, products for room type VCTs have spread all over the world due to technological innovations over the last few decades and lower costs resulting from more competition among system vendors in the marketplace. Room type includes the more traditional videoconferencing systems aimed at global corporate users that appeared in the 1980s, and spread in tandem with the new worldwide media developments of the time, and were mainly adopted by big international companies. Users were limited, because these products were designed with projected increases in the spread of the ISDN network in mind, and were extremely expensive, costing more than $100,000 each to deploy. Room systems were also a driver that pushed the global spread of the ISDN network and expansion in worldwide communications equipment markets after 1990. Around this time, there were many system vendors participating, and products also began to appear in the market from companies other than communication equipment makers (Kodama, 1999a).

It was also during this period after 1990 that the desktop type "desktop teleconferencing systems (DTCs)" for PC appeared as a result of dramatic developments in video encoding technologies. Compared to the room systems, desktop types were cheaper and also allowed collaborative functions such as data sharing, which greatly distinguished them from the earlier room systems and triggered their popularity in small- and medium-sized businesses as well as in large corporations. The last half of the 1990s then saw the arrival of high-performance videophone types targeting the general public. Nowadays, broadband-compatible products are readily available in worldwide markets for around $50, and in recent years, video communications have progressed even further with the inclusion of functions in iPhone and other types of mobile telephone, while in the corporate world, the market for web conferencing with inexpensive and easy-to-use videoconferencing systems continues to grow steadily. On top of that, new ways of communicating in the consumer sphere (C2C) such as Skype and other types of video chat (SNS, etc.) hold great promise as huge market potentials, and with fiber-optic broadband and wireless broadband available with next-generation mobile phones steadily emerging, the market for video communications is rapidly on the rise.

In the video communication market, usage gradually permeated businesses with the rapid spread of ISDN after 1995, but the broadband and IP developments of recent years and the arrival of low-cost systems have further accelerated the spread of video tools. This movement has been characterized by new users and older users deploying IP-based (H.323/SIP) teleconferencing in a shift away from the older ISDN (H.323 systems).

The IP technology and video communication fields not only have shortened product cycles and sweeping improvements in performance and quality delivered terminals that are easier to use, but have also brought prices down and advanced terminal diversity. This is because the use of video communications themselves has brought about favorable cycles in the market. As well as these factors, video communications have become remarkably more convenient thanks to permanent "always on" connection capabilities, dramatic cost reductions with the introduction of flat fee structures, improved quality with faster broadband transmission rates and the advent of global connectivity across high-speed Internet.

The use of video communications has also dramatically increased due to the diversification and specialization of video communications such as meeting room-based conferencing with full videoconferencing systems, web conferencing, PC-based groupware and collaboration, and small-scale conferencing and personal videophone applications, along with video chat services (using webcams), mobile telephones,

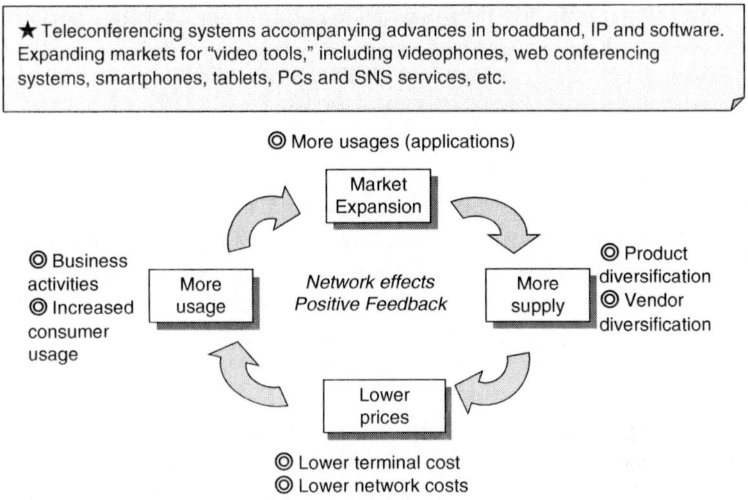

Figure 3.1 The expanding video communication tools market

smartphones and tablet PCs. These broadband and IT developments have triggered positive feedback loops by continuing to bring down the costs of products and communications even further, which has promoted more widespread use and expanded the market (See Figure 3.1).

From the point of view of technological innovation, system vendors had focused on ISDN or dedicated line VCTs enabled by high quality audiovisual encoding and compression with circuit switching technologies. Systems were constantly being developed to meet ever-increasing demands for more reliability and stability, and it was necessary to continually pursue compression technologies to bring about even higher-quality multimedia transmission (video/audio/data) over narrow bandwidths. In addition to the high initial cost of systems, the metered fee structures of communication costs presented huge hurdles that users had to overcome in implementing these systems.

However, innovations in video communication technologies were radically transformed by the IP technology of the Internet. The advent of this disruptive technology (Christensen, 1997) brought with it the arrival of high-speed, high-quality VCTs at lower costs (permanent connections with flat fee structures) compared to the tools that were available through switching circuits based on ISDN. Also, the hardware-based product lineup of the ISDN era diversified into software-based products that became available through the more modern IP technologies and faster, more functional semiconductors.

In particular, the free-to-use client videophone software Skype (eBay, later acquired by Microsoft) uses a format not compliant with the International ITU-T standards, and nevertheless has enjoyed rapid popularization in the C2C sphere. Also "software as a service" (SaaS model) multipoint connection services in which all processing is carried out by software such as WebEx (acquired by Cisco Systems) and other web conferencing systems are becoming prevalent. These low-cost, software-based product architectures (also disruptive technologies) offer greater functionality thanks to the evolution of microprocessor units (MPUs), and have already overtaken hardware-based products (sustainable technology) and brought about the shift from ISDN products to IP products at the global level (roughly between 2000 to 2008) (see Figure 3.2). This means that gradual improvements in the performance of disruptive technology IP-based products have eroded away the market for older videoconferencing systems that used ISDN and dedicated lines—once considered conventionally sustainable technologies.

As mentioned, the emergence of IP-based VCTs have not only brought with them new types of traditional room systems for full videoconferencing, but have also branched out in response to demands from users with different needs to become groupware and collaboration systems,

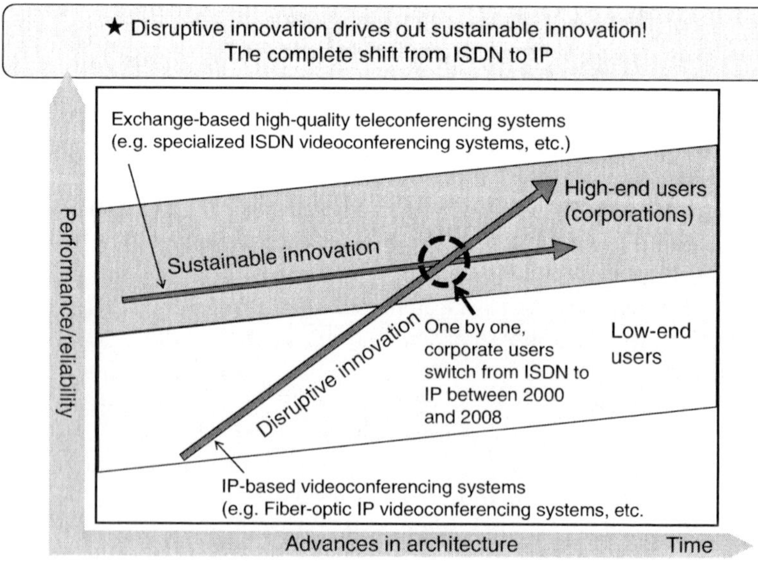

Figure 3.2 IP video communication tools: A disruptive innovation

chat type PC videoconferencing systems, and integrated videophone systems. The lower cost of software-based multipoint control units (MCUs) has also driven deployment in user businesses; however, corporate users who focus on reliability and high quality of the IP network have begun to actively outsource their multipoint connections to ASPs (application service providers).

3.3 The changing product architecture of video communication tools

At the beginning of 1990, manufacturers and developers of VCTs mainly focused on high-quality audiovisual encoding and compression with switching circuit technologies for their ISDN and dedicated line-based products. Systems were constantly being developed to meet ever-increasing demands for more reliability and stability, which meant it was necessary to continually pursue compression technologies to achieve higher-quality multimedia data over narrow bandwidths. New specialized LSI (large-scale integrated circuit) technologies had to be developed as the hardware needed to achieve higher audiovisual quality and encoding and compression capabilities demanded (Step 1 in Figure 3.3). To improve the processing power of these specialized LSIs and lower power consumption, engineers in individual companies pursued higher performance in their own unique hardware architectures. In the 1980s specialized LSIs were created through the adoption of a hardware architecture in which functional blocks were designed with logic circuits designated for audio and video encoding.

However, from the latter half of the 1980s through to the first half of the 1990s, processors consisting of multiples of individual functional blocks and multiple specialized hardware blocks (also known as system LSIs) began to be adopted. This evolution from specialized hardware LSIs to system LSIs in which the CPU (central processing unit) was configured internally meant that the software components began to be added as part of the architecture.

Specialized LSIs were created differently by different makers, and engineers in individual companies honed their core technologies to achieve VCTs with high-quality video and audio. However, the prohibitive high costs of the VCTs at the time meant that the consumer market only really consisted of major corporate users. And in addition to the high cost of these systems, communication costs also followed metered fee structures, which also presented high barriers to users who wanted to implement these systems. Looking at the global market of the time

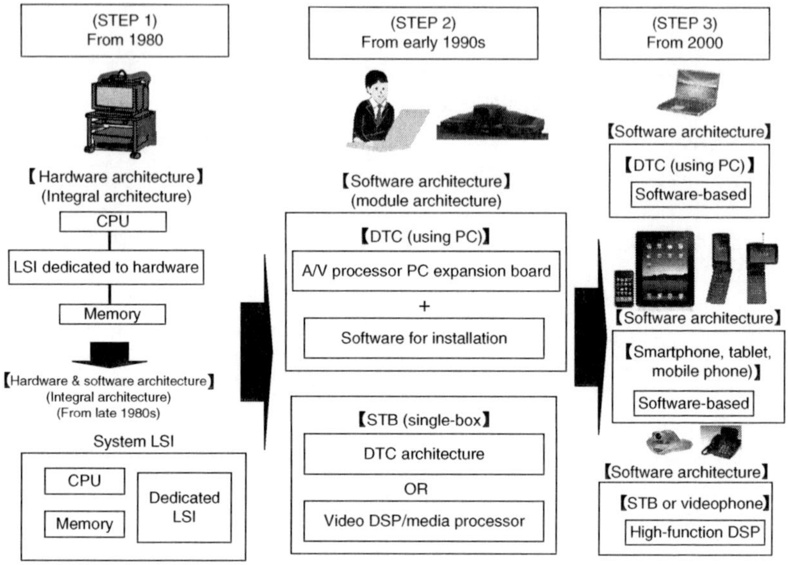

Figure 3.3 Advances in video communication tools architecture

PictureTel in the US (later acquired by Polycom) held 40% of the market share, while Sony in Japan held a 20% share.

After that VCTs began to follow a course toward lower prices (Step 2 in Figure 3.3). Products with new architecture that did not use specialized LSIs began to emerge, notably from companies in the US. This shift was typified by PictureTel's 1992 commercialization of a desktop conferencing product with video functions (DTC) running on PC (Windows 3.1). Then Intel released its "ProShare" DTC product, and then in 1995, NTT in Japan released a DTC product called "Phoenix." With the appearance of these new products, companies in Japan and all around the world began to adopt DTC systems, including small- and medium-sized companies and even individuals, in contrast to the big-business-only market of the past.

As well as audiovisual exchange, DTC systems also enabled data sharing on PC (via the T.120 international standard for communications between application software such as PowerPoint, Word, Excel and so forth). Also, special boards with general-purpose processors such as digital signal processors (DSPs) could now be inserted into the expansion slots in computers, and audiovisual data transmission was carried out through the PCI bus in the computer (enabling high-speed data transmission).

In Step 2, American manufacturers stopped using the specialized LSIs of Step 1, and began creating computers with low-cost, general-purpose processors and expansion ports, and created inexpensive VCTs by developing software drivers that could be used with the Windows 95 operating system. These manufacturers also managed to create system architecture that enabled much simpler settings and control of parameters for PC expansion boards via a graphical user interface (GUI). What's more, these universally compatible expansion boards and bundled software could be used with computers from any manufacturer, which was a revolutionary technology at the time.

PictureTel also adopted architecture similar to the PC architecture and developed non-PC integrated specialist VCTs, and released their set-top box (STB) product into the market—a much cheaper product than the older specialized LSI devices.

The development of these software architecture-based DTC and STB products is also an achievement of modular innovation. With modularization, there is lower interdependence between structural elements, and the individual interfaces are well defined. Modular innovation achieved through modular architecture is important because it gives a company a flexible and strategic advantage in upgrading its products and diversifying its lineup (Sanchez, 1996; Worren, Moore and Cardona, 2002).[2]

In a departure from highly structurally interdependent hardware-based VCTs developed through integral architecture using specialized LSI technologies described in Step 1, DTC and STB products were created through software running on general-purpose processors (CPUs and DSPs). Moreover, data-sharing functions could be added to DTCs as software modules, which meant that these software-based DTC and STB products enabled product upgrades without having to change hardware.

In this way, product architecture shifted away from the traditional hardware-based products to software module architecture using general-purpose processors. If we focus on the videoconferencing system as audiovisual signal processing and communications processing functions, although there were no big changes to architecture in Step 1 and Step 2 (changes to the couplings between structural elements), the core concept behind the structural elements of architecture had changed dramatically, meaning DTCs and STBs can also be called modular innovation (Henderson and Clark, 1990). This is why PictureTel and Sony downsized their high-cost specialized system operations and dominated the global market in one fell swoop with their low-cost DTCs and STBs.

With the exception of Sony, Japanese VCT manufacturers at the time had to back out of the market. One reason why Japanese manufacturers failed is because they were slow in responding to the new modular innovation technologies. In 1995, ISDN was rapidly spreading throughout Japan, and Japanese manufacturers were pursuing technologies oriented toward high-quality video transmission over the narrowband ISDN network. Japanese makers were involved in developing highly functional VCTs by focusing on their expertise in hardware and specialized LSIs, and system LSIs software elements, while on the market side, Japanese manufacturers ran down this particular track because the popularity of VCTs was not as great as in the West, and was limited to deployment in large corporations which meant that good video quality would mean sales even at a high price, since Japanese corporate users are naturally fussy about video quality.

In contrast to Japan, ICT was quickly becoming profuse throughout the West, and the use of VCTs was rapidly increasing year by year. In these Western markets, the chorus of demand from corporations for low-cost VCTs with added PC-based data-sharing applications became louder and louder. Western corporations' needs focused on audio- and data-sharing capabilities rather than a need for high video quality. Therefore in pursuit of low-cost VCTs, American teleconferencing vendors reviewed the capabilities demanded of image compression technologies and adopted new modularized, software-based architecture in which general-purpose parts are used. These companies also made efforts to outsource hardware assemblies of boards, among others, to lower production costs even further. With the exception of global giant Sony, this second point was something Japanese makers hardly did at all.

One important thing corporations focused on in deciding whether to deploy a teleconferencing system, was whether companies in overseas locations or international sales and manufacturing partners had deployed their own teleconferencing systems. This is one reason why American vendors such as PictureTel and Polycom achieved high international sales and market superiority. On the other hand, Sony has had good brand penetration for its VCTs in the global market from the outset, and compared to American manufacturers who have responded to new architecture, even though they are a little bit behind in this respect, Sony currently holds the number two position in the Japanese market behind Polycom. Internationally, Sony holds a 13% share of the world market and is in the third position behind Polycom and Tandberg of Finland, and is currently forging ahead with the Step 3 phase toward the broadband era (see Figure 3.3).

As mentioned, due to the improvements in performance of PC CPUs and the arrival of disruptive IP technology, VCTs much cheaper than the older style videoconferencing systems had begun to appear. Because improvements to CPU performance follow Moore's Law, real-time encoding of both audio and video has become possible without the need for any kind of specialized processors, and just by simply picking up a commercially available camera and audiovisual processing software, anybody can videoconference using their existing PC and the CPU therein (Skype and SNS video chat services are categories that apply this technology).

Right now, global vendors are in fierce competition with each other to develop and sell products that adopt this software-based architecture. Software-based products have the disadvantage of being slightly lower in audiovisual quality compared to the specialized processor types described in Step 2, and are disadvantaged in that they are limited to use on PC. Also, with software-based products that follow this low-cost route, manufacturers must pursue economies of scale and scope or they won't be able to make much of a profit.

On the other hand, high-functionality, low-cost DSP systems are also spreading, and low-cost STB-type videoconferencing and videophone systems that use these technologies are also becoming more popular, and charging ahead as the new VCTs are smartphones, tablet PCs and next-generation mobile phones that use general-purpose hardware (see Figure 3.3). Video communications are supplied as standard functions with these products, and are mostly achieved through software. To put it bluntly, these wirelessly connected, broadband IP devices make it possible to communicate in high-quality video with anybody, anywhere, anytime, and can eliminate the need for a specialized teleconferencing system, STB or videophone.

In the few decades between Step 1 and Step 3, the cost of VCTs has come down dramatically. Alterations to core technology and architecture accelerated the manufacture of lower-cost, more compact products while prompting more intense competition. Also, the MCUs that enabled people in a range of locations to hold meetings were rapidly being replaced by even lower-cost software architecture-based products that used high-performance servers and PC. These newer, low-cost software-based MCUs encouraged use within corporations, although other corporate users who focus on the greater levels of reliability and quality with IP networks have been actively pursing outsourcing for their multipoint connections with ASPs.

The dramatic advance of core technologies such as semiconductors and broadband brought with it changes to core components and technological architecture which determined the competitiveness of products (Henderson and Clark, 1990). Many Japanese companies were unable to quickly adapt to these changes, and withdrew from product development and sales. Currently, there are some Japanese corporations who are pouring effort into Step 3-type product development and sales of software architecture PC-based DTC products, smartphone, tablet and mobile telephone products, and even MCU products. Even though it is wise to invest business resources in the development of software products that are designed to run on generic hardware, the fact that there is fierce competition between a large number of players involved in price wars makes it difficult to decide how to respond, and although Skype and SNS services need not necessarily be compatible with every single manufacturer's products, vendors cannot ignore the existence of these free-to-use services.

Even Polycom and Sony who are proud of their share of the integrated specialized device market will not be able to avoid being affected by software architecture-based products that run on general-purpose hardware (smartphones, tablet PCs, etc.). These software architecture-based products using even more advanced processors are bound to remain competitive well into the broadband era.

Markets should also be focusing on the wireless 3.9G, 4G, wireless LAN and WiMAX technologies of the future. As these wireless networks deliver even more bandwidth and terminal performance increases while prices continue to fall, the quality of wireless VCTs will become indistinguishable from fiber-optic communications systems, and systems will be configured to converge fixed-line and mobile video communications ("visual FMC," coined by the author, meaning visual Fixed and Mobile Convergence) that have the potential to give rise to new product architectures and business models.

Another type of new architecture that has emerged is known as unified communications (UC). Unified communications not only provide the flexibility to link up different communications methods but also enable seamless communication between IP telephone, PC, mobile phone, smartphone and tablet computer devices. Linking these multiple communication methods will enable companies to enjoy the benefits of more efficient business and improved productivity. Currently, companies are using unified communications for cloud computing as strategic tools to achieve better business efficiency and a greater level of staff creativity.

In addition to the old telephone and fax devices, modern corporations and organizations use an array of communications methods, including

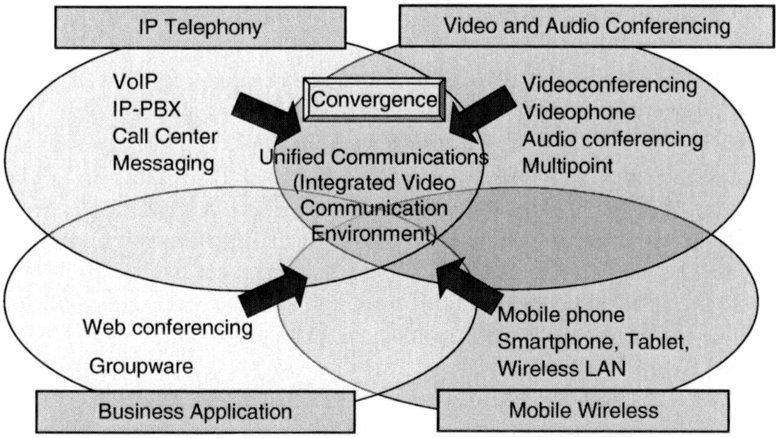

Figure 3.4 Unified communications

e-mail, instant messaging, and video and web conferencing. Ordinarily these communication methods have been applied as necessary, and are achieved through separate devices/terminals/applications and so forth. In contrast, UC offers flexible and interactive communications by bringing together these different communication methods and devices and integrating them in the IP network (see Figure 3.4).

These days many companies have introduced a range of groupware applications, ERP tools, etc. to encourage communications and information sharing between organizations and drive best practice. However, as described in Chapter 2, a problem can also surface—companies deploying these tools to upgrade organizational culture are not always able to improve internal and external communications or speed up decision-making processes by the sole implementation e-mail and groupware. So, these cloud-based, highly practical unified communications ICT tools can to lead to business revolutions in companies by enabling people to overcome the sense of being cloistered and closed off due to the fact that e-mail and groupware do not sufficiently convey an individual's thoughts and intentions. In other words, these video tools enable more fulfilling discussion and prompt decision-making.

Captured from the view point of the knowledge-creation process that is central to business innovation activities in companies, companies have been able to dramatically increase capabilities by linking and adding efficiencies to explicit knowledge (e.g. knowledge in existing documentation) with groupware, application sharing and databases.

On the other hand, the integration of video, voice and text data in unified communications has the hidden potential to spark ideas, thoughts, perceptions and feelings as tacit knowledge (knowledge that is not easy to put into words such as human beliefs and thoughts, perceptions and images, etc.) through dialogue and collaboration in the world of converged cyberspace and real space. Therefore, UC of the cloud era have the potential to enable collection, analysis and linking up of the vast array of information and knowledge unevenly distributed throughout the world, and bring into being an era of "creativity" in which new knowledge and values emerge (i.e. the emergence of rich tacit knowledge, or the conversion of tacit knowledge into explicit knowledge).

That being said, hardly any research findings into the relationships between UC and people and organizations have been published either in Japan or internationally. This is probably because UC are cutting-edge ICT tools, and it isn't easy for social science researchers who are external to corporations to access data about these corporate strategically positioned support tools (because it involves accumulated corporate know-how). Therefore, in the broadband and ubiquitous era of the future, research into UC, with its high potential to play a leading role in the business innovation processes of "knowledge and creativity," will be of great significance as it moves to clarify the practical implications for business and expand and develop this social science research area. One of the purposes of this book is to present how UC of the cloud era is an encouraging platform that can invigorate societies and economies through networked circulation of knowledge and know-how that results in new knowledge and value.

3.4 The diverse usages of video communication tools

Looking at the ways VCTs are used, one can see that particularly in recent years, the use of video terminals implemented to raise productivity and creativity in corporate global business by encouraging collaboration among disbursed project teams and the like has been remarkable. One company, Japanese software developer Sky, regularly uses videoconferencing to connect together the many dispersed bases of its project team. Holding meetings in which participants can see each other's faces enables smooth discussions between people in separated locations, because they are able to engage in more nuanced communication than telephone-only contact. This company also has communication systems in which regular communications are performed by teleconferencing

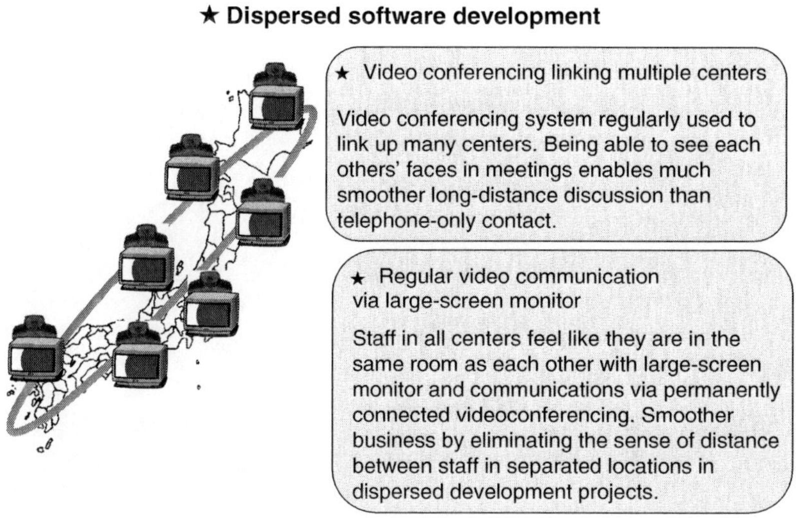

Figure 3.5 Sharing a *Ba* in real time
Source: See http://www.skygroup.jp/software/organization/

using large-sized monitors, which enable staff in its various centers to talk with each other as if they were all in the same room. Characteristically, these systems eliminate the sense of distance between people involved in dispersed development projects and enable smoother execution of business. Another important feature of VCTs is their ability to facilitate a *Ba* that can be shared in real time (see Figure 3.5).

As well as that, these tools are also spurning the spread of educational applications for staff and personnel training, encouraging telework, and are bringing forth a range of virtual businesses that use video communications to provide services such as e-learning, e-health care and sign language support in the education, health care and welfare fields. For example, American hospital and nursing facilities have introduced VCTs between nurse stations and hospital rooms that enable nurses to monitor and communicate with people in hospital rooms (see Figure 3.6), while in Taiwan, Chunghwa Telecom commenced multimedia services in 2011 with a view to replace existing office and domestic telephones with next-generation communications devices. These new multimedia services provide video and voice telephone, whether in major global cities, public transport timetable, hospital booking, lottery purchasing, calendar, SMS, taxi booking, medical care, video recording, clock and music clip replay functions, and can potentially provide domestic

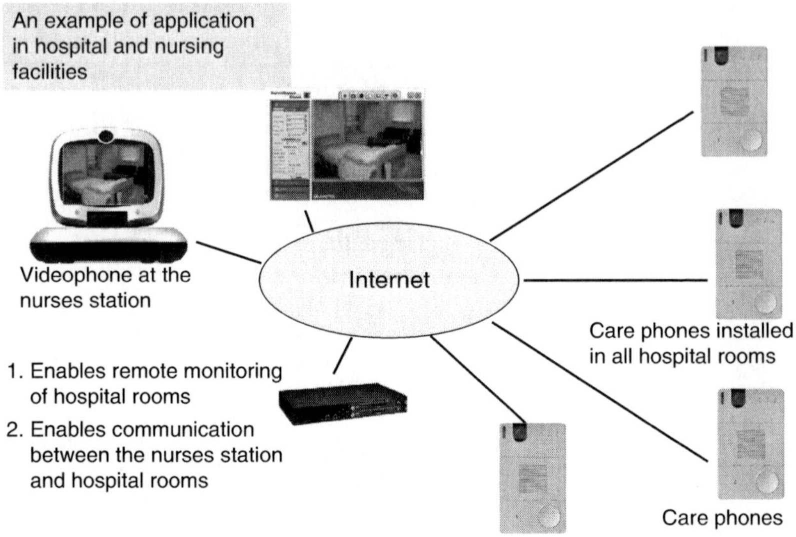

Figure 3.6 An American example: A care phone system
Source: Based on information published by Leadtek (Taiwan), http://www.leadtek.com

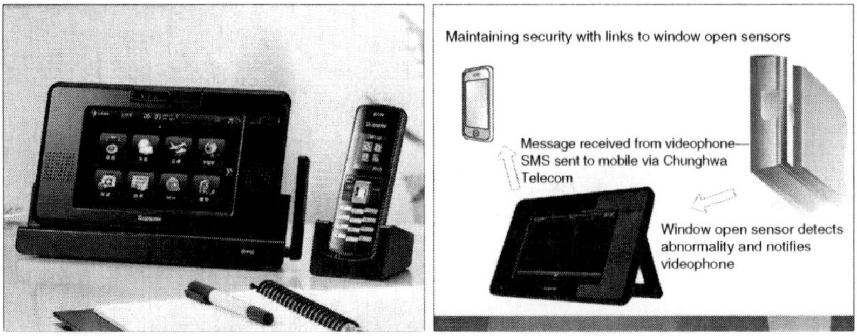

Figure 3.7 Applications from Chunghwa Telecom (Taiwan)
Source: Based on information published by Leadtek (Taiwan), http://www.leadtek.com

video surveillance applications through linkages to sensors that check whether windows are open or shut (see Figure 3.7).

Riding on the third-generation broadband and mobile telephone developments in Europe, a range of mainly French-centered broadband video services are developing through partnerships between switched server gateway vendors such as France Telecom, Alcatel, Siemens, Lucent and Radvision (Israel); and IP-based videophone company Leadtek (Taiwan) and others; while in Italy a new entrant, fixed-line operator Fastweb, is offering VoIP and video communication services through its triple-play services (video on demand, VoIP and high-speed Internet). Bredbandsbolaget of Sweden also has been pioneering demands for services to high-density housing complexes, expanding their corporate user market and offering triple-play services that include video and VoIP.

As already mentioned, the market VCTs triggered by the broadband network (fixed and mobile) is bound to become even more challenging in the future.

3.5 Adapting organizational systems (technologies) for video communication tools

Figure 3.8 classifies ways VCTs can be used for communications in all forms of business (B2B, B2C, C2C). As usage forms become more and more clear, VCTs usage will move away from simpler forms and become more and more diversified. Apart from human–human interactions such as education, training and consultation, these tools can also be used for video transmission such as surveillance and hook-ups that link people with things (products and equipment). This means that ubiquitous business involving video networking between non-human things is likely to become even more prevalent in the future.

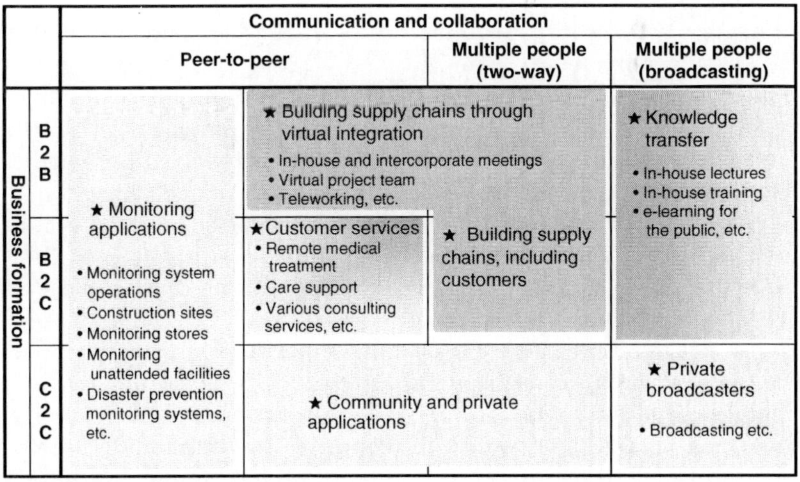

Figure 3.8 Application domains for video communication tools
Source: Compiled from interviews.

These are the reasons why applications for diverse video communication uses arise:

- The first reason is the creation and embedding of business applications through organizational learning mainly by end users themselves (corporate and various organizations such as communities). Then, results of this user learning are passed as feedback to the system vendors and ASP (SaaS) services, which in turn trigger new practice in those companies.
- The second reason results from the formation of knowledge communities and mutual learning processes through coordination and collaboration between system vendors, ASP (SaaS) companies and end users.

Thinking about this from the Agency perspective (e.g. Barley, 1986; Robey and Sahay, 1996; Orlikowski, 2000; Orlikowski and Barley, 2001), actors in different companies in different businesses using the same VCTs have different strategic and organizational contexts, which means that they use tools differently, and the resultant structures (business routines and systems that emerge as the results of actors' routines in using VCT and ICT tool) enacted are also different (e.g. Orlikowski, 2000). Therefore, implementing the same type of VCTs results in structural changes enacted in different organizational settings (Barley, 1986). In short, the effects (structures) of VCTs' usage that result from actors thinking and behaviors are diversified, as are the actors themselves (the organizations involved).

Even for tools with the same technical functions, the video communication usages described in Figure 3.9 illustrate the various usages for the business category or industry that a company is involved in (whether it be education, health care, welfare, consultation, surveillance, broadcasting, etc.) and the actors' intentions and strategic objectives that in turn also affect ICT habits and business forms.

Also, as described in Figure 3.8, VCTs do not only have a range of corporate uses for communicating between businesses (B2B), but also enable B2C e-businesses (e.g. e-learning, e-health care), and even new C2C usages among consumers. System vendors need to improve and upgrade the technical functions of VCTs to create new VCTs in response to market circumstances and user demands. In addition, ASP (SaaS) work to develop new network businesses and operational technologies that they offer to corporate users, and corporate users in various

	All industries Shared	Manufacturing	Distribution	Transport and travel	Services	Broadcasting	Finance	Medical care and welfare	Education	Security	Construction and real estate
Meeting	• In-house meetings • Management meetings • In-house training	• Design meetings • Interworking • Trial product training	• Shared knowledge of trial product (convenience stores, etc.)						• School exchanges		
Education Training Guidance		• Technical guidance • Engineering support	• Product explanation • Display guidance (arrangement) • Sales supervisor guidance	• Health check prior to starting work	• Sales methods and service guidance	• Training	• Guidance and work support from HQ to branch offices	• Medical training • Operation guidance	• Remote lessons	• Training	• Construction site monitoring work
Monitoring		• Monitoring system operation	• Store monitoring • Unmanned facility (store) monitoring	• Link with crime-prevention monitoring system	• Store monitoring (eating establishments such as taverns and revolving sushi)	• Broadcast equipment (unmanned) monitoring	• Monitoring of ATMs, etc.	• Patients, hospitals and patient's homes	• Link with crime-prevention monitoring system	• Link with crime-prevention monitoring system	• Construction site monitoring work
Discussion		• Support service	• Consulting/ support service	• Consulting/ support service	• Consulting/ support service		• Financial negotiations (retail)	• At-home medical care • Health discussion • Link with care support system	• Consulting/ support service	• Consulting/ support service	• Remote operation of model rooms
Relay			• Perishable goods auction (flowers, food, etc.) from market to retailers • Pet shops		• Wedding location hook-up	• Intermediary between TV program and actors	• Seminar distribution	• Academic meeting relay	• Seminar distribution		• Display distribution
Other		• Confirming purchases (manufacturing to distribution)	• Direct sales	• Health check	• Worship (religious organizations)	• Video server connection provides support for sportspeople, etc.	• Customer consulting				• Establishing apartments and newly built homes

Figure 3.9 Usage structure of video communication tools
Source: Compiled from interviews.

business categories and industries create different usages and business models. In other words, citing the structuration theory (Giddens, 1984) and agency theory (e.g. Emirbayer and Mische, 1998; Jones, 1999), even though confined to physical structures such as a communications network and VCTs, the human agency serves to effect mutual transformation through the interactions of individual human will and action with VCTs (the actual physical functions and usage methods of the VCTs, and human beings themselves), and bring about new structures (the emergence of new products or services, or new usage forms, business routines and business models and so forth using these).

It is the development and use of VCTs and network services through the recursive practices of actors, especially their thinking and behaviors, that transform habitual routines and give rise to structures as new social systems (Orlikowski, 2000), and then, as illustrated in Figures 3.8 and 3.9, a diverse range of usages is created by users.

In this interaction between "practice" and "structure," the formation of "knowledge communities" (communities of practice and innovation communities) is an important factor in promoting mutual coordination and collaboration between companies (system vendors and ASP, SaaS companies) and end users (other companies or consumers). And these collaboration and coordination factors deliver the awareness, power, motivation and ICT capabilities to all actors to effect transformation and innovation, whether they be working in companies or operating as end users.

As actors aim for co-creation and co-evolution for new business models, the resulting organizational learning through user feedback, and boundaries innovation that crosses over different industries and technologies mentioned in Chapter 1 brings about new VCTs and network service developments, which in turn users then use. This enables routine transformation and new business transformations (the creation of new structures) to emerge (or to be created) (see Figure 3.10). The key to these processes (organizational learning and boundaries innovation) is the formation of "knowledge communities."

New business model co-creation and co-evolution is enabled through the formation of knowledge communities by organizational learning with coordination and collaboration between companies and end users (Robey, Boudreau and Rose, 2000), and built through boundary innovation. The mechanism of this establishment process, when viewed from the human agency perspective can be explained by Giddens' (1984) structuration theory (Orlikowski, 1992; Orlikowski and Robey, 1991; DeSanctice and Poole, 1994) and actor network theory (Walsham, 1997; Jones, 1999),

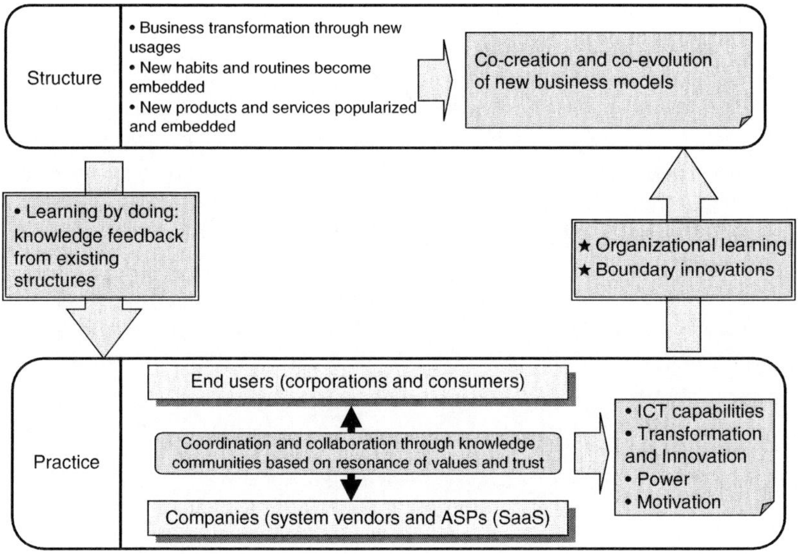

Figure 3.10 Recursive interplay of structure and practice through video communication tools

and can be basically thought of as inherent in the execution of organizational learning and boundary innovations that arise through the interactions of human agencies and institutions in the medium of ICT.

3.6 New virtual businesses

Communication businesses operating through broadband and wireless provide new and interactive knowledge to their customers by offering services that integrate collaborative tools with the contents and networks achieved by boundary innovation in business formations between different business categories. As mentioned earlier, the recursive interplay process between structure and practice enabled by forming knowledge communities with the coordination and collaboration between businesses and end users is of importance. Coordination and collaboration through the formation of knowledge communities between different types of businesses create new businesses, pioneers new markets and customer bases, and, moreover, serve to create new knowledge communities around those customer bases, which results in the development of new virtual businesses—a phenomenon observed in the education, health care and welfare fields.

In the ICT field, communications carriers and ICT vendors all over the world are under pressure to establish increasing returns business models that focus on video with broadband and wireless Internet; and (to reiterate) the formation of various knowledge communities between companies and organizations from different fields of expertise and business categories (communities of practice and innovation communities) raises the potential to create new business for cyber companies by fusing ICT collaborative tools, network, contents and a whole range of applications.

Knowledge communities formed between different companies and organizations can pioneer and expand markets—and even form new ones—and have the potential to bring increasing business returns to all sides of partnerships.

4
Collaborative ICT Tools and Organizational Development

4.1 Video communications as strategic business tools

Video communications through such means as PCs, smartphones, mobile videophones and tablet PC underpin the potential to create new work styles, lifestyles and daily habits that together make up the new "imaging culture." Thanks to the expansion of broadband and emerging ubiquity, means of communication ranging from voice and data to still images and video are rapidly developing in conjunction with the diversification of person-to-person communications and collaboration. This chapter takes a systematic look at the relationship between video communication tools (VCTs) and organizational transformation over the past ten years, and delivers new insights into the impact of VCTs on corporate ICT and knowledge-creation strategies in this broadband and ubiquitous era.

As mentioned in Chapter 2, a great number of corporations are currently incorporating all kinds of groupware, ERP tools, weblogs and web-based tools to encourage communication and information sharing across and between organizations to promote best practice and knowledge management. But among the companies that are already using these tools to reform and innovate corporate culture, the failure of e-mail and groupware to adequately strengthen communication inside and outside the organization and accelerate the decision-making process has already been brought to the fore.[1] In this regard, VCTs can be considered the ultimate practical ICT tool to lead a company down the road to transformation and resolve the "closed-off" feeling that results from the inadequacy of e-mail or groupware to satisfactorily convey the will and sentiment of individuals, because VCTs enable richer discussions and more efficient decision-making.

Historically in the world of communications, the video medium was generally high priced, often poor quality and difficult to use, and designed for specialized corporate applications. Recently, however, the remarkable development of broadband and mobile multimedia communications infrastructure[2] and video and voice digital encoding technologies have led to the rapid emergence of highly functional, low-cost, compact and user-friendly VCTs, including video and web conferencing, smartphones, mobile videophone, video chat services and IP multimedia phones. Furthermore, the unified communications that integrate these functions have resulted in more diverse possibilities with video communications that are suited to both business and consumer use. In addition to the technological drivers, market drivers including applications as collaboration tools for advancing global business, strategic outsourcing and off-shoring and business models involving dispersed product development project teams have also become key factors in accelerating penetration and market expansion. There are soaring demands for multimedia communications not only from big businesses but also from small office/home office (SOHO) businesses, education, health care, welfare and so forth.

VCTs enable flexibility with different means of communication (voice, text and video, in real and non-real time), and seamless communications between different terminals, including IP phones, PCs, dedicated video terminals, smartphones and mobile phones. Connecting these multiple means of communication benefits companies by boosting business efficiency and production, and encourages creativity (including creating new ideas). Thus, VCTs are becoming recognized as strategic ICT solutions that hone the competitive edge.[3] The world's most advanced companies today are proactively applying these tools in B2B and B2C settings as described in Chapter 3.

This chapter illustrates how VCTs become enablers that transcend space and time to promote the creation of new business "knowledge," and delivers new findings and managerial implications vis-à-vis practitioners and academics specializing in business and management, based on survey analysis of usage structures in a range of business fields (manufacturing, IT, finance, retail, education, medical treatment and welfare, etc.) and in public institutions in Japan, the US and Europe. The chapter also presents new insights drawn from a decade of field research (including participant observation, ethnography, and interviews) (see Appendix: Research Methodology).

4.2 ICT and corporate innovation

Broadband networks now feature bandwidths that have enabled "always-on" connections to become commonplace, and have dramatically improved user convenience. Operational response speeds have spectacularly improved, download times have become remarkably shorter, and it has become inexpensive to be online all the time, which have made bidirectional communications incorporating video such as video mail, video chat, video blogs (vlogs), videophones, videoconferencing and video distribution much more accessible. These ICT broadband VCTs have made extraordinary advances in the last few years, which has not only improved the efficiency of business, but has also radically transformed existing supply chains.

Cisco Systems CEO Mr. John Chambers reflected on these developments. By enabling staff in Cisco's bases all over the world to work together in a virtual environment, management of large-scale projects at Cisco Systems has moved away from a top-down managerial style to a much more cooperative teamwork approach. Cisco has held about 10,000 teleconferencing sessions since deploying its videoconferencing systems. Illustrating the efficiency of these systems, when Cisco Systems acquired WebEx (a web conferencing development and sales company) for $3.2 billion, it took a mere eight days from the beginning of negotiations, which were all carried out by videoconferencing, to the signing of contracts.

As already mentioned, as a large proportion of meetings with global customers are also carried out via videoconferencing, these ICT technologies are radically transforming business supply chains through online collaboration that includes customers.

There is also great potential for new content and usage forms such as music distribution, games, remote health care and e-learning to become available with products like iPod, iPhone and iPad. As described in Figure 4.1, a market is emerging in which consumers can access not only entertainment, but also range of online services such as health care and consultancies, while in the business domain the advance of ICT has greatly contributed to supply chain and business process efficiencies and the creation of new businesses across a wide range of industries and business categories (see Figure 4.2).[4]

The diverse communication means brought about by large-capacity, high-speed, high-performance broadband technologies and large database information systems combined with mobile phones, smartphones and Web 2.0 technologies is increasing business opportunities and accelerating transformation, and having a huge impact on business activities and individual lifestyles to become a foundation of socio-economic activity. ICT brings competitiveness by enabling companies to make their business activities run more smoothly and expand their

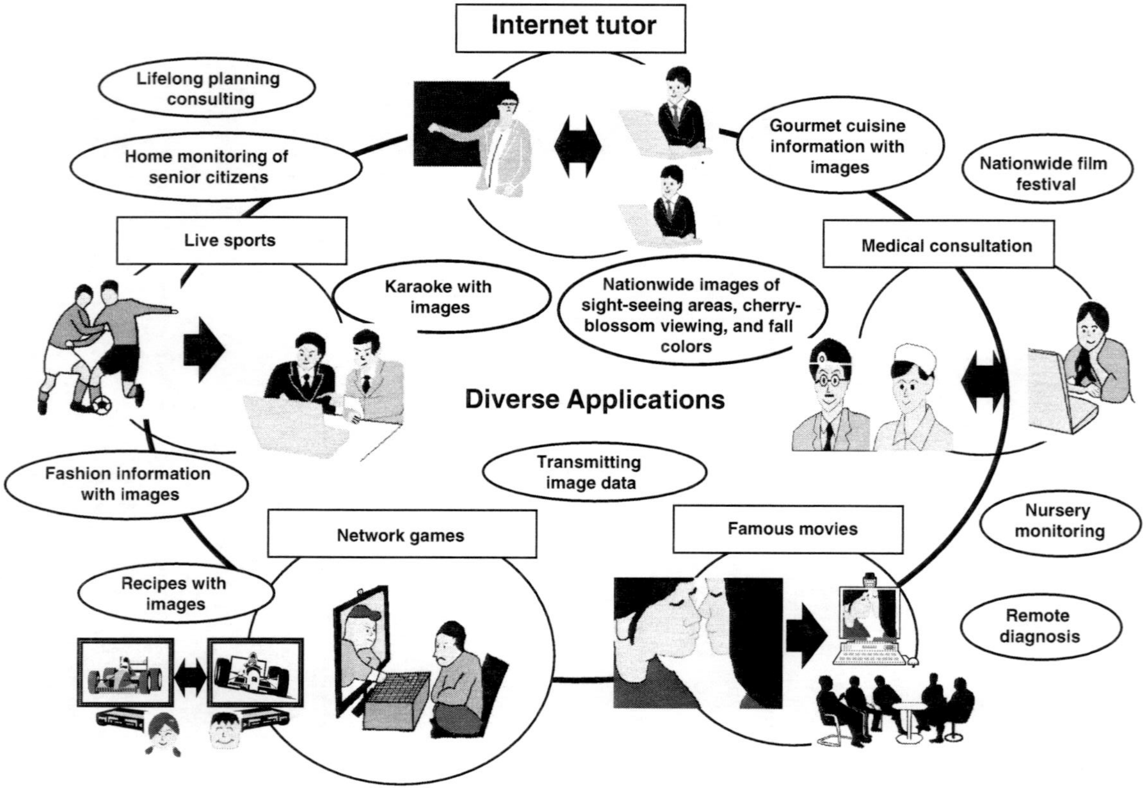

Figure 4.1 Areas of use in the consumer market

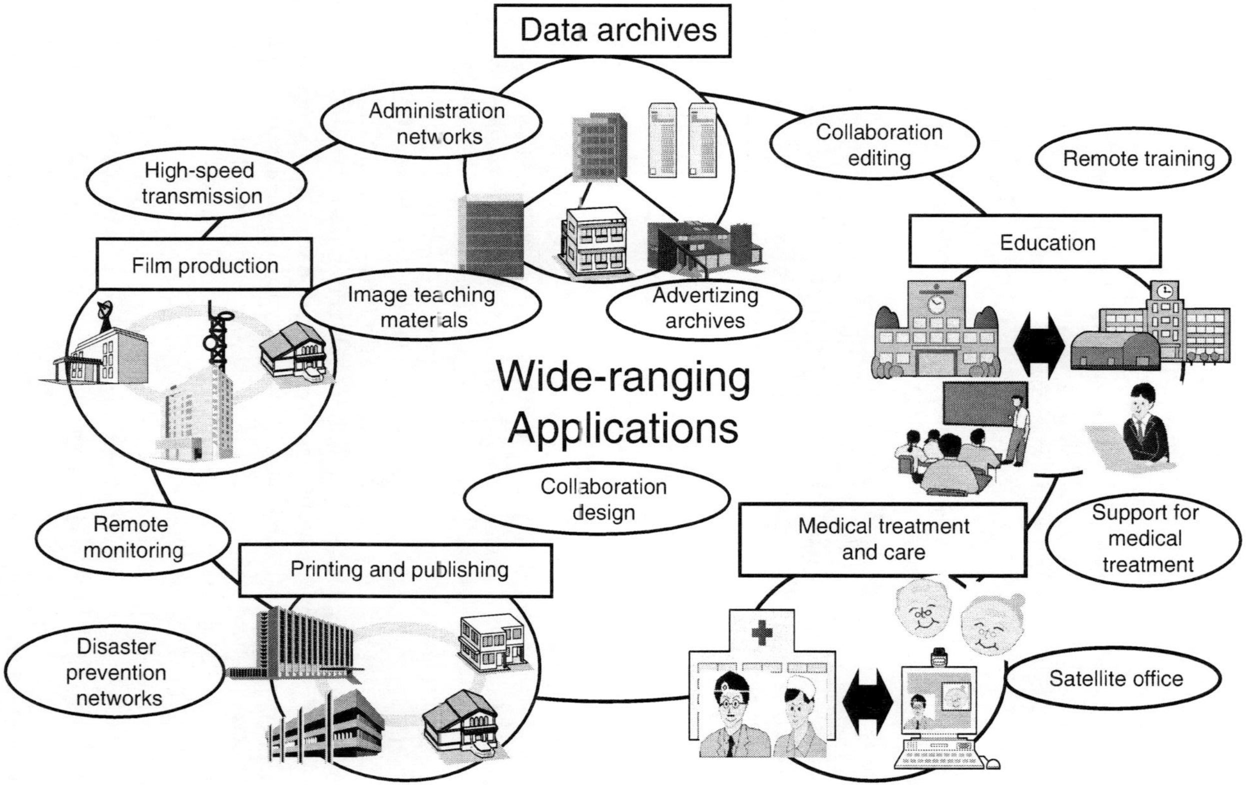

Figure 4.2 Areas of use in the corporate market

global operations, and can offer an environmental solution by encouraging work-at-home lifestyles that reduce the amount that people have to physically commute.[5]

As stated at the beginning of Chapter 1, the implementation of ICT as corporate strategy to give rise to innovation and new business models is becoming an increasingly important consideration for companies. The author has identified fixed frameworks for business models of success (or failure) from 20 years' experience in the ICT industry and field research in the area of management studies. The clarification of these frameworks is the major motivation for involvement in these studies. These are key topics that will both contribute to scientific study and help companies deploying ICT to acquire a competitive edge.

Figure 4.3 describes the results of a survey of Asian and Western companies (500 companies in ICT, manufacturing, finance, distribution, broadcasting, etc.) carried out through questionnaires and hearings regarding corporate resources, competencies and ICT. The companies surveyed expressed that it was important to implement ICT to encourage the sharing and use of information, to speed up decision-making processes, make business processes more efficient, increase productivity and raise the level of efficiency and precision in development. All of these aspects—objectives of raising business productivity and increasing efficiency through the use of ICT—have been identified by much of the existing research (e.g. Brynjolfsson and Hitt, 1995, 1998). However, many of these companies pointed out that the implementation of staff training programs to improve ICT capabilities, rethinking business processes, organizational structures and decision-making processes were more important than the physical deployment of ICT systems themselves.

In other words, to make an investment in an intangible asset succeed, simply spending money on new technology itself does not transform employees' minds. This means that decisive action needs to be taken to transform the corporate landscape in conjunction with the introduction of ICT. What is most important is to build mutually complementary relationships incorporating ICT into a company's strategic and organizational contexts. Both top-down and bottom-up approaches are essential to achieve this. In principle, the top-down approach can transform the corporate landscape. For example, some companies introduced collaborative tools such as videoconferencing systems and prohibited business conference trips. This had the major effect of speeding up decision-making while cutting transport costs. What was significant in these cases was that management, especially the CEO, broadened the opportunities to apply ICT within the company. This was done to create a workplace

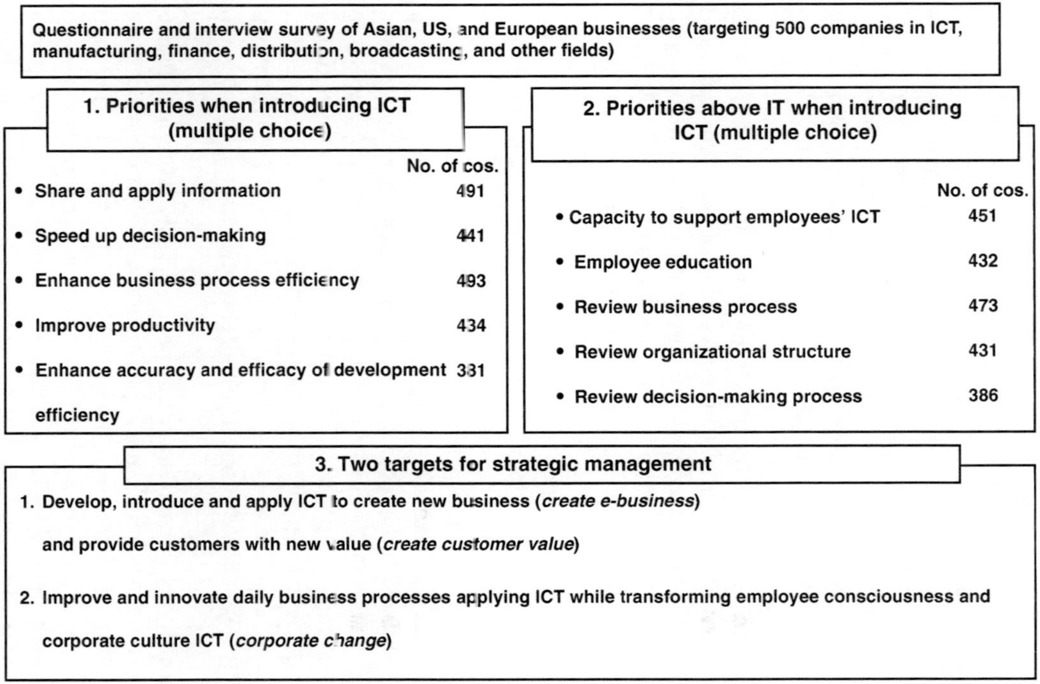

Figure 4.3 ICT and resources/capabilities

Note: The demand potential for mobile phones has hitherto been put at around 360 million, but is now projected to rise by an additional 210 million due to the addition of such factors as information appliances and packages to total 570 million.

Source: Survey results (2004 to 2010).

atmosphere in which work could be carried out with or without technical skills in ICT, especially through the use of collaboration tools, and company staff could be instructed through ICT activity. The banning of business trips alone would have ended with an adverse reaction from employees, but by transforming the corporate landscape through fostering ICT activity at the same time, the sense among employees that they had a fight on their hands was alleviated. In other words, by speeding up decision-making while cutting transport costs, they managed to kill two birds with one stone.

In contrast to those top-down decisions, management also hoped that ICT would enable staff in each workplace to build human networks across organizational boundaries from the bottom-up, because the sharing of common aims and values in this way leads to the formation of dynamic human networks within the company, which enhances the creativity needed to bring about new products and technologies, and thus helps to give the company a competitive edge. There is also existing research that illustrates the intrinsic relationship between ICT and productivity in companies that invest in the intangible assets of organizational and business processes, human resources and so forth upon their deployment of ICT (e.g. Brynjolfsson, 2000).

In their systematic research of ICT and productivity, Brynjolfsson and Hitt (1995, 1998) identified the necessity of transforming business processes with supplementary investments into intangible assets as organizational resources, in order to improve productivity with ICT. They suggested that this interlocking of ICT investments with investments in these human and organizational intangible assets has the potential to impact on a company's productivity. This research clearly showed that it is the investment in these intangible assets that determines whether a company will improve its productivity or not, even if similar companies invest the same amount on the ICT technology itself (Brynjolfsson, 2000).

The relationship between ICT and business processes can be interpreted as follows: Generally, individual companies in the same industry or same business category have different strategic contexts (strategy formulation and implementation) and different organizational contexts (business and decision-making processes, organizational structure, political power structures within the company, and corporate culture, etc.). Therefore, implementing ICT in individual companies to supplement inherent corporate strategy and organizational contexts can deliver a company a distinguished and difficult-to-copy organizational capability, and thus raise the potential to sustain a competitive edge (e.g. Clemons, 1991a,

1991b; Clemons and Row, 1991; Weill and Broadbent, 1998; Weill and Ross, 2004). In other words, as a strategic tool for business operations, introducing ICT tools internally into a company and encouraging synergies between strategic contexts and ICT tools can produce organizational capabilities that set it apart and enable it to maintain its competitiveness. These organizational capabilities have also been described in Chapter 1 as "ICT capabilities."

The "digital organizations" that Brynjolfsson (2000) describes can also be interpreted as organizations that are able to produce ICT capabilities through mutual and complementary ICT, strategic and organizational contexts. In digital organizations, business processes are transformed, decision-making is dispersed, and information sharing and communication are invigorated by ICT. These organizations focus on organizational and personnel education strategies by investing in staff training, recruiting the most skilled people available and sharing the objectives of performance principles in their distilled business domains.

From surveying these companies regarding ICT development, deployment and use, the author has identified the following two critical core components of strategic management (two strategic objectives) (see Figure 4.3).

The first of these is the creation of new business models (establishing e-businesses), which enable ICT-related product planning and development, and the creation of new customer value through the use of ICT. Of the companies surveyed, 75 ICT vendors and distribution companies, including communications carriers, commented that being able to offer new products and services to their end-user customers (corporate and consumer) was a crucial factor in reinforcing their competitiveness. Furthermore, 93 businesses involved in the contents industry (broadcasting, publishing, film, music, game and software businesses, etc.) said they were able to offer new services and expand services through the deployment and use of ICT. These companies say that ICT has strengthened their ability to improve the quality, quantity and diversity of their content services, especially for the consumer market. The second core strategic component was also identified as common to all companies—the deployment and use of ICT (in some cases its development) enable these companies to upgrade their existing business processes and bring about sustainable organizational transformation. In other words, for continued expansion of existing business (exploitative activities), and pioneering the businesses of tomorrow (exploratory activities), these two strategic approaches must be simultaneously executed by a company (March, 1991).

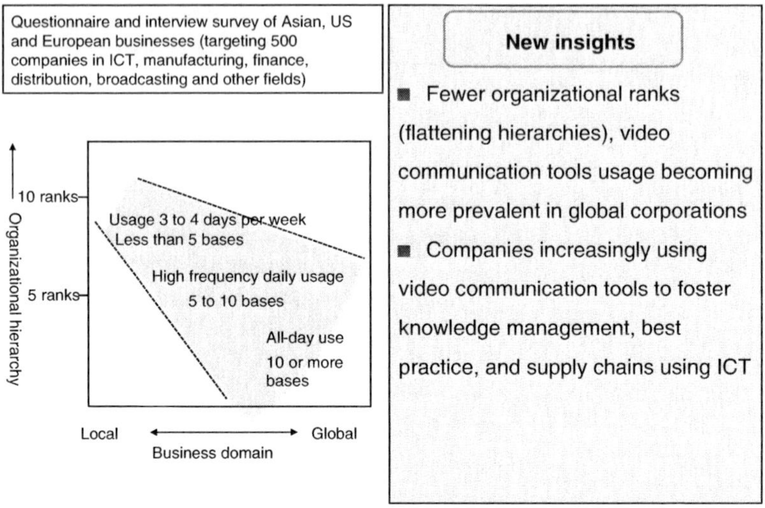

Figure 4.4 Flattening hierarchies through video communication tools

Many companies clearly recognize the importance of ICT as a strategic corporate tool, and thus the deployment and use (or independent development) of ICT to achieve corporate strategic objectives is a serious consideration. What this really means is that ICT is indispensable for achieving business objectives.

Also, from the author's research into "collaborative ICT tools and corporate transformation," it is clear that the use of VCTs is advancing in global corporations such as the Cisco Systems (mentioned earlier) and organizational hierarchies are becoming flatter (fewer ranks exist).

Companies like Cisco energized by the use of VCTs clearly raise the level of their performance principles, engage in internal knowledge management, hone their best practices, and optimize their supply chains through the use of ICT, and as illustrated in Figure 4.4, the more global a company is, the more striking this pattern becomes. Put differently, the more a company encourages interactions between its strategic and organizational contexts with ICT, the more it raises its performance.

4.3 Designing new knowledge communities and promoting knowledge management activities

VCTs are not just a "substitute for business trips" as is widely thought by many in the business world. On the contrary, VCTs are fundamentally a significant new form of communication. New, unique and inimitable styles of discussion emerge among people who participate in meetings via VCTs.

Illustrating this point, one factory manager (from company A) stated, "In the set meeting format where the number of participants from headquarters outnumbered other participants, naturally talk coming from headquarters' staff would dominate. However, with videoconferencing, participants from our factory are able to contribute more to the meeting. These tools have also enabled people to overcome reservations and talk more freely. Videoconferencing seems to enable people to communicate more comfortably with each other. It enables people to talk with more composure, and seems to alleviate the bad feelings that often remained after a conventional meeting."

He continued, "It also has other advantages. For example, if the business division communicates with the factory because there has been some enquiry from a customer about a particular component, we can use the video to show the actual components themselves. It means we know what we are talking about straight away. We never had meetings like this before. As the saying goes, 'a picture paints 1000 words.' It certainly makes it much easier for us in production to take measures if we can actually see things with our own eyes."

VCTs do not eliminate set meetings; rather they increase the frequency of meetings. This doesn't mean that they cause an increase in unnecessary meetings. On the contrary, video communications are advantageous because they enable meetings like the factory manager's example that were previously not possible. VCTs can also spark and deepen new social relationships that would not otherwise occur.

One of the supervisors in the business department of company A said, "Well, we in general affairs don't often go over to the factory, so by communicating with the people over there by teleconferencing, we have been able to hold face-to-face conversations with people who we normally wouldn't get to meet or talk to; so thanks to this system, we are able to more closely understand each other's personalities."

These sorts of interactions with VCTs were not predicted. Although basically necessary, these social relationships would not have surfaced without the interactions through VCTs. Therefore, one cannot really say that VCTs are just a simple replacement for real-world face-to-face communications.

One important observation is that things are said in meetings that can only be said via VCTs, even between people who meet regularly in real-life. Information that cannot be gained through face-to-face and set meeting styles can be brought to the fore with VCTs, which is an important factor in the formation of knowledge communities that arise from the foundation of a *Ba* (Nonaka and Konno, 1998). Through his research, the author has observed that all active users of VCTs recognize that the VCTs themselves are not a simple replacement for real-world meetings. These users also understand that knowledge communities can form as a result of these new meeting styles, something that isn't possible with other ICT tools such as groupware or e-mail.

The deployment of VCTs has the potential to trigger new behaviors in actors as they distribute new knowledge and information among themselves via this medium, and begin engaging with each other as knowledge communities in which much denser interactions than those of the past can take place. And while it may seem odd, VCTs can also increase the amount of meetings, but of great significant is new communications between actors; these meetings are in fact necessary, but were impossible prior to the deployment of these tools and the convenience that they brought.

Figure 4.5 describes VCTs' use in a large retail company for its internal meeting system. This figure illustrates the various knowledge communities that originate from a *Ba* – a time–space in which regular and irregular meetings are held in the top management level, the middle management level for product development, and at the on-site level among store managers for store management and meetings between stores. The actors in these meetings do not have to move to some predetermined location—all they need is the VCTs environment to engage in concentrated communications among themselves and set up flexible knowledge communities that enable a new design for conferencing. Actors with necessary information and knowledge can also quickly move to where they are needed in this virtual environment (including wireless video communication environments in which devices can be used anywhere, anytime), and promptly set up knowledge communities. Thus, the proactive use of VCTs is an enabler that actors can use to design new knowledge communities.

The author has observed from this research that clearly these condensed meetings through VCTs create knowledge communities that originate from the *Ba*, and the more video communications are used, the more the variety of categories of meetings increases. In the large retail company mentioned, development and product meetings, and on-site-level meetings among store managers for in-store management and interstore conferences are some of these categories of meeting. Each of these particular categories of meetings has a context formed by staff

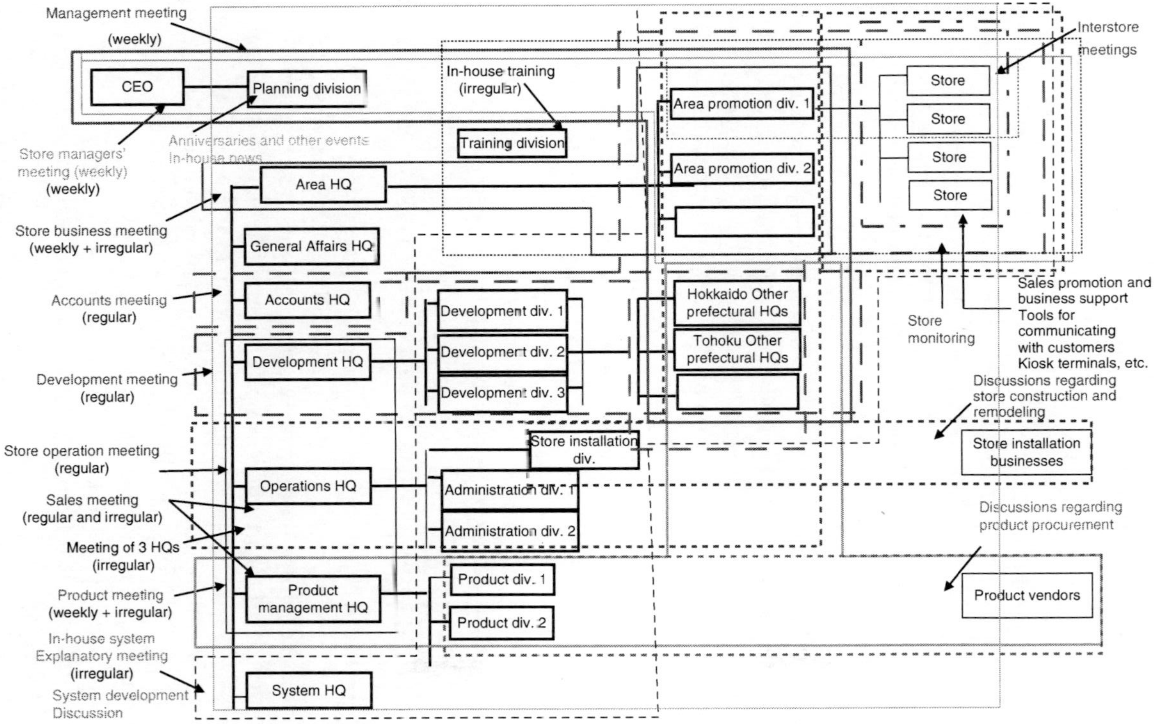

Figure 4.5 Setting and design of all types of meetings as knowledge communities (example of company C)
Source: Compiled from interviews with NTT Bizlink and presentation materials for use outside the department.

from the knowledge that they hold, and they enable the smooth allocation of business resources to deal with individual issues and problems and to drive particular areas of business. This is consistent with the idea that the more VCTs are used the more that the categories of knowledge community expand. For example, one major IT solutions company authorizes different meeting bodies as knowledge communities within the company, and members are called upon regularly or as necessary to share and use a wide range of information and knowledge over the network. From the observations made, it is clear that these increases in networked knowledge communities do not involve knowledge communities being created in one fell swoop; rather they are born through accumulated organizational learning that takes place through ICT use over a long period of time.

For instance, Sony, a company that develops and sells VCTs, also uses these tools to form many different meeting bodies as knowledge communities (also described as a case study in Chapter 6). However, in Sony's case, the organizational learning processes through VCTs that led to the formation of these knowledge communities took many months from the outset. These organizational learning processes increase the level of staff (actors) ICT capabilities, and give rise to a wide range of usage forms as new business structures are enacted using VCTs. Chapter 8 describes the four ICT capabilities that actors need to form various knowledge communities to respond to these diverse usage forms. These four organizational capabilities are enablers that encourage the formation of knowledge communities through the use of VCTs to bring about new knowledge.

4.4 Video communication tools as network strategy

As described in Chapter 2, many modern companies have adopted a range of different types of groupware and ERP tools to encourage communications and information sharing between the different organizations to promote best practice. However, corporations that are already using these tools to transform corporate culture have found that e-mail and groupware alone are not sufficient to reinforce communications within and between organizations and speed up decision-making processes. Many managers and information supervisors have complained that it is difficult to make quick decisions and judgments using only unidirectional non-real-time communications and consultation methods such as e-mail.

The reason is that face-to-face communications between individual staff members in which people are able to empathize and resonate with each other is a crucial element of organizational communications.

Thus, VCTs have the potential to drive transformation in companies by enabling people to overcome the sense of being cloistered and closed off due to the fact that e-mail and groupware do not sufficiently convey their thoughts and intentions. Put simply, VCTs enable people to have much richer discussions and engage in much faster decision-making processes, but that is not the only function of VCTs—as we move into the future, businesses will form more and more wide-ranging knowledge communities involved in strategic affiliations, strategic outsourcing and mergers and acquisitions and so on, that include the company's partner businesses and customers. VCTs are strategic network tools that will enable knowledge management in these future knowledge communities (See Figure 4.6).

Between 1999 and 2010, the author surveyed a total of 500 leading Japanese and Western companies (220 IT, 180 manufacturing, 40 distribution, 20 financial, ten advertising, 20 educational and ten health care organizations) that have already adopted VCTs and actively use them for a range of individual business processes, including planning and development, design, manufacturing, sales and distribution. Figure 4.7 sorts the results of the questionnaires and hearings gained from high-level administration staff, including general managers, project leaders, group leaders, team leaders and so forth who are involved in strategy, development, operations and service departments, etc.

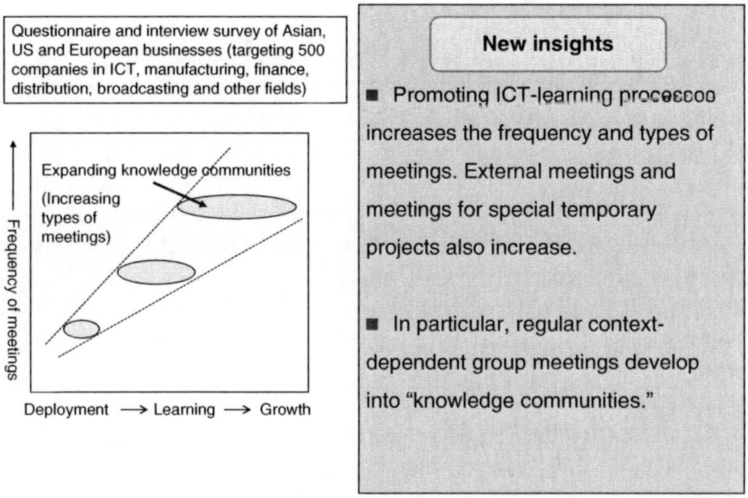

Figure 4.6 Knowledge community formation through video communication tools

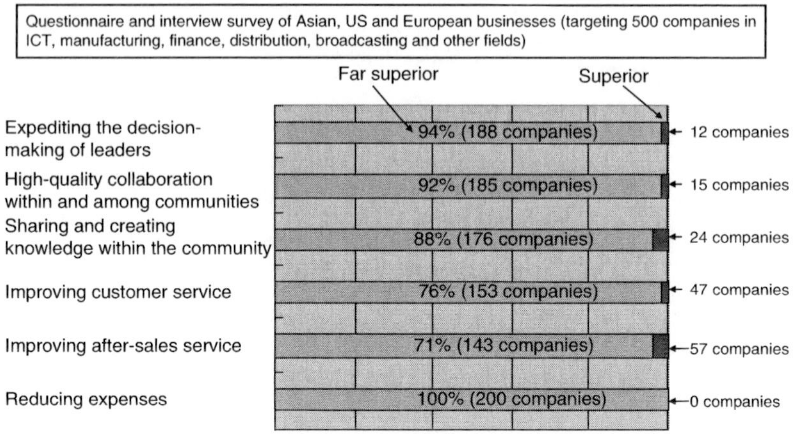

Figure 4.7 Superiority of video communication tools over groupware and e-mail

This illustrates why companies find that VCTs are superior to conventional e-mail and groupware in driving strategic business activities. Firstly, these tools accelerate business by speeding up managerial decision-making processes, and bring more efficiency to business processes by encouraging better quality communications and collaborations among individuals within and between organizations, and are much better at transforming business because they enhance the sharing and creation of knowledge and know-how in the business community.

Secondly, these tools offer strategic marketing superiority in creating customer value, as they enable improved customer services and more fulfilling after-sales services in the business communities formed from companies and their customers. Thus, it can be concluded that VCTs can play a central role in supporting corporate strategic activity and speeding up business transformation in regards to management innovation and customer value creation.

VCTs' users made the following types of comments about the effects of these tools: "The more you use these tools the richer the experience becomes!" "I couldn't do my job without these tools!" and so on.

The author has also had a lot of involvement in verifying the effectiveness of VCTs applied as e-learning for staff training and so forth in companies, and from these studies has confirmed that group training or home learning through satellite classrooms delivers satisfying educational results (increases in skill levels) (Kodama, 2002b, 2005). Thus, remote training via VCTs can greatly contribute to improving staff abilities—the knowledge assets of a company.

At their core, VCTs are not just an efficient mechanism for distributing the information that people and companies have, but are also dynamic knowledge and information instruments that enable the creation of new value in corporate activities and human lifestyles, and therefore can invigorate economies and society in general. VCTs are an important ICT platform that holds the promise of giving rise to new knowledge and value, because the knowledge and know-how of diverse people can be distributed across the network not only as text, but also as audiovisual multimedia.

4.5 Video communication tools supporting corporate business activities

This section describes aspects of the approaches taken to VCTs' deployment in the 500 companies surveyed that promote the use of VCTs (Asian, US and European companies in ICT, manufacturing, finance, distribution, broadcasting and other fields). As already mentioned, digital organizations set up mutually complementary ICT systems, strategies and organizational contexts, which give these organizations ICT capabilities that are difficult to copy, which enables them to sustain a competitive edge (Brynjolfsson, 2000). These organizations use ICT to disperse decision-making processes and energize communication and information sharing to transform their business processes, while focusing on organizational and personnel education strategies by investing in staff training, recruiting the most skilled people available and sharing the objectives of performance principles across their distilled business domains. More than 80% of the companies surveyed were able to transform their business processes, simplify their decision-making, streamline their delegation of authority, flatten their organizational structure and further their ICT training and knowledge management, all through the implementation of VCTs.

As a result of the 500-company survey, three main effects of VCTs' use became apparent (these were common characteristics inductively extracted from interviews and hearings) (see Figure 4.8).

First is the achievement of "speed business." VCTs provide leaders and management with support in information gathering, and thus help to speed up decision-making processes. Because this bidirectional medium enables managers in upper levels to communicate their thoughts and intentions directly with all staff, they also enable managers to obtain fresh information directly from the source, and exchange information with that source, and as a knowledge management enabler, these are strategic tools that make it possible for all staff, including management,

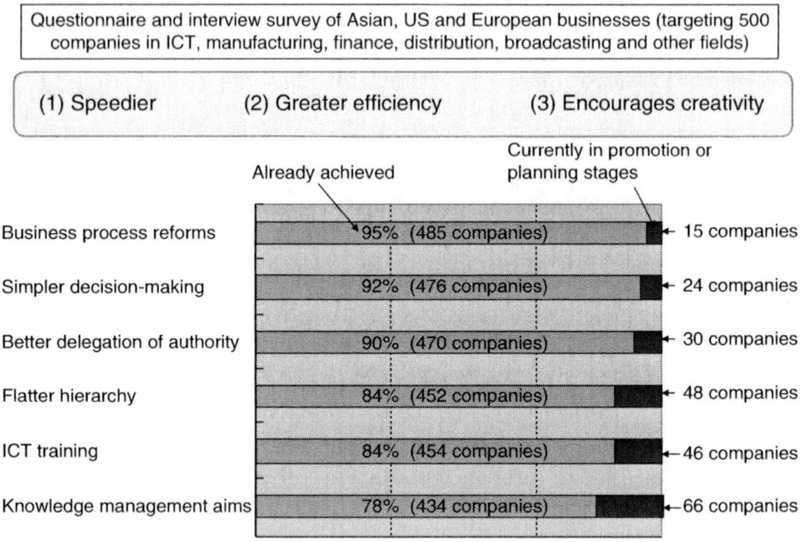

Figure 4.8 Corporate objectives for video communication tools' usage

to disseminate information and knowledge that they have and share it among themselves.

These tools enable instantaneous and profound sharing of knowledge and information because the unadorned "nuances" of the spoken words of people in business can be communicated to their counterparts in other locations as they discuss reports and business results, for instance, and because VCTs also give business leaders the ability to intentionally share information and contexts with third parties, they are also third-party communication tools.

Second, because they bring more efficiency to business, VCTs are an important strategic consideration that can transform business processes and help companies achieve even better improvements in productivity. In concurrent engineering and frontloading processes for new product development (Khurana and Rosenthal, 1998) for example, companies need to radically rethink their business processes, and in the chain of business processes from product design and development through to production technology and manufacturing, it is VCTs that the actors in each of these specialized business areas (development, manufacturing and so forth) use as their ICT support tool to solve problems and issues at a distance, and in real time. In particular, the combination of CAD (computer-aided design) and VCTs enables actors in different specializations to share common knowledge (Star, 1989; Cramton, 2001; Carlile, 2002), which demonstrates the role that these tools play in reinforcing the linkages between organizations by enabling clearer understanding of individual business processes among the actors involved.

Many companies also place great importance on raising the skill levels of individual actors through training in order to improve efficiencies and business processes, and raise productivity. As mentioned in Chapter 2, much emphasis is placed on explicit knowledge sharing in ICT-based knowledge management that makes successful transfer of tacit knowledge such as techniques and know-how a rarity. In general, tacit knowledge—the techniques and know-how of skilled laborers and specialists—is acquired by regular practice in on-the-job training and apprenticeships, etc. However, the recent advances in ICT and precision engineering mean that production processes traditionally based on skilled labor and know-how can now be substituted with ICT. Die-making businesses and so forth are good examples of this. In contrast, some areas of specialization do not lend themselves to substitution with ICT, and the actors in these areas can only learn skills and know-how from masters through on-site practice.

It is here that VCTs can offer an efficient and effective platform for remote study. For instance, Toyota is one company that not only makes use of the real-time functions of VCTs but also accumulates video material of real-life work processes of its skilled workers, which it uses to create visual manuals that other workers use as educational materials. These visual manuals, available through video-on-demand functions, are just one beneficial aspect of VCTs. Toyota even provides multilingual translations for its visual manuals, which enables the company's workers in production lines around the world to improve their skills. Thus, Toyota's efforts in this area can be interpreted as converting the tacit knowledge of skills and know-how into explicit knowledge stored as a video database. Encouraging knowledge management by using ICT in the processes of converting difficult-to-transfer tacit knowledge into explicit knowledge is a major issue in high-tech corporations.

Former Panasonic CEO Kunio Nakamura who once stated that without ICT there would be no transformation in business also said:

> The importance of IT is not just placed on the factory floor. We are always having to rethink a whole range of business processes. If we use IT, we can change invisible tacit knowledge into explicit knowledge that we can actually see. Tacit knowledge exists in people's brains which makes it difficult to share, but by converting this into explicit

knowledge with IT we can universalize it, which can transform all kinds of business processes."

Nakamura (2005)

Third is the "driving creative business" idea of bringing about new business models and innovations. This third point is fundamental to maintaining a corporation's competitiveness. As discussed in Chapter 1, the dramatic increases in fusion between different technologies in recent years and flourishing of diverse network businesses is bringing convergence across a wide range of industrial fields, although at the same time, technological domains in business and industry are becoming more specialized with more segmentalization, and organizations are becoming more divisional. For companies to respond to this kind of business environment, companies need to be able to merge the wide-ranging knowledge that is scattered within and beyond themselves (Kodama, 2007b), and are thus under pressure to integrate the boundaries between these even more complex organizational layers (both in and out of the company). To do this, leaders and managers need to share knowledge and information more deeply and make quicker decisions, and bring about powerful ICT capabilities that enable the birth of creative new technologies and products.

To drive this kind of creative business, the old sectionalist department structures of yesterday need to be swept aside, and communications between different departments must be encouraged and intensified.

Sectionalism is common in major companies between marketing, product design and development, and manufacturing divisions. Paradoxically, however, the knowledge and organizational boundaries that exist between actors in different specialist areas are both battlefields of conflict and friction and wellsprings of innovation (Leonard-Barton, 1995). Existing research has identified the fact that new ideas and innovations are easily borne through the friction and dialogue that occurs when actors from unfamiliar fields assemble (e.g. Kodama, 2007a). Thus, the formation of a *Ba* across the different business organizations and divisions involved is the key to raising the chances of successful product development.

New knowledge—new ideas and concepts needed to develop new products—arises out of dynamic contexts (relationships of time, place and people). As discussed in Chapter 2, a *Ba* is a metamorphic place in space–time that changes as contexts are changed through the interactions of individuals, as they share their contexts with each other. A *Ba* can be a physical place (offices or dispersed business locations), a virtual place (in cyberspace), or an existential entity (such as a project team), but the common purpose of these *Ba* is to act as a source of tacit knowledge that members can share to foster commitment, share values and build trust with each other.

In formal organizations identified as actual sectionalized organizations, members tend be aware of the fixed and dispersed nature of resources, which also tends to dramatically lower creativity and efficiency in new product development. In contrast, *Ba* created across and between organizations to foster fusion of the best knowledge available (core technologies and skills, etc.) encourages the efficient and creative development of new products. VCTs also give rise to new *Ba*, and are a contributor to the formation of knowledge communities (see Figure 4.9).

In the interviews conducted by the author with corporate users, many comments were made about the effects of VCTs.

For instance, one Japanese component manufacturer commented by saying,

> Video communication tools promote smooth collaboration between designers and engineers. They enable designers to engage in real-time exchanges in the course of their work, and new ideas and approaches emerge from their dialogues with engineers while sharing design drawings and so forth using video communication tools. Put simply, video communication tools erase the boundaries between people in their business dealings!

Another major Japanese manufacturer (company B) said,

> In the past there was a great deal of sectionalism between the marketing and product planning, development and design, and manufacturing departments, but with video communication tools we have been able encourage communications between people in different departments and reduce the adverse effects of sectionalized structures. Since we originally had a sense that new ideas and innovations easily arose from the dialogues between a diversity of people when they assembled as part of our new product development process, we can certainly confirm that the role played by video communication tools in invigorating communications and collaboration between departments has been huge.

Thus, VCTs can be seen to be promoting networking and energizing cross-boundary communications among the actors in different departments and areas of specialization. VCTs encourage the formation of

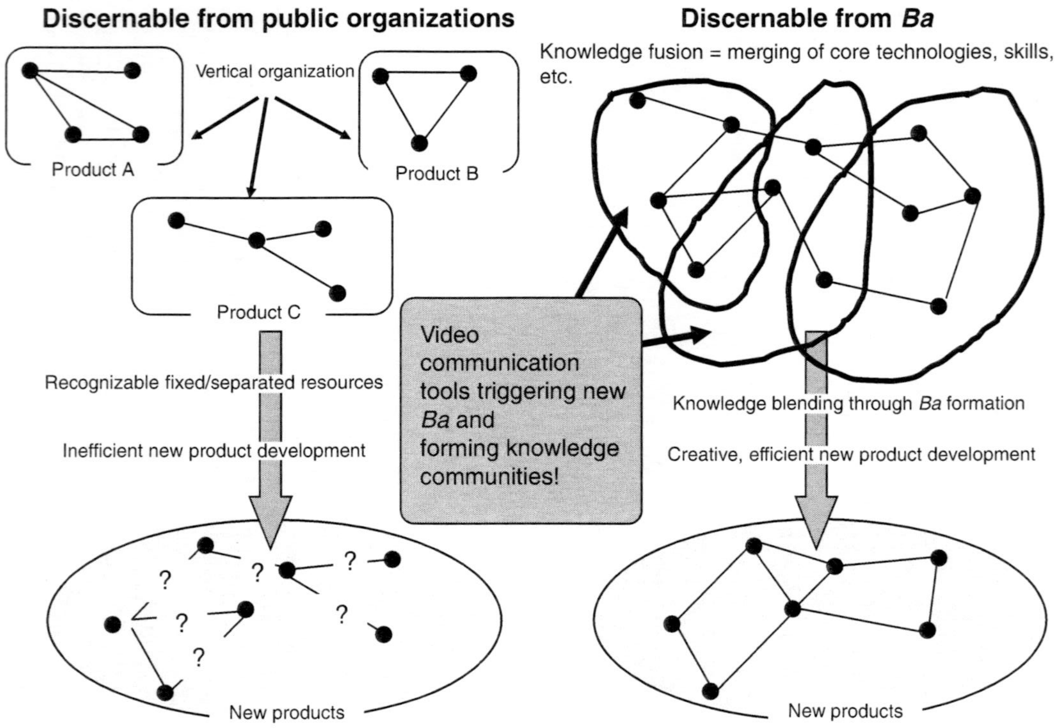

Figure 4.9 Video communication tools and knowledge community formation leading to *Ba*
Source: Based on materials provided by Professor Nonaka.

knowledge communities, and bring with them more concentrated collaboration and faster decision-making processes, and are therefore a powerful enabler for actors to achieve the creative business style needed to bring about new products and new business models.

Next Chapters 5 through 7 present detailed case studies of companies that use VCTs, and discuss new practical and theoretical implications.

5
Product Development and Collaborative ICT Tools

5.1 Development process context and temporal changes

This chapter offers two new views and implications regarding collaborative ICT tools usage forms in product development processes, through analyses of case studies in the IT, communications, electronics, automotive (including component), machinery, semiconductor, chemical, medical and distribution fields. The first of these views illustrates how collaborative ICT tools are used in the two development processes of developing new and novel products, and upgrading existing products—in other words, ICT tools' usage is dependent on the product development context. The second of these views describes how ICT tools' usage differs in each of the phases (or steps) of the new product development process, by focusing on the temporal changes in business processes to see how ICT tools' usage changes.

Existing Information Systems (IS) research does not describe a lot of experimental study or case analysis from these two points of view. Much of it only consists of empirical studies of usage form snapshots or fixed business details, while research into the relationship of ICT tools to the temporal changes in product development and the contextual details therein remains scant and undeveloped.

This chapter clarifies how diverse project organizations consisting of multifunctional teams spanning different specializations and business functions proactively use collaborative ICT tools to spurn the creative and efficient development of new products. It also identifies a pronounced increase in collaborative ICT tools' usage between various organizations as the pace of change and new product development risk increases.

Furthermore, the chapter describes how companies engage in "ambidextrous R&D management" involving simultaneous "uncertainty management (exploration)" for new product development, and "management of existing business (exploitation)" for upgrading existing products, and in so doing use different types of collaborative ICT tools to respond to temporal and circumstantial changes that occurred during the development process.

5.2 Organizational and ICT tools' usage forms in product development

Of course, exploratory activities aimed at new product development present challenges for a company in maintaining its competitiveness. Many high-tech corporations in high-risk industries are directly faced with the challenges of executing imaginative and efficient management to develop new products and services where markets, technologies and the competitive landscape are rapidly changing (uncertainty of success, development costs etc.).

One solution that many high-tech companies have used to promote their exploratory activities is to flatten company hierarchies and form cross-functional teams (CFTs) and project-based organizations with a high degree of integration, into which resources for product development are invested. Although market conditions and the state of technology is contingent to successful new product development with project based organizations or CFTs, it has been reported that a high level of organizational integration is an effective method of product development when attempting to develop new products in risky or uncertain circumstances (e.g. Gemser and Leenders, 2011).

Multinational corporations (MNCs) (e.g. Bartlett and Ghoshal, 2000; Forsgren, 1997; Nohria and Ghoshal, 1997) create project-based organizations as horizontally integrated structures that are more flexible and flatter than the hierarchies in conventional organizations (e.g. Child and McGrath, 2001; Child and Rodrigues, 2003), because in highly volatile markets and fluctuating technological circumstances, these flexible and autonomous project-based organizations are a suitable system for integrating knowledge both inside and outside the company to bring about new products, services and business models (e.g. Lundin and Midler, 1998; Hobday, 2000; DeFillippi, 2002; Lindkvist, 2004). In these systems, project team members work toward common objectives by collaborating under a fixed timetable (e.g. Henrie and Sousa-Poza, 2005).

As an organizational form, the project team has been applied in a wide range of industries to date. Classic examples include the construction business (e.g. Gann and Salter, 1998), IT and communications industries (e.g. Kodama, 1999d), the automotive industry (e.g. Clark and Fujimoto, 1991), media industries (e.g. DeFillippi and Arthur, 1998; Windeler and Sydow, 2001) and consultancy and service businesses (e.g. Alvesson, 1995).

Essentially, as temporary organizations, project-based organizations are formed from specialist staffs within a company, who work together over a fixed period on a mission to bring about new products in response to specific customer demands. However, in organizations like consultancy firms in which there is hardly any routine business, the entire company can be thought of as a collection of project-based organizations.

5.2.1 Organizational form and product development performance

This section describes the relationship and level of integration between organizations involved in product development and related organizational forms.

Much has been reported about the relationship between product development performance and organizational integration (e.g. Allen, 1970; Gupta, Raj and Wilemon, 1986; Song, Montoya-Weiss and Schmidt, 1997). Allen (1970) showed that the structure of company communication networks and the level of communication through them influence the performance of R&D organizations. Notably, the communications interfaces between marketing and R&D are a factor in determining the success of a product development (Griffin and Hauser, 1996). Furthermore, in cases of high-risk product development or highly uncertain circumstances, strong integration between organizations raises the chances of success with new product development, although it has been reported that the degree of interorganizational linking should be selected according to the difficulty of product development (Gomez et al., 2003; Gemser and Leenders, 2011). This is because knowledge boundaries exist between different departments, and the way in which business people behave in response to the disparities (Lawrence and Lorsch, 1967; Dougherty, 1992; Griffin and Hauser, 1996) that accompany these knowledge boundaries influences the process of developing a product, and thus influences performance.

In relation to the degree of organizational integration, Kahn (1996) describes the behavior of business people in organizational relationships in product development as "interaction" and "collaboration."

5.2.1.1 *Interaction and the community of practice (CoP)*

"Interaction" indicates a relaxed level of integration between functions of structured organizations, in which organizational and personal interrelationships include routine business such as communicating company rules or business manuals, and communications by telephone, e-mail and business meetings. In the context of product development, these interactions are equivalent to the traditional sequential model (Cooper, 1988, 1990) of a product development process—product development processes as routine innovation to improve and upgrade existing products. Interpreted differently, these are routines that are born from the interactions of the "communities of practice" (CoPs) in each functional organization.

A CoP is a group of "people who share a concern, a set of problems, or a passion about a topic, and who deepen their knowledge and expertise in the area by interaction on an ongoing basis" (Wenger, McDermott and Snyder, 2002, p. 4). Put differently, a CoP involves a group of actors rooted in the company community who have the same specializations and job functions. A CoP has the character of a "learning community" (Brown and Duguid, 1991; Lave and Wenger, 1991; Orr, 1996) comprising a group with the same basic specializations (actors possessing fixed domain-specific knowledge in fields such as management, development or production).

In practice, vital knowledge in the community of practice resides as "decentered" knowledge in the system of activities, and the tacit, communal background knowledge contained in the practice and narratives of the community.

The CoP does not rely on specific individual knowledge. Members create a communal and coherent knowledge platform through sustained cooperation and coordination over an extended period of time. This is advantageous because knowledge accumulated through sustained learning plays a part in organizational growth.

Since the actors in CoPs work in the same job functions and specialist fields, the members possess similar "thought worlds" (Dougherty, 1992), and the knowledge boundaries between them (Brown and Duguid, 2001) are not great, and because the work revolves around daily business routines project-work elements of novelty and uncertainty do not play a major role. Thus, it follows that there is little conflict and abrasion among the actors.

In CoPs, new meaning is created through daily business routines, and incremental improvement is promoted through the learning and deep knowledge sharing among members.

A CoP whose members are geographically separated can also be encouraged to share and use knowledge using ICT. This type of CoP has been referred to as a "virtual community of practice (VCoP)" (Pan and Leidmer, 2003; Fuchs, 2007; Taifi and Passiante, 2012).

5.2.1.2 Collaboration and strategic communities

In contrast to "interaction," "collaboration" involves relationships between formal and functional organizations and informal and unstructured ones. Project organizations operating as cross-functional teams with a high degree of integration are examples of this.

Collaboration is also an important factor in bringing about creative friction and productive discord in which negative behaviors and ideas that emerged between businesspeople in different organizations and specializations are controlled. Therefore, the key to promoting creative and productive collaboration is the formation of "strategic communities" (SCs) (Kodama, 2007a) by highly integrating organizations as project teams and CFTs that traverse communities of practice and cross the boundaries between diverse organizations. In the broader sense, SCs are examples of "collaborative innovation networks" and "innovation communities" (Taifi and Passiante, 2012).

The new knowledge that emerges from the various organizational boundaries (see Box 5.1) both inside and outside the company is the very source of organizational capability. The integration of new knowledge that emerges from various pragmatic boundaries within and outside the company, including customers and partners (or the integration of those boundaries) in particular, is a source of innovation—a source of new product development and organizational capabilities that sustain a company's competitiveness.

The new ideas proposed in this book concern a dynamic and practical method that corporate managers can use to integrate diverse knowledge distributed on networks, whether real or virtual, in order to develop new products and business models. At the core of this framework is a concept known as the strategic community (SC; see Box 5.2) (Kodama, 2003a, 2003b, 2005, 2007e), a theory of a practical method of accelerating innovation in a corporation.

To obtain diverse and valuable knowledge, it is important to have a process in which managers from various strata of management both inside and outside the corporation can dynamically form SCs along pragmatic boundaries with participation by internal and external actors, who are not restricted to existing formal organizations.

Box 5.1 Organizational boundaries and strategic communities

In their daily business activities, practitioners become aware of a variety of organizational boundaries. Here, "organizational boundaries" mean the boundaries between work in formal organizations dedicated to such areas as research, development, production or sales; boundaries between layers of management within the company; or boundaries between customers, external partners or various other industries. Boundaries exist among actors with different backgrounds or knowledge. These boundaries are characterized by the following three layers (Shannon and Weaver, 1949; Jantsch, 1980; Carlile, 2002, 2004; see Figure 5.1).

The first layer is the syntactic or information-processing boundary for ensuring that information or knowledge is accurately transferred between actors. This may involve the commercialization of a product through development and production methods, or established routines and business processes. The function of syntactic boundaries within a company is to enable focus on rules such as internal procedures or manuals to govern operations in order to increase efficiency and productivity.

The second layer represents the semantic or interpretive boundary, along which new meaning is generated, and new knowledge is translated. Specifically, the incremental actions that an organization

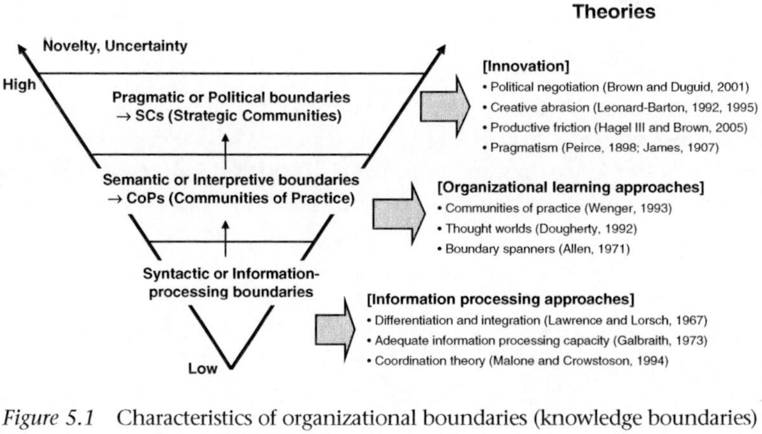

Figure 5.1 Characteristics of organizational boundaries (knowledge boundaries)
Source: Based on Kodama (2007a).

takes to improve existing business processes or development and production methods occur at this boundary. In addition to internal procedures and other rules that are important in the syntactic boundary, the semantic boundary also includes a variety of organizational learning such as TQM that promote best practice and improve business within the company.

The third layer consists of the pragmatic or political boundary that transforms existing knowledge through friction and conflict among actors, or through political pressure, thus enabling actors to address completely new issues and achieve new goals. This is the creation of completely different business concepts, including products and services that achieve new business models, the development of new technology architectures, components and production methods, while as the source of innovation the new knowledge needed to achieve these objectives is much more likely to be generated along these pragmatic boundaries.

These three-tiered boundaries, however, are mutually dependent, and their characteristics change significantly in response to changes in the business environment, such as customer needs or the actions of competitors, or are changed by the intentions or interests of actors. Notably, if these changes are more influential in terms of innovation or corporate reform, the relationships between actors will shift to a more pragmatic boundary (syntactic boundary → semantic boundary → pragmatic boundary) (Carlile, 2004).

5.2.1.3 Organizational integration and risk

Gomes et al. (2003) argues that "collaboration" with a high degree of integration is a necessary factor for the success of new products that carry a high risk (uncertainties and technical difficulties), while "interaction" is important for the success of routine developments such as improving and upgrading existing products. This means that teams collaborating along boundaries or collectives of communities of practice are not suitable for low-risk and routine upgrading of existing products, while existing routine organizations are not suited to dealing with high risk and technical difficulty (Gemser and Leenders, 2011).

From the previous discussion, and with reference to the studies carried out by Gemser and Leenders (2011), Figure 5.2 describes the suitability of organizational forms in terms of the level of integration of CoPs and SCs, and risk (uncertainty and technical difficulty). In other words,

Box 5.2 The concept of strategic communities

The SC is characterized by four basic concepts.

The first is that the SC possesses the element of *Ba* as a constantly changing shared context that enables corporations to respond to dynamic changes in markets and technologies (or to create markets and technologies) (Nonaka and Konno, 1998). Knowledge needs a context to be created, as it is context-specific. The context is defined by both participants and the nature of the venture, and can be social, cultural or even historical, and provides a basis for information to be interpreted, and thus a basis for knowledge and meaning to be created.

Ba is a place offering these shared contexts, but is not necessarily just a physical space or even a geographical location or virtual space in ICT. Rather, it is a time–space nexus as much as a shared mental space. Any form of new knowledge can be created regardless of the business structure, as *Ba* transcends formal business structures.

The second concept is that the SC is a community of practice (Wenger, 2000) rooted in the resonance of values (Kodama, 2000, 2001a, 2002b, 2004) among the actors that form the SC. This aspect promotes mutual learning within the community as actors come to understand shared contexts and common values to continually generate new knowledge.

In the strategic community, the community membership and community leaders directing activities are gradually established. These people dynamically produce the context as they work toward fulfilling the community's mission. This results in the development of new products and services as community members create new knowledge by learning from one another and sharing.

The third concept is that the SC has a pragmatic boundary characteristic that enables actors with different contexts to transform existing knowledge (Carlile, 2002, 2004). (Since pragmatic boundaries are positioned above the syntactic and semantic boundary layers, SCs are not necessarily only characterized by their pragmatic boundaries.) The underlying concepts of *Ba* and the practical communities therein cause new meaning to be generated and shared among members at the boundaries (e.g. Dougherty, 1992), while promoting organizational learning and best practice (a semantic boundary characteristic—the second layer mentioned earlier; see Figure 5.1).

At organizational boundaries where high-level novelty or uncertainty inherent in innovation emerges, however, new meaning must be generated through the sharing of contexts within the *Ba* or practical communities, new knowledge that transcends organizational learning must be created, and existing knowledge must be transformed (pragmatic boundary characteristics—the third layer mentioned previously), as various problems and issues are raised at this boundary, and actors must face the accompanying challenges of finding solutions and creating new knowledge.

Actors at these organizational boundaries engage in practical, creative abrasion (Leonard-Barton, 1992), productive friction (Hagel III and Brown, 2005) as well as political negotiations (Brown and Duguid, 2001) (see Figure 5.1).

The fourth concept is one in which the actors, as hubs or connectors in an organization, dynamically bridge multiple SCs (or pragmatic boundaries) and form networks (or links) among different SCs (Barabasi, 2002; Watts, 2003; Kodama, 2005, 2006). In this way, multiple SCs (or pragmatic boundaries) become integrated and enable corporations to create new knowledge.

In order to develop new products or business models, the actors consciously network the SCs along the pragmatic boundaries among various corporate organizations to integrate them. If needed, the actors also form SCs through strategic alliances with external entities including customers, and bind them deeply with the SCs in the corporation (Kodama, 2003b).

an appropriate organizational form must be selected for exploration for new product development when there is a high level of uncertainty, or exploitation for routine development to upgrade and improve products. Thus, appropriately allocating resources necessary for the organizational form (CoP or SC) increases the potential for "parallel development" as ambidextrous R&D strategy using exploration and exploitation, depending on the nature of the target product development.

5.2.2 The relationship between product development context and collaborative ICT tools

5.2.2.1 Methodology and analysis of case-study surveys

Surveys and interviews (with some companies) were conducted about the types of ICT tools and their actual usage for the two types of product development processes of "developing new products" and "upgrading existing products." A total of 174 companies in the IT, communications,

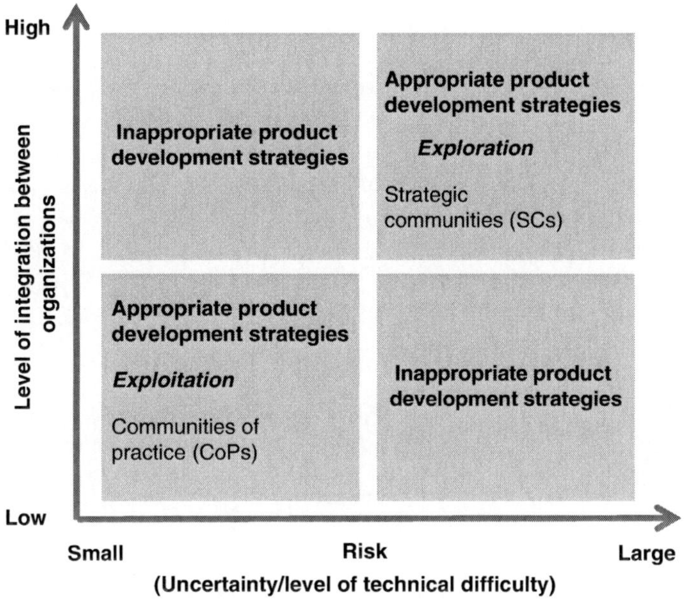

Figure 5.2 Product development strategies with the two organizational systems
Source: Based on Gemser and Leenders (2011).

electronics, electrical, machinery, automotive (including component), semiconductor, chemical and medical fields were surveyed (36 in Japan, 15 in Korea, 16 in Taiwan, 12 in China, five in India, 41 in the United States, 12 in Great Britain, 15 in France, 16 in Germany, two in Israel, two in Finland and two in Norway). The types of ICT tools identified were telephone, e-mail, voice conferencing systems, web conferencing systems, and videoconferencing systems (including TV phones).[1]

Table 5.1 describes the degree to which video communication tools (VCTs) were used in product development and organizational systems. Additionally, Figure 5.3 describes the ways ICT tools are used to respond to the details of product developments.

For Table 5.1, data was collected through the company surveys about what type of ICT tools were used, and how often they were used in the course of carrying out business for the two types of product development (developing new products or upgrading existing ones). The results clearly show that in general, all of the companies adopt different organizational forms to deal with new product development or existing product upgrades.

Table 5.1 Video communication tools' (VCTs') usage level in product development/organizational systems

Development content and organizational system	VCTs usage frequency (single SC or CoPaverages/no. of companies)				Comments
Appropriate product development strategies	Always connected	7 or more times a day	Used 3 to 6 times per week	Used once or twice per week	All 174 companies surveyed use VCTs in their SCs.
SC *Exploration*	12	106	41	15	
Appropriate product development strategies	Always connected	7 or more times a day	Used 3 to 6 times per week	Used once or twice per week	VCTs use almost nonexistent in CoPs in 71 companies
CoP *Exploitation*	0	0	61	42	

Number of companies surveyed: 174.

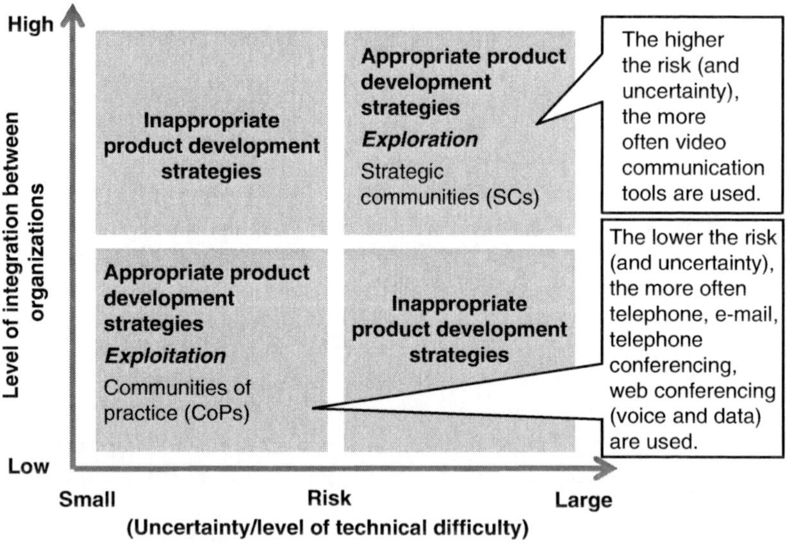

Figure 5.3 ICT tools systems to address product development details

As mentioned, CoPs are formed from existing production line or business functional organizations to carry out upgrades on existing products, whereas supervisors involved in existing product business come together to form pan-departmental CFTs or special project teams to develop new products, and the larger the company the greater the number of CoPs and SCs that exist within it.

In conducting this survey, for the sake of simplicity, data was collected for average frequency of usage for the different types of ICT tools in a typical SC or CoP. Even though telephone, e-mail and teleconferencing are used on a daily basis regardless of the organizational form (whether it be a CoP or an SC), the survey was designed to gather quantitative data about the degree of VCT use in relation to product development and organizational form.

The results clearly suggested the following:

(1) In challenging new product developments where there is a high level of risk and uncertainty, there is a high degree of integration between organizations (CFTs, etc.).
(2) In upgrading existing products where there is a low level of risk and uncertainty, there is a low level of organizational integration (existing routine organizations).
(3) When there is high risk and uncertainty, there is also a high level of VCT usage.
(4) When there is a low level of risk and uncertainty, there is a high usage level of e-mail, telephone, voice and web conferencing systems (data and voice exchange to share documents and other materials etc.).

What can be interpreted from these results?

The following observations can be made about the "level of organizational integration and business objectives", and the "media richness of ICT tools."

5.2.2.2 Organizational integration level and business objectives viewpoint

As stated in Section 4.5 in Chapter 4, there are three main business objectives for VCT usage. The data obtained from company interviews and surveys were categorized according to these three business objectives. Table 5.2 describes the key business drivers for organizational forms in the strategic and organizational context (1), while Table 5.3 describes the key business drivers and organizational forms in terms of ICT tools usage forms (2).

- **The speedy business viewpoint**

The first key business driver is the need for speed. The main product development business in CoPs (including VCoPs) is the speeding up

Table 5.2 Key drivers of organizational systems and managerial factors (1): Strategic/organizational context

Key drivers	CoP (including VCoP)	SC
Speed management	• Faster version upgrades for existing products and services • Shorter life cycles for existing products ⇒ Linking up and sharing information in related organizations and existing trading partners, quick decision-making.	• Faster new product development • Faster information gathering for decision-making for new product planning ⇒ Collaboration and information sharing with related organizations and new partner corporations, quick decision-making.
Efficient management	• More efficiency through improvements to existing supply chains • Improved internal business processes ⇒ Efficiently linking up information with related organizations and existing trading partners.	• Efficiency in product planning and establishing manufacturing technology • Establishing platforms/ standardized technologies • Establishing efficient high-mix, low-volume production ⇒ Collaboration to set up new and efficient supply chains.
Creative management	• Learning processes through improvement activities ⇒ Few creative business factors.	• Promoting innovation activities through imagination and new ideas ⇒ New company-wide and intercompany collaboration.

of upgrading for existing products and services, or the shortening of life cycles of existing products. Important considerations here are the sharing and linking of information with related organizations and existing trading partners, and prompt decision-making. The ICT tools mainly used to achieve these objectives are telephone, e-mail, voice and data conferencing etc. for checking routine processes and making decisions.

In contrast, in SCs, data is rapidly gathered for decision-making about new product planning or fast-tracking product development, and sharing this information and collaborating with related organizations or

Table 5.3 Key drivers of organizational system and managerial factors (2): ICT tools' usage forms

Key drivers	**CoP (including VCoP)**	**SC**
Speed management	• Linking up and sharing information in related organizations and existing trading partners, quick decision-making. ⇒ Proactive use of telephone, e-mail, telephone and data conferencing, etc. for checking routine processes and quick decision-making.	• Quick decision-making through dialogue encouraged between new staff members and new partner companies. ⇒ VCT use increases as it encourages real-time dialogue and practice among users including top management.
Efficient management	• Linking up and sharing information in related organizations and existing trading partners. ⇒ Proactive use of telephone, e-mail, telephone and data conferencing, etc. for efficient routine checking of processes and decision-making.	• Dialogue and collaboration with new partners dispersed around the globe to build new and efficient supply chains. ⇒ VCT use increases as it encourages real-time creative dialogue and practice among users.
Creative management	• Sharing information and linking with related organizations in the learning process. ⇒ Proactive use of telephone, e-mail, telephone and data conferencing, etc. for routine checking of processes and decision-making.	• Encouraging collaboration in mixtures of staff, between different businesses and joint development dispersed around the globe. ⇒ VCT use increases as it encourages real-time creative dialogue and practice among users.

new partner companies for prompt decision-making, which is a chief concern. For this reason, the use of VCTs for real-time dialogue and practice among users, including top management in SCs, increases out of necessity, because VCTs enable business people to collect data more quickly, and enable management to make decisions more speedily.

Of course, precise and speedy decision-making is required throughout all aspects of business management, regardless of whether it's related to an uncertain or risky product development. However, when issues do emerge with high-risk new product developments, VCTs provide an important capability because they enable users, including top management, to work on problems face-to-face, and in real time.

- **The business efficiency viewpoint**

The second key business driver is efficiency. In CoPs (including VCoPs) importance is placed on sharing information with existing trading partners and related organizations to improve in-house business processes and raise efficiency by reforming existing supply chains.

Similar to the speedy business viewpoint previously mentioned, the dominant ICT tools in these cases are telephone, e-mail, teleconferencing, data conferencing and so forth, which are used for checking up on routine processes and making decisions.

In SCs, however, collaboration is required between related organizations and between companies to establish efficient design and production technologies, or platforms and standardized technologies, and, moreover, new supply chains and well-organized production systems capable of high-mix, low-volume production. For these reasons, VCTs are the dominant ICT tools because similar to the speedy business viewpoint, they enable and encourage cross-organizational real-time dialogue and practice between departments, and between companies.

In low-risk product development where existing products are upgraded, reforming a company's business processes with the aim of improving productivity is a particularly important goal; however, developing more efficient design platforms for high-risk product development, and reflecting these with subsequent design standardization, is also an important way to transform business processes.

For instance, in concurrent engineering and frontloading in new product developments in which companies have to radically rethink existing business processes (the process chain from product design and development through to production technology and manufacturing), business people need to be able to share information in real-time across physical distance to come up with ways to solve problems and issues that arise with the individual specializations (development, manufacturing, etc.) involved in these processes, and it is VCTs that provide the ICT support for this business.

One notable example is the combination of VCTs and computer-aided design (CAD) that enables people in different areas of specialization to share their knowledge (Carlile, 2002; Cramton, 2001; Star, 1989), and fortify the linkages between organizations across diverse knowledge boundaries by enabling participants to deepen their mutual understanding of the different aspects of the business processes involved.

Contrasted with the CoPs mentioned earlier, this example illustrates why there is a necessity for a high level of integration in SC formations.

In addition to that, many companies place great importance on skills training to improve productivity and processes and raise efficiency. VCTs also offer an efficient and effective support tool for this type of training because they enable the tacit knowledge, techniques and know-how of specialists and craftsmen to be handed down remotely in the course of routine practice, on-the-job training or apprenticeship systems.

- **The creative business viewpoint**

The third key business driver is the promotion of creative business to bring forth new business models and innovations. In CoP-type organizations, there is not as much emphasis placed on creativity, as learning processes are geared mainly toward improvement and upgrading activities. For this reason, the main ICT tools that are used in CoPs are telephone, e-mail, telephone and data conferencing, which are used to check routine processes and make decisions.

On the other hand in SC formations, the emphasis is on getting mixtures of company staff to collaborate and form new concepts and ideas to drive innovation activity, and coordinate globally dispersed joint developments both in and between companies. Accordingly, much more importance is placed on use of VCTs in SCs, because these ICT tools enable face-to-face dialogue and practice in real-time, since executing business for new product development and creating new business models in SCs often involves very high levels of risk and uncertainty.

These risks and uncertainties have emerged with the rapid developments, technological convergence, diversification of business models and accelerated pace of network business in recent years, which have caused an increase of technical specialization and segmentation, and have thus forced the pace of organizational division in corporations and industries to accelerate.

For these reasons, companies are under pressure to integrate knowledge dispersed both inside and outside of themselves, and integrate the increasingly complex boundaries between organizations—processes that demand higher levels of integration in and between companies than that of CoPs. Therefore, business people use VCTs because they enable greater amounts of knowledge and information to be shared more thoroughly, and decisions to be made more speedily, and thus reinforce the organizational capabilities needed to give birth to new and creative products and technologies.

To drive this kind of creative business, the old departmentalized and vertically structured hierarchies must be swept aside, and communications between a variety of departments encouraged.

However, the organizational and knowledge boundaries among individuals in diverse professional fields are both paradoxically places of conflict and friction while simultaneously having characteristics of *Ba* that act as sources of innovation (Leonard-Barton, 1995). New ideas and innovations can come about more easily when business people from unfamiliar backgrounds meet up and communicate (e.g. Kodama, 2002a). For this reason, since VCTs offer a way of networking business people in different departments and areas of specialization (in other words, raise the level of integration), they have the effect of invigorating creative communication and collaboration—they are support tools that give people an advantage in pursuing the creative business of achieving new products and business models.

As described, the proactive use of VCTs can be interpreted as a corporate means to raise the level of organizational integration needed to foster the key business drivers of speed, efficiency and creativity in high-risk, high-uncertainty new product development.

In contrast, the use of VCTs can be interpreted as being comparatively lower for processes involving upgrading and improving existing products where there are low levels of risk and uncertainty, and lower levels of creativity required, and ICT tools are mainly used for speed and efficiency in routine business (telephone, e-mail, telephone and data conferencing etc.).

In this way, it can be seen that corporations use different types of collaborative ICT tools for different product development situations. They do this by executing "ambidextrous R&D management" in which they engage in both "uncertainty management (exploration)" to develop new products, and "existing business management (exploitation)" to upgrade existing products.

5.2.2.3 The ICT tools media richness viewpoint

VCTs enable much greater information transfer than telephones because they offer a level of media richness that is much closer to real-life face-to-face communication than regular telephony (Kydd and Ferry, 1994).

Richness refers to media capabilities and characteristics that enable actors to engage in bidirectional information sharing to build understanding and reach a consensus (Daft and Lengel, 1984). Naturally, face-to-face communications offer the highest level of media richness.

Because VCTs have a media richness level that is closest to actual face-to-face communications, they offer a higher level of information and context sharing in a range of circumstances, and thus enable users to transfer larger amounts of information. Particularly in risky or uncertain new product developments where an increased amount of issues and problems arise, there is a greater need to share complex organizational and technical contexts.

It was clear from the interviews conducted that the high media richness of VCTs had positive effects on communications and collaboration among business people. It was also clear that there is a need for users of these tools to acquire "new media literacy"[2] and "video producer capabilities"[3] to get the most out of VCTs in new product development ventures.

Business people working on-site in risky and uncertain new product developments need to raise the level of their skills through learning processes with VCTs to acquire these media literacy and video production capabilities (discussed in detail in Chapter 8).

In general, the richness of electronic media is not inherent in each type of media, but can be raised as people engage in "learning by doing" and gain experience (Carlson and Zumd, 1999). Therefore, skills training can enable users to raise the richness of VCTs and thus reduce equivocality or misunderstandings (Weick, 1979) when using these tools to communicate.

5.3 ICT tools' usage forms and product development processes

The previous section discussed and analyzed ICT usage forms in terms of the context of the product development (whether it is for an existing or new product). In other words, the different ways that ICT tools are used is dependent on the product development context.

This section considers and analyses the different aspects of collaborative ICT tools' use in each of the phases (or steps) in new product development processes. Put differently, this section focuses on the different ICT tools' usage forms that emerge at different times in different stages of business processes.

First of all, this section constructs a new framework using existing research as a yardstick to enable consideration of what sort of phases (or steps) exist in new product development processes.

To acquire a competitive edge and sustain it over a long period, it is clearly important that companies constantly need to create new products, services, and business models (e.g. Jelinek and Schoonhoven, 1990; Morone, 1993; Markides, 1999). Creating and implementing new business models that radically transform conventional products and services and shake up existing business rules have induced major strategic changes in the historical flow of large traditional corporations. The major transformation of the mobile phone business with NTT DOCOMO's i-mode (e.g. Kodama, 2002a; Peltokorpi, Nonaka and Kodama, 2007), Nintendo's DS/Wii game business and Apple's US-developed music distribution business are examples of the creation of the co-evolution model, which is a new value chain often found in the ICT industry.

A succession of academic research in recent years on radical (e.g. Leifer et al., 2000), breakthrough (e.g. Hargadon, 2003), discontinuous (e.g. Kaplan, Murray and Henderson, 2003) and disruptive (e.g. Christensen and Raynor, 2003) innovation has provided numerous examples of companies taking on challenges strategically oriented to explore new markets and create technologies, the accompanying difficulties and the numerous reasons for success or failure. The conclusion is that acquiring the organizational capabilities needed to respond rapidly to circumstantial changes, develop new technologies and promote business development is crucial (e.g. Tushman and Anderson, 1986; Brown and Eisenhardt, 1997; Teece, Pisano and Shuen, 1997).

In the past, a major source of competitiveness for large traditional corporations came from releasing new version of products by exploiting path-dependent capabilities and gradually improving existing products for existing markets (incremental innovation), thereby generating profits. However, radical and breakthrough innovations have caused a paradigm shift in markets and technologies, and have given rise to a dramatic expansion of product function, dramatic transformation of existing markets, the creation of new markets and major cost reductions (Leifer et al., 2000; O'Connor and Rice, 2001). These kinds of radical innovations and breakthroughs differ substantially from the path-dependent incremental innovations in the past.

To achieve radical innovation, a company requires new knowledge distinct from existing skills and expertise (e.g. Dewar and Dutton, 1986). The reason is that companies and individual projects undertaking radical innovation face uncertainty and discontinuity in markets, technologies, organizations and resources, and while some projects may be able to surmount these hurdles and succeed, many others are highly likely to stall or fail midway (e.g. Leifer et al., 2000).

To acquire a radical innovation capability, a company needs different capabilities (including strategy, organization, resources, technology, processes and leadership), as well as the practical management elements nurtured through incremental innovation (e.g. Kodama, 2003b, 2007a; O'Reilley III and Tushman, 2004; Vanhaverbeke and Peeters, 2005).

The following section describes a theoretical framework for the temporal processes needed to bring about new product development as a strategic innovation, and considers and analyses the relationship between the changes to organizational forms in the course of business processes, and the ways ICT tools are used to support these organizational forms at different times.

5.3.1 Product development processes and the capability map

Resource-based theories that have focused on independent capabilities for companies and organizations (e.g. Wernerfelt, 1984; Barney, 1991) have developed theoretical frameworks for strategy in terms of micro and organizational economics. These resource-based theories and Porter's (1980) competition strategy theory enable a detailed analysis of strategic positioning and the relationship between competitiveness and the internal resources already owned by companies in slowly changing environments and industries. However, from these studies, it is difficult to analyze how companies create new competitiveness in highly competitive and rapidly changing high-tech industries such as the ICT and digital sectors.

In contrast, dynamic capability (Teece, Pisano and Shuen, 1997) is an existing resource-based theory that attempts to describe how competences inside and outside the company are dynamically integrated and reconfigured in response to circumstantial change.

The word "capability" refers to business processes for integrating and rebuilding assets inside and outside the company for the purpose of creating and maintaining competitiveness. Dynamic capability is the process of improving existing routine capabilities for transforming and exploiting existing corporate assets in response to changing circumstances (e.g. Zollo and Winter, 2002; Winter, 2003), while process management of existing routines and operations contributes to the incremental innovation of existing business (Benner and Tushman, 2003).

With dynamic capability under relatively stable or slow-moving conditions with little business uncertainty, companies systematically and analytically formulate and implement strategies such as "learning before doing" (Pisano, 1994). This means they formulate and implement detailed strategies and policies—a key characteristic of dynamic capabilities in market structures with clear corporate boundaries in which the players in value chains are easily known.

Later on, a number of researchers amended and reinterpreted their views of dynamic capability. The most relevant was Eisenhardt and Martine (2000), who made adjustments for tautology problems relating to the interpretation of capability, and clarified the relationship between dynamic capability and competitiveness. They argued that dynamic capability is the strategic and organizational processes and the routines of companies that use (integrate, reallocate, acquire or eliminate) internal and external resources in order to respond to or create market change, and they inductively derived concepts of corporate dynamic capabilities essential in both slow- and fast-moving market circumstances. These researchers stressed the importance of "learning by doing" with simple rules to emphasize results rather than prior training and process implementation, especially in fast-moving environments, where uncertainty is high, and industrial and corporate borders are vague (Eisenhardt and Sull, 2001).

This interpretation of strategy theory has evolved toward a dynamic structure that reflects current corporate activity. Furthermore, O'Connor (2008) agrees with the dynamic capability theory of Eisenhardt and Martine (2000), and asserts that a large number of major innovations (strategic innovations), including the radical innovations mentioned earlier, developed gradually from slow (or very slow) market environments, and were implemented over a period of several years to several decades.

Thus, the concept of dynamic capability is described as a theory characterized by strategic innovation that can be expressed and evaluated on the axes of both market speed and business uncertainty (including risk).

O'Connor (2008) used the term "MI dynamic capability" for capability that promotes the "exploration" process (March, 1991) to achieve strategic innovation under conditions of uncertainty and high risk. MI dynamic capability differs from the dynamic capability theory that emphasizes the evolution of the original "exploitation" (March, 1991) process, in that it is the capability to respond to highly uncertain situations, regardless of the speed of market movement, while embracing the concept of dynamic capability in the high-speed (or high-uncertainty) markets discussed by Eisenhardt and Martine (2000).

In reality, many strategic innovations start out as discovery or invention in slow- or very slow-moving basic scientific research and technological development environments. Subsequently, the core technologies and provisional business models discovered or invented are adopted and exploited in products and services through improvisation and trial-and-error processes (including the weeding-out process) involving manufacture, experiment and incubation. Product and service markets are gradually established, and then the new products and services anticipated or forecast as growth markets become competitive markets for other companies (just when other companies enter the market depends on individual businesses). At this point, the market environment becomes fast-moving, and companies accelerate their investment in necessary resources.

O'Connor and DeMartino (2006) undertook long-term observation and analysis of radical innovation in major US corporations, and stressed the importance of three-phase management (discovery, incubation and acceleration) as a radical innovation (strategic innovation) developmental framework. They then named the ability to implement these processes the "breakthrough innovation capability," and argued that building this capability into the company is a key business objective that can lead to successful radical innovation (O'Connor et al., 2008).

Previous research such as dynamic capability and MI innovation capability positioned around the two axes of uncertainty and change is described by the capability map in Figure 5.4. This shows the relationship between the previous research and the three development phases described by O'Connor and DeMartino (2006) previously mentioned. Here, strategic uncertainty beyond the four elements of markets, technology, organization and resources mentioned by Leifer et al. (2000) also exists, and change is not limited to the external elements of market speed and industrial technology speeds, but also includes the internal elements of a company's own strategy, organizational revamping and concentration of resources.[4]

The initial stage of strategic innovation (domain I) where there is slow or very slow circumstantial change with high uncertainty is the creation stage in which new ideas, business concepts, discoveries and inventions are brought forth. This corresponds to the "discovery phase" described by O'Connor and DeMartino (2006). In this domain, the exploration process is driven by the MI dynamic (or breakthrough innovation) capability mentioned before.

As the basic source of strategic innovation, the creation of ideas and research in domain I require (depending on the field) a longer period of time as the proportion of scientific factors and technological difficulties is more pronounced, and success depends greatly on the creative

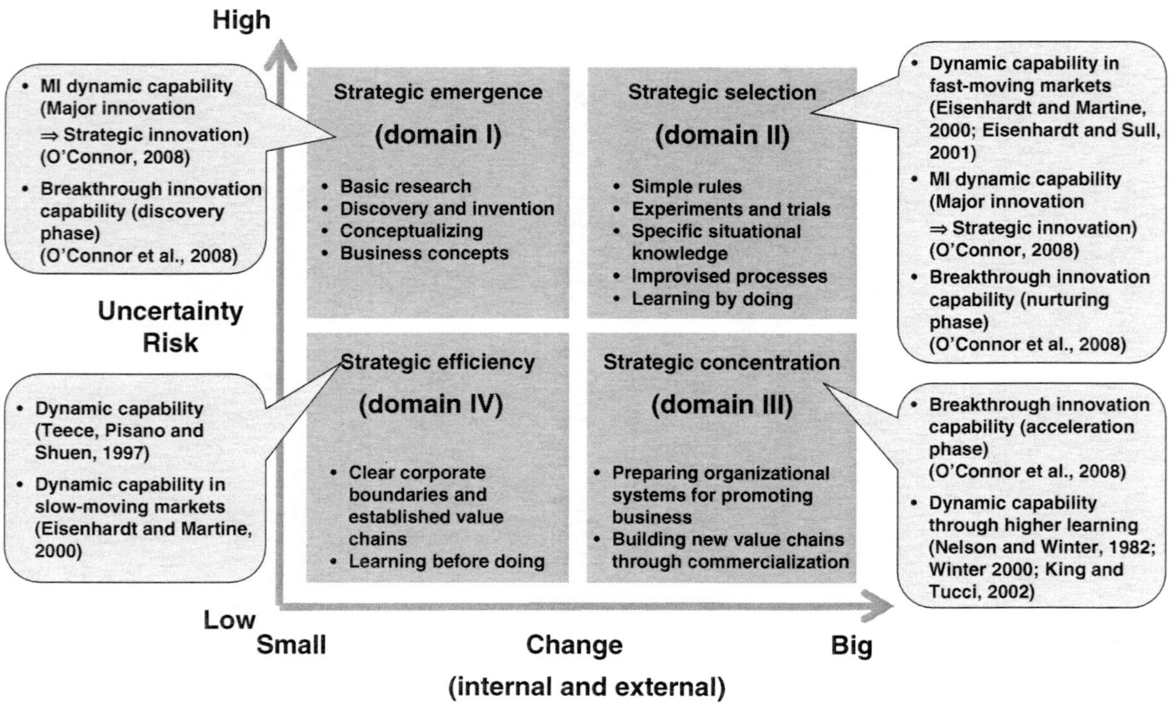

Figure 5.4 Capability map

thinking and action of middle managers and lower-ranked staff in a company's R&D and business development divisions, although there is also participation and commitment from top and senior management. The author calls the phenomenon observed in this domain "strategic emergence."

Next, with accelerated reshuffling of in-house (or external) human resources, personnel recruitment, and the maintenance and upgrading of organizations oriented to business incubation, the core technologies and business concepts migrate from the slow-moving environment of domain I to the dramatically transforming domain II environment in which rapid change and uncertainty dominate. This domain promotes the exploration processes enabled by dynamic capability (MI dynamic or breakthrough innovation) based on the simple rules discussed by Eisenhardt and Martine (2000) and O'Connor (2008), and corresponds to the incubation phase of hypothetical setups, experiments and assessments discussed by O'Connor and DeMartino (2006).

Learning through trials and experiments during incubation aimed at achieving strategic innovation also lowers the risk and uncertainty in markets and technologies and raises the probability of success (O'Connor et al., 2008),[5] and in turn, this enables top and middle management to make the decisions needed to select and bring to market rigorously tested and evaluated products, services and business models.

O'Connor et al. (2008) confines this incubation domain to trial experiment and assessment models, but in many cases where uncertainty and dramatically changing, fast-moving environments are coexistent, some current business activities transcend this definition in launching commercial businesses, because companies may gamble on risky ventures with a high degree of uncertainty.

In this domain, there are numerous cases where the high levels of confidence and commitment of the leaders and managers has lead to strategic activities and business creation through trial and error, in spite of the fact that it is unclear at the outset whether the newly developed ideas and prototypes will enable the building of new business models and value chains.[6] Examples of these can be found in the new online business world where products are both trialed and launched in dramatically changing markets of prevailing high risk and uncertainty. A key point is how to select and implement a promising and valuable business. The author calls the actions in this domain "strategic selection."

Having become more firmly established, the new businesses (including new products and services) chosen through strategic selection in domain II for their future potential shift to domain III, where uncertainty is further reduced to some extent, although external (environmental) and internal change continues. Domain III is the stage where the products incubated (or partially commercialized) with strategic innovation in domain II enter a growth orbit. This corresponds to the "acceleration phase" discussed by O'Connor and DeMartino (2006). According to O'Connor et al. (2008), this is where breakthrough innovation capability begins to promote the exploitation process: it is in this domain that the building and optimization of processes and value chains for the selected new businesses is achieved. New business functions are then wholly or partially transferred to the appropriate business divisions to accelerate commercialization (or new business divisions are established, or made independent as external ventures), and further resources are intensively invested through the strategic commitment of top and middle management. The author calls the actions in this domain "strategic concentration."

In the past, a large number of product and service development projects in major corporations have involved resource investment for commercialization through this shift from strategic selection to strategic concentration (Floyd and Wooldridge, 1999).

Capabilities found in domain III can be interpreted as encompassing the notion of inherent dynamic capability for incremental innovation, and enabling strong responses to internal and external change to create profits by evolving and diversifying operating routines through high-level learning (Nelson and Winter, 1982; Amburgey, William and Barnett, 1993; Winter, 2000; King and Tucci, 2002; Benner and Tushman, 2003).

There are, however, a great deal of existing businesses positioned in domain IV—in slow-moving market environments with low uncertainty and low rates of change. Here, incremental innovation is promoted by systematically enhancing business efficiency through the exploitation process, which includes activities to improve existing business with mainstream organizations that demonstrate inherent dynamic capability (Teece, Pisano and Shuen, 1997; Eisenhardt and Martine, 2000). Fostering these domain IV business processes reinforces an organization's abilities to innovate incrementally (Benner and Tushman, 2003). The author calls the actions in this domain "strategic efficiency."

As described previously and by the capability map illustrated in Figure 5.4, business processes related to product development can be classified by the four aforementioned domains, in which the processes proceed from domain I through to domain IV in sequence. In other words, the crucial processes for new product development occur in the procession from domain I to domain III, whereas the processes for upgrading and improving existing products are executed in domains III and/or IV. Looking at this capability map, then, we can observe and analyze what kind of organizational forms are adopted, and why certain ICT tools are used in the individual domain I–IV phases.

5.3.2 Organizational forms in the capability map

When considered in terms of corporate exploration and exploitation processes, strategic and incremental innovation, and the time axis of business contexts, the four domains form a continuous loop (see Figure 5.5: the author calls this the "strategic innovation loop").

The core exploratory processes for strategic innovation are found in the strategic emergence and selection domains. Risk and uncertainty are high in these exploratory domains, and there are demands for new products and businesses to be developed through new ideas and concepts. Therefore in these domains, multilayered SCs can be formed easily both in and out of companies to meet the needs for coordination and collaboration among business people both within and between companies.

"Strategic concentration" is the acceleration phase described by O'Connor and DeMartino (2006). In this phase, new product, service, business models and markets are rapidly set up through the exploratory processes of strategic emergence and selection, which is followed by the shift from exploration to exploitation. Strategic concentration then becomes the origin of newly generated strategic innovation that differs from the businesses established in the strategic efficiency domain.

In this strategic concentration domain, a newly generated business always undergoes major initial internal or external changes—internal elements aimed at building optimal value and supply chains to respond to external change are subject to major change. Strategic concentration businesses that succeed in establishing themselves in the market and achieve stability as mainstream operations then shift to the slow-moving (less variable) "strategic efficiency" domain, further hone their operational and business efficiencies, and either become part of the existing mainstream lineup or undergo business integration (which promotes still greater business process efficiency).

However, businesses subject to erratically changing markets and technologies, or major internal changes in areas such as strategy, organization, resources and operations (e.g. ICT industries involving broadband and mobile phones, online businesses, and digital consumer electronics)

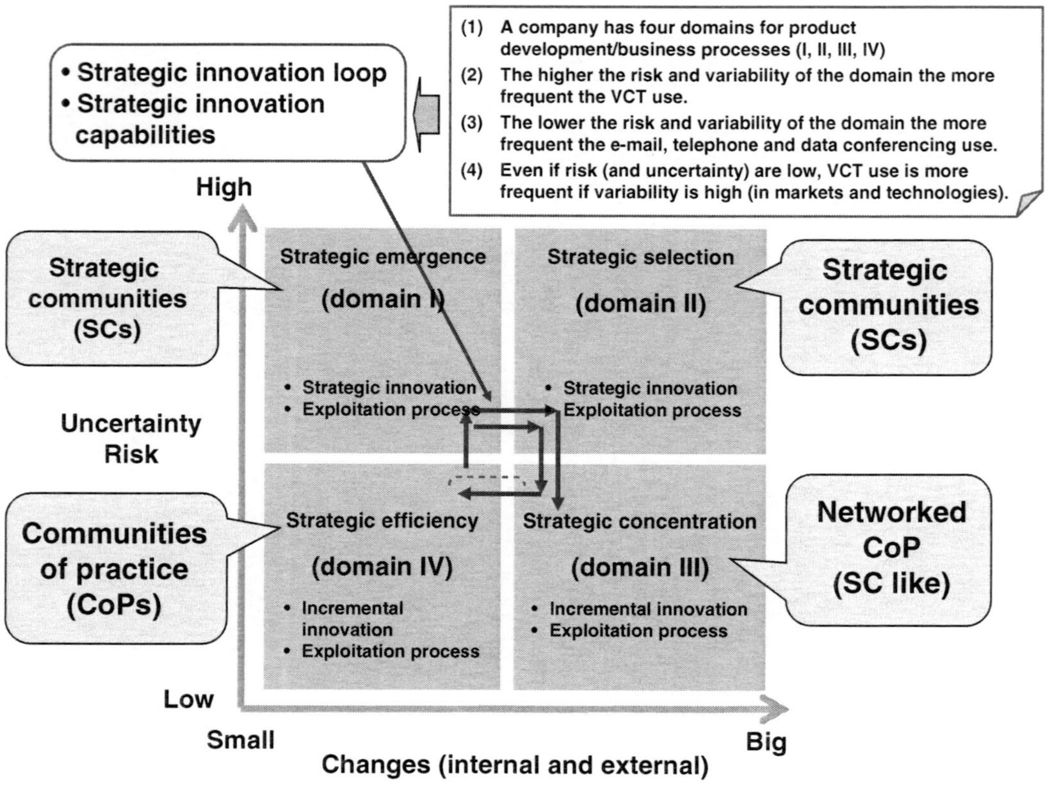

Figure 5.5 ICT tools' usage in the product development process

that are followed by mainstream growth, always become positioned in this strategic concentration domain. Put another way, businesses growing in a mainstream direction fall into one or both of the strategic concentration and efficiency domains.

Although new business in the strategic concentration domain is the "mainstream reserve," it does not mean that all businesses in this domain can grow in a rapidly changing mainstream environment, and some businesses have to withdraw. This is especially true of the ICT industry.

In the domains in which strategic concentration and strategic efficiency processes operate, where there is reduced risk and uncertainty, business people are required to both engage in activities to create new products and upgrade and improve existing ones. Therefore in these domains, CoPs form easily through organizational linking and information sharing activities based mainly in existing formal organizations (or established new organizations). On the other hand, however, when circumstances are rapidly changing in the strategic concentration domain, organizational forms take on the characteristics of highly integrated SCs formed along pragmatic boundaries from different CoPs as illustrated by Figure 5.1. This is triggered by "boundaries synchronization" among CoPs, which is described later.

In this way, the flow of strategic innovation for major corporations shifts from domains I to domain II, and on to domain III (where some businesses undergoing major changes maintain their position), and finally to domain IV (see Figure 5.2).

Amid this movement, businesses in the strategic efficiency domain may undergo old/new business conversion on the strategic concentration path (or shift from strategic concentration to strategic efficiency domains), which began with strategic innovation. Thus, the simultaneous management of existing positions and new strategic positions discussed by Markides (1999) involves co-establishment in domains III and IV. In this case, transferring from old to new positions involves existing business transformation in domain IV to accelerate, and new business in domain III to expand.

Realistically, however, although major corporations promote various strategically innovative projects, only some of them succeed after surviving the natural selection process that occurs in the shift from domains I to III.

Amabile and Khaire (2008) note a number of cases where outstanding ideas and business models born in domain I have been diluted and ended in failure after a major corporation employs a different managing organization to realize (commercialize) them.[7] This is one issue surrounding strategic innovation in a major corporation.

The most important interdomain shift is that from III and/or IV to I. This is the path to new strategic innovation (see Figure 5.3), and is characterized by accelerating environmental and internal interaction, followed by the creation of new ideas, technological inventions and discoveries based on high-quality tacit knowledge (Nonaka and Takeuchi, 1995). Tacit knowledge is cultivated through the practice of researchers, engineers, marketers and strategy specialists during the shift from domains I through to IV (accumulating and integrating new practices through both existing business and strategic innovation) via the "transformational experience" (King and Tucci, 2002; Amburgey, William and Barnett, 1993; e.g. Kodama, 2007a).

King and Tucci (2002) argued that the "transformational experience" of practitioners involved in continual (Katz and Allen, 1982) and large-scale (Tushman and Romanelli, 1985; Amburgey, William and Barnett, 1993) organizational innovation in product development teams removes rigid organizational inertia and leads to sustained new product innovation. Put another way, the transformational experience enhances the potential to embed new capabilities in organization members, thus enabling them to create new routines, transform organizations and achieve strategic innovation.

Although excessive adherence to existing knowledge in creating new knowledge integration can be a hindrance, the absorption of knowledge from different specializations and industries from scientific, technological, and marketing viewpoints, combined with the knowledge integration process, can trigger new strategic innovations (the i-mode and Nintendo game developments are cases in point) (Kodama, 2011a).

Various innovation theories including the importance of shedding the "mental model" (e.g. Spender, 1990), the focus on "peripheral vision", the challenge of achieving "cross innovation" (Johansson, 2004) and "destructive innovation" (Christensen, 1997) offer valuable insights regarding innovators, but more detailed theory building is yet to be undertaken.

The author considers, as a working hypothesis, that the evolution and diversification of high-level routines through advanced learning in domains III and IV fundamentally promote sustainable innovation (Christensen, 1997), while inducing a shift from domains III and/or IV back to I, by continually integrating new knowledge inside and outside the company to raise the probability of acquiring and integrating the new knowledge needed for strategic innovation.[8] The author calls the capability to achieve this spiraling "strategic innovation loop" "strategic innovation capability."

5.3.3 Collaborative ICT tools and product development processes

5.3.3.1 Methodology and analysis of case-study surveys

Before investigating the relationship between collaborative ICT tools and product development processes, it was necessary to understand how the phases (or steps) of product development processes in business change are executed. For this reason first of all, the capability map was created as a four-part matrix framework based on previous research. The validity of this framework was verified through interviews with 37 companies.[9]

These results confirm the existence of the aforementioned "strategic innovation loop" and the way that major, highly resourced and profitable corporations balance their exploitation and exploration activities. However, it could be seen that some companies experience difficulties shifting from domain III and/or domain IV to domain I.

Clearly, activities in domain III and domain IV are mainly exploitation processes for product development, and there is only a low level of exploration for new product development.

In order to analyze the relationship of ICT tools with the phases of product development in each of the domains, this research aimed to find out about the actual state of ICT tools usage in each of the domains by conducting interviews with 18 companies (eight Japanese, two Korean, four Taiwanese, two American, one French and one German) that have demonstrated a balance between exploitation and exploration. As mentioned, ICT tools were identified as telephone, e-mail, voice, web and videoconferencing systems.

Table 5.4 offers extracts of interviews about the usage of VCTs in each of the domains (general comments found to be common among all corporate users). In addition, Figure 5.5 has described the ways ICT tools are used in the product development process in each of the domains.

These results clearly indicated the following:

(1) Corporations have for domains for their business processes (I, II, III, IV).
(2) The use of VCTs is more frequent in domains where risk (or uncertainty) is higher and/or there is a high degree of variability (in markets and technologies).

Table 5.4 Video communication tools' usage systems in different domains

Domain	VCT usage forms (extracts of corporate user comments)
Domain I	• Often used in the research process to discuss problems and issues (medical product maker) • Often used to discuss prototypes and designs (automotive parts maker) • Used for brainstorming and ideas sessions (IT company)
Domain II	• Often used to discuss problems and issues with incubation (communications carrier) • Often used in the product development process both in and out of the company (electronics maker) • Used for supply chain-related meetings (electronics)
Domain III	• Often used to discuss interdepartmental problems and issues (automobile maker) • Often used for regular business process meetings and urgent meetings (chemical company) • Used for confirming schedules and milestones (IT company)
Domain IV	• VCT not often used (machine manufacturer) • E-mail and web conferencing mainly used to confirm progress (chemical company) • Non-urgent communication mostly by phone or e-mail (electronics parts company)

Number of companies interviewed: 18.

(3) In domains where risk (or uncertainty) is lower and there is a low degree of variability (in markets and technologies), the use of e-mail, telephone, telephone and data conferencing is higher.
(4) Even if risk (or uncertainty) is low, but there is a high degree of variability (in markets and technologies), the use of VCTs is more frequent.

Thus it can be seen that as a corporation moves through the temporal changes in a product development process (as the content of business processes change in the different domains), it executes ambidextrous R&D management with both "uncertainty management" (exploration) for new product development and "existing business management" (exploitation) for existing product upgrades, by responding to those changes with the types of collaborative ICT tools it uses.

What can be interpreted from this?

In processes in domain IV described in Figures 5.3 and 5.4, where there is a low level of risk, uncertainty and volatility, activities executed are mainly version-up activities for existing products carried out by

CoPs with low levels of organizational integration. Characterized by low levels of market and technological change, the main ICT tools that are used in domain IV are telephone, e-mail and telephone/data conferencing, which fits with the content of the development and its level of risk and uncertainty (upgrading existing products or developing new ones).

In contrast, exploratory processes in domain II in Figures 5.3 and 5.4 are high-risk, high-uncertainty and volatile processes in which SCs are formed with a high level of integration to mainly carry out new product development activities.

Notably in domain II, experiments and incubation activities for conceptualized new products, services and businesses are more intensified, and SC members have to discuss and combat the various problems and issues that arise in the course of these activities. With diverse participation from members both inside and out of the company, these SCs engage in information and knowledge sharing both globally and in real time, and are thus spurned toward maximized use of VCTs.

Also, in the initial R&D stage in domain I, where there is high risk and uncertainty without much volatility, participants from diverse backgrounds need to be able to engage in creative and productive dialogue to generate new ideas and concepts; and even though the level of urgency for solving problems and issues is lower, this is why VCTs play an important role in globally dispersed R&D project management.

In contrast, in domain III where risk and uncertainty is lower, but there are rapidly fluctuating market and technological factors, it can be clearly seen that the use of VCTs also increases.

Why is this?

With activities to upgrade products in high-speed markets, and shortened product life cycles like those found in domain III, products (upgrades and improvements) have to be released into the market one after the other in quick succession (e.g. the smartphone, TV and digital product markets).

This is why there are many more linkages between functional organizations (product planning, design, manufacturing technology, manufacturing, district, sales, support, etc.), which appear as raised levels of collaboration between different CoPs.

What this means is that the pragmatic boundary characteristics that emerge in the networks of different CoPs transform to take on the characteristics of an SC. Therefore, as business people in different areas raise the level of integration between CoPs, they have to share and use knowledge and information in real time more and more often, which means they increase their use of VCTs. Following from this and as a result of further interviews held in relation to this type of domain III product development led to the "boundaries synchronization" framework discussed next.

5.3.3.2 Boundaries synchronization

In domain III-type markets where technological and market circumstances are rapidly changing, diverse participants implement business through deep interaction across organizations such as sales, product planning, design, production technology and manufacturing. For example, digital and ICT businesses in this domain face highly volatile circumstances in which markets rapidly change and technologies speedily advance. In these situations, companies have to bring new products to the market in a timely and sustainable manner (including upgrades of existing products) or they will forfeit their global market share.

To counter this risk, deep sharing of context and knowledge is an important action that participants in differing organization and areas of specialization take by forming networked CoPs. These are the "R&D–CoP," "product development and production–CoP," "product development–CoP" and "sales–CoP" linkages that form the networked CoPs illustrated in Figure 5.6.

As participants work to bring about core product technology in R&D–CoPs, they discuss ways to pursue and acquire superiority with difficult-to-copy technologies, whereas product development and production CoPs are mainly concerned with executing development and new production technologies based on new product design ideas, and thus engage in discussions about how to achieve superiority over competitors through quality, cost and speed. These individual CoPs are engaged in learning processes for both regular improvements and upgrades, and innovation, and are characterized by the semantic boundaries mentioned earlier, and the strong linkages between these two CoPs bring about overall optimization of the R&D, development and production processes.

As well as that, binding ties in product development and production–CoPs, product development–CoPs, and sales–CoPs do not only serve to reinforce the connections between sales and marketing power, but also achieve both speed and diversification with products brought about by technologies created from the new product concepts based on latent customer needs that are distinguishable from competitors, and as these networked CoPs are characterized by pragmatic boundaries, they are similar in nature to SCs.

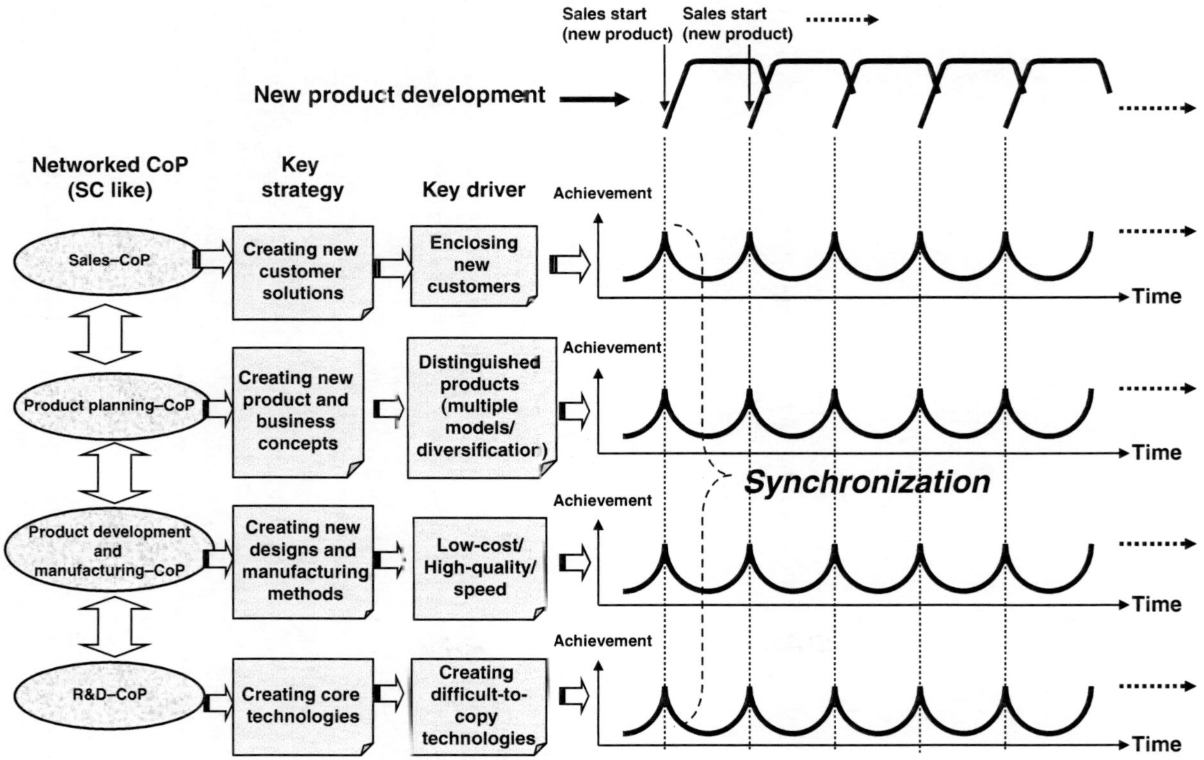

Figure 5.6 Boundary synchronization in domain III

The product development capabilities of leading high-tech companies are born through the formation of these CoPs, and the subsequent networking mechanisms formed among them.[10]

Participants from diverse organizations work mainly in their CoP right up until a new product is released, and the individual CoPs and individual roles are broken down as part of specific strategic and tactical decision-making, and the staff work in their individual capacities toward the product release.

However, if the business time frames for each individual CoP were completely scattered and inconsistent, there would be no optimization of overall business processes. Notably, this is why high-level managers in CoPs often have to participate in a number of different CoPs, different organizations and share and create information and knowledge deeply with staff members in different areas of specialization.

In other words, there is dynamic sharing of knowledge and context between CoPs, which not only serves individuals as they work towards targets, but also triggers "creative collaboration" (Kodama, 2007c) that engenders mutual support between CoPs. In this way, creative collaboration serves to optimize individual CoPs, as well as enables overall optimization the rigid linkages between networked CoPs.

In short, progress toward business targets in individual CoPs is achieved by optimization in individual CoPs as well as overall optimization of networked CoPs through mutual and rhythmical synchronization. Figure 5.5 illustrates this.

What is the concept behind this synchronization?

To achieve a new product, staff members in the diverse organizations discuss specifics about what needs to be done. And, the enormous number of actions that form overarching strategy and tactics are broken down into specific tasks in numerous sections such as marketing, advertising, sales, product design, development, production technology, manufacturing and distribution.

Of particular importance among this massive number of actions are actions that cannot be self-contained in the business framework of a single organization. These include actions that must be executed through coordination and linkage with other organizations, or actions that are completed by an organization but are dependent on the output of another organization and so on.

All actions that cannot be completed within the framework of a single organization must be achieved through the formation of networked CoPs that transcend knowledge and organizational boundaries. In these networked CoPs, the staff reaches consensus by discussing specific targets, meaning, methods and time frames about who will do what (what actions need to be taken), why, when, with whom and how things should be done. These are the practical strategic actions that staff members take at the micro level to carry out specific strategic and tactical measures.

Moreover, these practical strategic actions are often characterized by a dynamism that entails trial and error as times change. Staff must always have a "dynamic view of strategy", that not only enables them to execute "deliberate strategies" but also enables them to deal with "emergent strategies" flexibly, and they must be able to improvise to deal with rapidly changing circumstances.

In networked CoPs, staff members deeply share context and knowledge through creative dialogue, and execute actions that have strong mutual dependencies with other organizations, and, as the staffers execute practical strategic actions once they have been decided upon in each CoP, the progress toward achieving objectives is continually monitored.

As mentioned, the practical strategic actions in individual CoPs are interdependent with those of other CoPs. This means that collaboration and coordination with staffs in different organizations is required to answer questions such as who, when and how.

Accordingly, as staff members often participate in numerous CoPs (particularly upper management) and commit to objectives, they must match up the time frames, pitch and rhythm of progress toward the objectives for each practical strategic action, as they aim for the goals of the entire project (the realization of a new product).

In executing business, staffers have to get in step with each other to match the rhythm and pitch in the CoPs. This synchronization is the mechanism that achieves concurrent "practical strategic action" in each of the CoPs, and thus to achieve these "time pacing strategies" (Brown and Eisenharadt, 1998) the mechanisms of "boundaries synchronization" are critical.

CoPs networked together are knowledge platforms that bring about new knowledge through the sharing of dynamic contexts among staff members: they are a place in space–time for dialogue and practice, and the creation and sharing of tacit and explicit knowledge.

The new insight gained from cases of new product development (or developments to upgrade existing products) in domain III is the fact that knowledge and contexts exist in diverse, different, multilayered and networked CoPs. These contexts form and are linked together as members work in their main business area (with customers, etc.), or as participants influence other members of their organizations. Staffers consciously form and connect CoPs (to network them), because networked CoPs can become collectives of staffs in different specialist areas, and these collectives are characterized by knowledge boundaries that can act as a source of regular learning and innovation.

As mentioned, knowledge boundaries feature a pragmatic nature, and the increased risk, uncertainty and novelty that accompanies new product development.

Additionally, however, this research has clarified that even if risk and uncertainty are low, there is a high level of circumstantial volatility, organizational and technological contexts change rapidly, and are most likely associated with a shift toward pragmatic boundaries that emerge as related information and knowledge diversify.

For the energy of these pragmatic boundaries to transform into innovation, staffers must have "a strong intention to share." As tools to spurn innovation, not only are "boundary objects" required and not only do staffers need common knowledge such as common language, shared meaning and common interests (Star, 1989; Cramton, 2001; Carlile, 2002) but even more importantly they also need a strong intention to share that is rooted in their common values (Kodama, 2001a). This "strong intention to share" is also a factor that leads to the formation of highly integrated resilient networked CoPs, and thus raises the potential for successful new product development.

As described before, as networked CoPs moving toward the overall goals of a project (the achievement of a new product), they must be able to coordinate in real time to match up the pitch and rhythms of individual CoPs engaged in practical strategic activities to achieve their business targets. For this reason, there is an impetus for business people to use video communications to get CoPs in step with each other and bring about the "boundaries synchronization" needed to effect concurrent business in the practical strategic activities of each CoP.

5.4 Knowledge characteristics and conversion speed for product development processes

These observations and analyses have shown that the usage forms of VCTs are dependent on the speed of changes, and levels of risk and uncertainty.

As described in Figure 5.5, the author confirmed that as the preferred ICT tool for product development processes, the use of VCTs increases in domains I, II and III. This is probably because as the speed of change in risky or uncertain developments increases, differences in knowledge among business people and their individual ways of thinking become more diverse, and the characteristics of these interactions begin to look more like those of pragmatic boundaries.

VCTs offer support for the formal and informal formation of new SCs (including networked CoPs) as pragmatic human networks founded as *Ba* or CoPs. These network formations then dynamically create new contexts and knowledge (and change existing context and knowledge), and these transformative contexts and knowledge give rise to new meaning for the business people in SCs, and spurn the creation of new knowledge needed to reach common strategic goals.

The increased speed of change both outside and inside the company causes business context and knowledge to change much more dynamically, and raises the speed at which tacit knowledge held by individuals and shared among business people is converted into explicit knowledge (SECI conversion speed) (Nonaka and Takeuchi, 1995). These are the types of thoughts and actions of business people found in domains II and III.

Furthermore, increased business risk and uncertainty reduces the amount of clear explicit knowledge that is shared both in and out of companies, and raises the level of knowledge differences among business people. When this happens, more weight is placed on the tacit knowledge held by individuals and shared among business people because it can trigger actions that lead to the achievement of innovation. In short, the new ideas and concepts that are sources of innovation occur as a result of the interaction and sharing of different tacit knowledge. These are the types of thoughts and actions of business people that can be found in domains I and II.

The aforesaid increased tacit knowledge and SECI conversion speed increase the knowledge differences in and between business people on knowledge boundaries, and thus raise the necessity for activity styles characterized by close dialogue and collaboration. For these activities to run smoothly, ICT tools with a high level of media richness are required, and VCTs are the ICT tools that can meet this demand (see Figure 5.7).

By using VCTs, business people are able to intentionally (or as a result of their use) transcend organizational and knowledge boundaries, create new contexts and knowledge, and formulate networked CoPs and SCs, and by overcoming organizational and knowledge boundaries, business people are able to dynamically create new contexts with the "ICT capabilities" that are induced into them through the new perspectives they gain. This in turn gives business people the capability of building SCs through networking of new contexts.

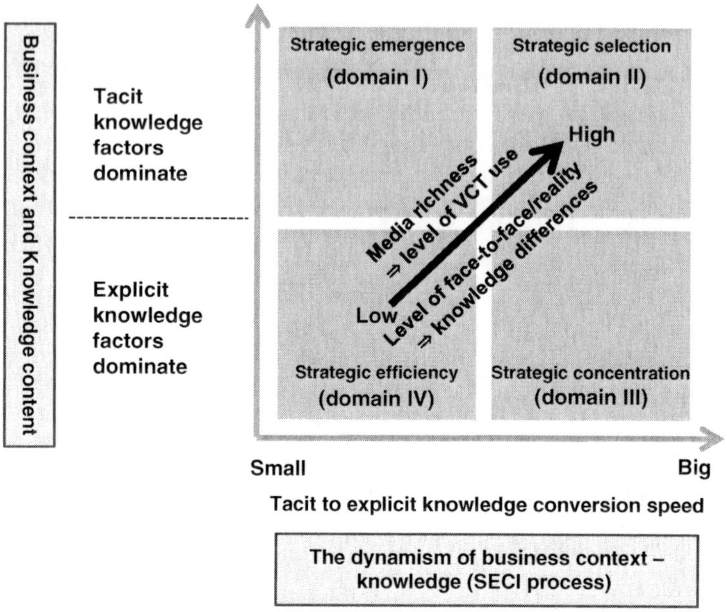

Figure 5.7 The relationship of knowledge context and knowledge transformation

Corporate ICT capabilities are core competences that enable business speed, business efficiency and creative business; and VCTs complement these ICT capabilities, because as a positive feedback effect the use of VCTs promotes ICT capabilities, which in turn encourages even more use of VCTs.

The new perspectives available through the proactive use of VCTs induce new understanding and awareness, and as these tools raise ICT capabilities, they also foster "SC building capabilities" through the new contexts brought about by the dynamic strategic and organizational contextual synergies that emerge inside and outside of companies—synergistic effects between ICT and "SC building capabilities" that drive even more the use of video communications, and thus raise businesspersons' ICT capabilities to new heights.

However, ICT capabilities are not just high levels of media richness, skill or know-how. As a technique, raising the level of raw media richness is just one aspect of raising ICT capability—the essence of ICT capabilities lays in businesspersons' creative awareness and productive interpretation that springs from the new perspectives gained (Wiseman, 1988). Chapter 8 describes "SC building capability" as an ICT capability in more detail.

6
Workplace and Collaborative ICT Tools

6.1 Organizational structure and office space

This chapter focuses on the organizational structures in businesses, their office spaces and the effects of ICT design on the formation of cross-organizational teams and human behavior.

Building on the observations described in Chapter 1, communications and collaborations patterns in organizations are determined by the interactions of the three factors of organizational structure, office space and ICT systems (Kodama, 2009a). Central to these interactions, however, are the interactions between human beings (dialogue and practice). Obviously, the structure of an organization influences the forms that communications and collaborations take within an organization, although the layout of office space and ICT systems also influence communications and collaboration in offices. This is because these spatial and ICT arrangements, including cyberspace, influence the interactions and pathways between people. Thus, office space and ICT systems design is just as important as the design of organizational structure, because it determines how people share knowledge and information, and how they communicate and collaborate while sharing dynamically changing contexts (creating *Ba*) to carry out business.

In the innovation process, creating new ideas and closely linking businesses in organizations is highly dependent on the quality and quantity of communication and collaboration, which is in turn dependent on the shared dynamic *Ba* among people. Therefore, organizational structures that are set up for real-time communications and collaboration to stimulate new ideas and brainstorming, and those supporting ICT environments and office space designs, are crucial for furthering innovation.

Thus as resources, the ICT systems in place, the organizational structure and the office environment influence whether the most suitable *Ba* can be formed to respond to changing circumstances, and establishing the appropriate organizational structures, office environments and ICT systems to promote human interaction and create *Ba* and "chains of *Ba*" will enable a company to respond to changing business circumstances, because organizational structures, office spaces and ICT systems are "workspace platform" resources that influence the formation of these *Ba*.

As described in Figure 1.3 in Chapter 1, the *Ba* form the foundations for the creation of knowledge communities, and it is through the human interactions mediated via the synergies in these human resource "workplace platforms" (organizational structures, office space and ICT systems in official organizations) that *Ba* are formed as new shared contexts that merge and transcend knowledge and organizational boundaries in response to changing circumstances, and from these *Ba* knowledge communities (or networked knowledge communities formed from "chains of *Ba*") are formed as new organizational systems.

6.2 Process and practice

What factors are required to maximize organizational capabilities using ICT? What managerial factors are essential for companies to establish organizational capabilities with ICT?

As stated in Chapter 2, these questions are largely related to the organizations and the knowledge boundaries among them from which knowledge originates. In academia, the relationships between officially established systems and business processes as procedures within a company, and the practice of organizational flexibility and prompt action in response to changing circumstances and business conditions have been discussed in much detail (Brown and Duguid, 2000: Lampel and Bhalla, 2007).

There must be some balance preserved between context-sensitive practice and manual and procedure-based processes. Management focused on processes aims to improve and bring more efficiency to existing businesses, while practice aims to pursue creativity as innovations and so forth that go beyond existing business, and in essence, corporate activity demands the simultaneous pursuit of both process and practice, and companies must have these different circulatory factors within their organizations.

How then should corporate business use ICT, and as a basic necessity, what is its relationship with process and practice?

Once again, the question of the best way to execute management that maximizes organizational capability using ICT is related to the various knowledge boundaries that exist in and out of companies.

Just as important as office space design, clarifying the mechanisms needed to make business more efficient through the creation and sharing of new knowledge by maximizing ICT use, while maintaining a balance between process and practice, is a major challenge for corporations, because it is the formation of knowledge communities across the physical spaces of organizational boundaries in which knowledge arises that encourages the triggering, creation and sharing of knowledge.

As mentioned in Chapter 2, it is human knowledge that lies at the heart of process, practices and ICT. In general, there are two types of knowledge—tacit and explicit—each with its own unique characteristics. However, both kinds of knowledge are important. Tacit knowledge is the source of explicit knowledge, and is therefore essential for the creation of new knowledge (e.g. products and services).

Individuals involved in business activities must be able to understand things and communicate them to other people, and they must also be able to put tacit knowledge into words and objectify it. This means that tacit knowledge and explicit knowledge are in no way independent of each other, and in groundbreaking companies they are mutually complimentary and in constant dynamic and circulatory interaction (Nonaka and Takeuchi, 1995).

Knowledge creation means creating new knowledge that goes above and beyond business circumstances at all levels, whether they be individual, group or organizational.

Obviously, the ICT revolution of recent years with its computers, mobile phones and smartphones has achieved monumental transformations through its support of socio-economic activity, and one major achievement of the advance of ICT technology is the higher levels of efficiency and productivity it has brought to business processes.

In the dimensions of human knowledge, the concepts of efficiency are related to explicit knowledge. One way ICT usage has pursued business process efficiency is by enabling explicit knowledge to be conveyed and shared—the ICT toolkit with its e-mail, web-based bulletins, blogs, groupware, data bases and so on has increased the efficiency with which people can disseminate and share explicit knowledge, and has thus become an important human aid in the processes of work routines and business activities.

However, when contrasted with the tacit knowledge hidden inside people's brains and embedded in human behaviors, knowledge sharing using

ICT has usually been thought of as mainly sharing explicit knowledge, although this is not necessarily the case—tacit knowledge creation and sharing by pursing creativity with ICT can be increased with practice. This is not same as sharing and dissemination of completed explicit knowledge; rather, it is the dynamic use of ICT to continually bring forth new business concepts. Continued practice with ICT enables the creation and sharing of tacit knowledge, and the achievement of creativity from which new markets, business and social structures emerge. While dissemination and sharing of explicit knowledge is of course possible with ICT, the creation and sharing of tacit knowledge cannot be achieved simply by applying the ICT processes used to manage explicit knowledge. It is the recursive ICT practices in which human beings engage themselves—accumulated trial and error and organizational learning—that raise the level of creativity, imagination, ideas and inspiration.

As stated in Chapter 2, companies need ICT to effect these spiraling synergies of tacit and explicit knowledge by forming knowledge communities and networked communities in cyberspace that include their customers, and thus acquire and maintain the organizational capabilities needed to spawn and sustain competitiveness. Recycling and integration of differing resources (knowledge transfer and convergence) becomes possible through these knowledge-interaction processes, which gives rise to ICT organizational capabilities that can be acquired as new and unique business resources for a company.

Sustained acquisition of organizational capabilities using ICT does not only require the physical ICT infrastructure itself and skilled ICT administrators, because it is the interactions among people and organizations in unique corporate contexts (changing business circumstances, strategies, groups and business cultures, etc.) that have the potential to result in improved organizational capabilities.

In general, individual companies have their own strategic and organizational contexts (decision-making processes, organizational structures, political power, corporate culture, etc.). However, the inclusion of ICT in a company creates synergies with those strategic and organizational contexts, which raises the ability of the company to maintain distinguished and difficult-to-imitate organizational capabilities and competitiveness (e.g. Clemons, 1991a, 1991b; Clemons and Row, 1991; Weill and Broadbent, 1998; Weill and Ross, 2004). These are also described as the "ICT capabilities" in Figure 1.3 in Chapter 1.

Systematic research into ICT and productivity (Brynjolfsson and Hitt, 1995, 1998) suggests that there is also a simultaneous need for supplemental investment in intangible assets such as a company's organizational resources, and reform of business processes in order to improve productivity with ICT. Therefore, this suggests that it is ICT investments that are intertwined with investment in human and organizational intangible assets that enable a company to demonstrate productivity effects. This is what distinguishes companies that greatly raise productivity from those that do not—even for the same capital investment in ICT.

Accordingly, the interconnection of ICT with human and organizational intangible assets can raise the quality of a company's ICT capability.[1] In other words, *Ba* are created in (and outside of) companies for the new contexts and meanings that arise through the interactions in the ICT environment, which triggers the formation of knowledge communities and networked knowledge communities as *Ba* that span the various organizational boundaries within and between companies.

Firstly, this chapter takes a look at the mechanisms that promote knowledge triggering, creation and sharing in the knowledge communities formed across various physical spaces in offices and in virtual environments through the achievement of dynamic and flexible organizational systems described in the case study of IBM Consulting Services KK (IBCS hereinafter) and its parent company, IBM. Then, the chapter observes and analyzes Sony's example of furthering its knowledge management across organizational boundaries in and out of the company through the use of ICT tools (video communications tools).

6.3 Case study (IBCS and IBM)

IBCS is a new company established through the merging of PricewaterhouseCoopers consulting division and IBM's IT consulting division, which aims to realize innovative ideas for IBM's business reforms and contribute to improving the value of its user businesses. IBM is a global IT solutions company operating in 160 countries and employs about 360,000 people (involved in this system hardware and software, maintenance, outsourcing, solutions and IT consulting), while PricewaterhouseCoopers is a global company operating in 150 countries and employing about 150,000 people involved in account and systems auditing, and management consulting. IBCS is a company that has been born through the convergence of these two companies' core competences. IBCS is mainly involved in implementing business all the way from the user's strategic visions and concept drafts through to research and systems specification design, which the company backs up

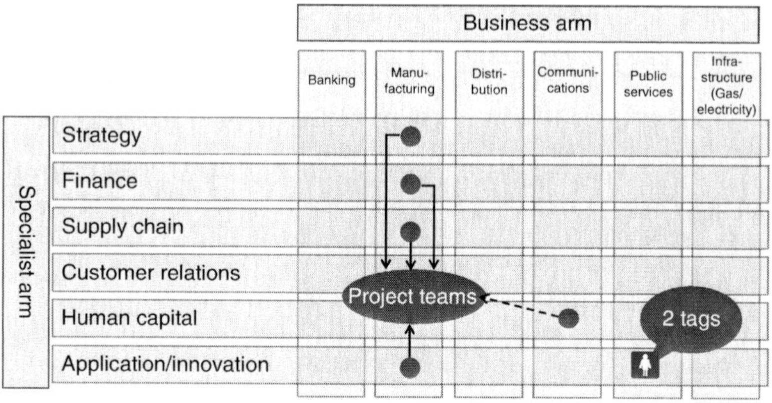

Figure 6.1 Matrix organizations in consultancy companies
Source: Interviews.

by providing users with seamless business linkages with IBM for system specifications creation and design through to deployment and operation. IBCS is one division of IBM, a globally integrated corporation, that takes advantage of professional business skills across the worldwide network, and offers users in a wide range of different services ranging from consulting through to systems development and implementation end-to-end support for sustainable transformation leading to business success. IBM and IBCS were merged on April 1, 2010 to strengthen their position as a "global business service."

At the outset, the organizational structure of IBCS was configured as a matrix organization consisting of its business arm (business fields) and its specialist arm (functional fields) (see Figure 6.1). In a matrix organization, two leaders in the business and specialist sections oversee the same staff, which means there are basically two chains of command. Matrix organizations in consultancy companies have the advantage of enabling timely matching of professional business knowledge with information about the target business and the needs of its users. This enables these consultancies to make the most of expert know-how, match technologies with markets and offer optimized solutions. However, the two leaders of the business and professional sections shoulder equal responsibility for the business that they are dealing with, and from the point of view of subordinates, the chain of command is somewhat complicated. This increases difficulties in managing human resources such as staff deployment, and increases the load on each other's business sections, and can also increase the load on subordinates and affect output.

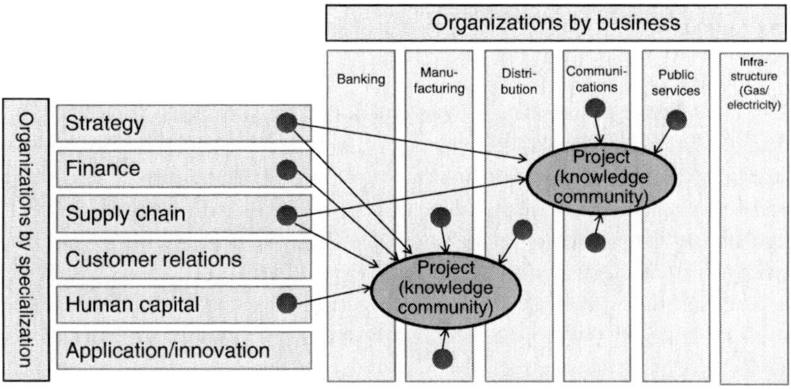

Figure 6.2 Organizations and projects by IBCS functions
Source: Interviews.

For this reason in recent years, IBCS has moved away from the total matrix organizational setup. The company now has a more flexible system in which the business and specialist sections are separated, and staff from these sections can be flexibly assigned to projects as required to meet user demands and their business objectives (business fields in the business arm of the company) (see Figure 6.2). Moreover, there are cases where specialist staffs in the company also simultaneously participate in multiple business projects (e.g. human resource development/personnel specialists take part in distribution and manufacturing projects at the same time).

As mentioned earlier, making the most of the strengths of the business and specialist sections in a matrix organization may seem ideal, but in reality an organizational system that enables the reassembling and merging of specialist fields needed to respond to changing circumstances, such as user needs, may be more appropriate (see Figure 6.2).

This is the type of system that gives IBCS its advantage, because it enables the company to foster knowledge sharing and knowledge-integration processes through the building and rebuilding of knowledge communities as project teams formed from the staff in its flexible business and specialist sections.

Through trial and error, IBCS has configured its office space so that staff can share and utilize information and knowledge openly to suit the type of business they are dealing with, and thus has strengthened its business and specialist arms to create an adaptable organization that can endure and absorb changing circumstances. Ideally, an organizational structure should be flexible to enable effective and efficient interaction between staff members, and respond by adjusting business activities to meet objectives. In addition, the organization's office space needs to be configured so that it acts as a mechanism to promote and support human interaction. Therefore, the best organizational systems and office environments are "workplace platforms" that enable new knowledge to be triggered, created, shared and accumulated, and those encourage communication and collaboration among staff members to raise the intellectual productivity across the entire company.

Consultancies basically offer intellectual property-based services to their customers. This means that as policy not only do these companies foster the sharing and use of the knowledge that staff already have but they also encourage the triggering and creation of new knowledge. IBCS recognizes its project teams as knowledge communities, and so makes sustained efforts to enhance communal intellectual productivity through knowledge community-based staff training. In turn, these efforts enable the company to offer value to its customers as new services.

To raise knowledge productivity, one aspect of office space design at IBCS is called "promoting communications through free address".[2] The consultants chair is not positioned in the traditional office manner; instead, consultants decide where to sit each time they report to work. Seating is only available for 20% of staff in the office. This forces consultants to think about where to sit in order to share information with other members of their current project teams (i.e. their knowledge communities). IBCS is also forging ahead with the switch to digital, paper-free offices, and complete digitalization of business processes. Accordingly, the ICT tools required to share information in these digitalized environments are laptop computers, mobile phones and the Internet.

The second point about office space design is "managerial transparency." The executive office (the "management cockpit") is also an open space that encourages executives to share information in real time to make speedier decisions.[3] Usually corporate executive offices reflect the vertical organizational style, with a wall (or partition, etc.) between each office. Partitioning office space like this does not invigorate communications between executives, and ends up reinforcing organizational boundaries, which is undesirable, because communications and collaboration among organizational leaders is the most important factor in enhancing the synergies of capabilities that exist in those organizations.

As mentioned in the introduction, and described by Figure 2.5 in Chapter 2, as the importance of new business models that cut across different industries and fuse together different technologies increases, collaboration among organizational leaders and synergy of leadership is becoming even more essential. The management cockpit at IBCS features a central meeting space that enables executives to easily engage in dialogue to exchange information to make decisions. IBCS is a textbook example of a company whose top-level managers have taken the initiative to promote knowledge sharing and real-time management with speedier top to bottom decision-making and transparency throughout the whole company.

The third point about office space design is "encouraging the triggering and creation of knowledge." Under the "promoting communications through free address" idea mentioned earlier, project team members are able to minimize the distance between themselves, which encourages the sharing of information and knowledge.

Furthermore in IBCS, there are many functional spaces (presentation and meeting rooms, etc.) in which staff members can meet with each other or with users outside the company to formulate new ideas, regardless of whether these meetings are formal or informal.

The first of these is the "Arena." In this space, many people—from within and outside the company, including users—can meet to share information and create ideas. This space is not only used for announcing the results of company projects or technical lectures, but is also used to conduct seminars with participation from users and experts external to the company. There are also presentation rooms called "Guest rooms" into which users can be invited.[4] The company also has "Studio" spaces available for staff to meet for brainstorming sessions to come up with new ideas. Not only do participants engage in information sharing with multiscreens, multiprojectors, Internet and database facilities in these rooms, they also use a range of applications and record the minutes of their meetings in real time. These Studio rooms are places where new ideas are triggered through dialogue and discussion, and are not just places for delivering reports and handing out information.

The company also has "Cube" spaces where two or three people can have a quick meeting (to discuss the progress of tasks and so forth) that are only equipped with a monitor.[5] As well as those, there are "Telecon rooms" that are equipped with a full range of conferencing tools (telephone and web conferencing, etc.) that are available 24 hours a day for meetings with global staffs (many participate in these international meetings from their place of residence due to time differences).

There are also "Collega" spaces for discussing personnel matters, staff appraisals or private consultations, and an informal open space called "Piazza" for quick chats and meeting with visiting business people and so forth. The open and common Piazza space also serves as a center of staff communications and information sharing, and as an exhibit space for various presentations (introducing IBM research technologies, technological exchange and so forth).

These office spaces determine the form that organizational communications and collaborations take, and also influence knowledge productivity. IBCS does not only reformulate its organizational systems flexibly into projects, but also devises and sets up a range of different types of office space to offer workplace platforms on which knowledge can be created and shared, by tailoring communications and collaborations and adjusting the focus of communications to the pathways between staff members. As a professional business committed to the use and sharing of knowledge within itself, IBCS uses its dynamic organizational structure and office spaces to engage in daily brainstorming and bring about the new knowledge needed to respond to latent customer needs.

IBCS fosters knowledge production activities in its daily business by creating these "workplace platforms" from flexible organizational systems and unique office environments. This real-time office environment enables people to easily form temporary teams and establish projects as they meet in these "free address" offices and studios whenever required, and for as much time as they need, and the Arena and Piazza spaces can also be used to announce project results or the latest technological trends. This type of office environment facilitates a shared experience in real space interlocked with an organizational flexibility in which people can communicate knowledge and express their ideas by engaging in dialogue. These types of workplace platforms are also knowledge infrastructure in which knowledge workers can engage in creative dialogue and practice to trigger, create and share new knowledge.

The diverse office spaces at IBCS encourage people to engage in dynamic exchange, and trigger the formation of dynamic knowledge communities to respond to the current status of company projects. Individual knowledge communities are always being formed in these office spaces as different participants meet up with each other to deal with project and customer issues.

These knowledge communities are not formed in some fixed way in a particular office space but are also created dynamically in virtual ICT space. IBM, and IBCS are proactive in their application of ICT collaboration tools on a global scale (see Box 6.1). Just like IBCS, the practice of trial and error through the formation of dynamic project teams (knowledge communities) from specialist and business organizations, and original office spaces (and ICT), can trigger the creation and deeper sharing of high-quality tacit knowledge among knowledge community members and bring about new business solutions. This creative dialogue and practice in knowledge communities can more thoroughly transform rich tacit knowledge into explicit knowledge as business solutions tailored to respond to individual customer needs.

Just like in IBCS, unified teams encircled by this kind of company environment are tied to the formation of knowledge communities, and the staff work to merge knowledge dispersed in and out of the company by dynamically adjusting these knowledge communities as adaptive and flexible human networks formed as *Ba*, without being snared by existing business processes in the company's official organizations (those based in the business and professional arms of the company).

One thing that twenty-first-century innovation companies like IBCS have to do is simultaneously make the best of their official organizational structures and the characteristics of knowledge communities. Knowledge communities give rise to the flexibility and creativity required specifically to express the work needed to realize individual organizational strategic objectives and corporate visions, whereas the official organizational structures ensure efficiency through their high-level expert capabilities in executing those tasks. The key to adapting to the uncertainties of the business solutions environment and changing customer needs is a total organizational system in which flexibility and improvisation can be applied, and official organizational structures and knowledge communities are adjusted to meet changing circumstances (see Figure 6.2). Office space design also plays a role as a medium in which these knowledge communities can be created, developed and recreated.

While "business process reengineering" (BPR)—the process of standardizing operations—was fundamental to the traditional white-collar worker, as knowledge workers one of the outstanding qualities of consultants is their extraordinary ability to respond with creative and impromptu practical actions that they enact through the formation of knowledge communities. What this really means is that business can never be fully standardized as processes, and over-standardization of business through process reengineering creates obstacles that prevent knowledge workers from exhibiting their full potential.

As in IBCS, knowledge workers autonomously use "workplace platforms" within the framework of relaxed business processes in the company's existing official organizational structures, and by forming knowledge communities as they engage in their business practice, they create the conditions in which new knowledge can emerge. In this way, knowledge workers are able to raise the level of knowledge productivity by harmonizing unique office spaces with official organizational structure.

Box 6.1 IBM's communication and collaboration environment and business reforms[6]

After a couple of major turning points in business transformation, IBM celebrated its 100th anniversary in 2011. These transformations were the result of policies that aimed to create a "globally integrated business," and have enabled the company to successfully revolutionize its business processes and achieve new work styles by encouraging communications and collaborations both in and out of the company.

The first of these business transformations took place in 1993 when Louis Gerstner was serving as CEO of the company, and the company branched out from its manufacturing operations to include service businesses. During this time, the information sharing mechanisms in the company were completely renewed to improve the company's ability to respond to customers, since this is the rock upon which service businesses are built.

At this time, IBM also aimed to integrate its operations in various countries to become a "multinational" business. The most noticeable feature of this period was the monumental changes that occurred with information flow.

In order to get information to all members of the staff, the company had to rethink paper-based communications and switch over to e-mail and groupware. This was the beginnings of the communications and collaboration environment that exists today.

The second business revolution at IBM took place in 2002 with Samuel J. Palmisano as CEO. The main objective of this transformation was to get each and every staff member to redefine value so that the company could pour all its efforts into ensuring the success of its customers, offer valuable innovations to the world, and build trust and individual responsibility into its relationships with all its stakeholders. As another of IBM's objectives, the company began to encourage bottom-up innovation based in market structures so that it could apply Internet technologies that had already become popular in the consumer market to new enterprise markets. At the time, many at IBM felt a serious threat from emerging venture businesses in the software and IT fields, and so embarked on a course of business transformation.

One of the symbols of this revolution was the company's global exchanges of opinion across the Web that they called "jam sessions." Through these sessions, IBM was able to gain insights and ideas from staff members, families and customers and derive three outlooks from the opinions and results of studying leaders in these areas (social trends: GIO—Global Innovation Outlook; market trends: GMV—Global Marketing View; technological trends: GTO—Global Technology Outlook), and thus set down new strategies for the company.

It was the business crisis facing the company in 2002 that triggered IBM to move toward this work style. Especially in top management, there was a feeling of danger that the company would not be held to keep up with global movements if it could not increase speed in all aspects of business.

Under the catchphrase of "One IBM," the company tackled this problem by executing sweeping shake-ups and rebuilding the company from the ground up with the aim of creating a company that could function as a globally integrated corporation formed from the 170 IBM companies that existed around the world.

The essential features of One IBM are as follows. First is the company's globalized use of knowledge and assets. This meant deploying the most skilled international personnel in the right place at the right time to create knowledge assets that can maximize value at the lowest cost (this also includes head-hunting), and encouraging the sharing and use of knowledge to contribute as much as possible to the success of the company's customers. Second is the global integration of the company's indirect functions. This meant creating indirect functions that are internationally consistent and uniform to realize highly supportive business functions, while at the same time, minimizing costs and maximizing value of the company's support services. Third is the company's ability to swiftly hone in on growth markets. This strategy involved building organizational systems and support functions that could respond to growth markets with a high degree of agility, while delivering IBM's experience as a global customer consultancy and its knowledge assets to its customers in the fastest possible time.

As an important practical challenge, and something that was necessary for the company to arrive at the One IBM goal, IBM also transformed a wide range of work styles, including the introduction of work-from-home systems, and laid the foundations for communications and collaboration such as unified communications (UC—see Chapter 3, Figure 3.4). For instance, it is impossible to speed up face-to-face meetings when staff members are scattered across the globe.

This means that as one objective, the company needed infrastructure that would enable it to overcome the barriers of time and place.

If IBM could consolidate its strategic and managerial businesses as One IBM, it would mean that the company would be able to share the business resources of personnel, materiel and capital across the boundaries between organizations and countries; use its knowledge resources more efficiently; and speedily shift its business resources into growth markets.

The key to achieving One IBM were the ideas of alertness, consistency and self-motivation. In particular, IBM created rules and policies as mechanisms for standardizing staff actions; managerial mechanisms for swifter grasping of progress; personnel mechanisms aimed for more effective employment of 400,000 people with a higher level of motivation; globalized One IBM operations (R&D, SCM, distribution, sales, services) and information systems to support those operations; and to achieve these One IBM business strategies, IBM built an information base as the groundwork for communications and collaboration. This is how IBM created a free and open-minded communication and collaboration environment, which placed emphasis on work style and dramatically transformed the work environment and the way jobs got done, leading to the work styles of the present day.

However, the order of these transformations was also a very important point for IBM. The company did not start from work-style transformations and unified communications. These corporate culture, business strategy and personnel systems transformations were constructed from a managerial base. This is because merely implementing UC—a set of IT tools—is limited in effectiveness. For example, depending on the manager, if the boss is only able to assess subordinates working right before his or her eyes, then business transformations across the whole company are unlikely to succeed; so IBM needed to introduce personnel assessment mechanisms that could interlock with the corporation's strategy and offer sweeping improvements.

Currently, IBM uses six general types of collaboration tools. These are portal sites, e-mail/middleware, mobile devices, UC, company telephony (FMC—Fixed-Mobile Convergence, IP telephony) and social networking services (SNS). Recently, the company has been linking these tools so that they are based on UC, and once a user understands the situation of the person he or she wants to contact, the user can choose the most appropriate communication tool, whether it be e-mail, instant messaging, telephone, web conferencing or videoconferencing and so forth.

"IBM Lotus Sametime" is a real-time communication tool that enables real-time communications from different locations with video—real-time communications that are not possible with telephone (one-to-one, voice only). Furthermore, the company is shifting toward using UC and SNS for external cloud communications with people outside the company using the company's LotusLive and Lotus Connections products.

These usages have dramatically changed the way that staff members share information. This "social" arm that extends across the company—its partners and customers—has served to strengthen relationships, and has led to the formation of the company's present-day knowledge communities and heightened the level at which staff can share information and negotiate. To find information, a user merely needs to find the related knowledge community, and adopt the method of extracting information from the community.

Staff time is valuable, so IBM pursues work styles that minimize the amount of time that staff members are in transit.

Furthermore using social and UC tools, staffers at IBM are able to work with people they have never actually met and borrow knowledge and wisdom from colleagues all around the world.

In its approach to workplaces, the company is shifting toward selecting locations that are closer to work, making better use of mobile and satellite communications, using regular office space as meeting space, and treating residences as a type of workplace. In this way many staff members are able to actively use collaboration tools both in and out of the company, and under the idea of "One Team for Client Work Style," staff across the entire company are able to take a unified approach to problem solving.

Managing Director of IBM Japan, Mr. Yoshio Kita, said, "As an individual, I really feel that the pace of work is completely different to the old ways, and at this rate time has become much more valuable."

To secure this valuable time, it is important to minimize the amount of time that staff members are in transit, so IBM has fully equipped mobile environments and satellite offices and uses UC and SNS communications.

Into the future, IBM plans to advance in two directions—linking various systems with its SNS arm to form new ways to collaborate and improve individual staff member's business performance, and fortify customer self-service capabilities.

IBM has also announced visions for next-generation products that integrate tools into its social arm. For instance, IBM's recently released Project Vulcan includes SNS functions designed to improve staff business performance, and has walled functions similar to Facebook that can handle e-mail and SNS on the same screen for seamless and integrated communications. Additionally, Project Northstar is a solution that offers easy-to-use and responsive SNS functions to provide customers with improved self-service capability.

As mentioned, the most important aspect of IBM's business transformations was not the tools that were originally introduced, but the results of trial and error and organizational learning that the company underwent to achieve the objectives of the One IBM business policy that led to the current shape of the company.

These UC and social tools also demonstrated their substantial effectiveness in the Great East Japan Earthquake of March 2011. IBM Japan was able to flexibly respond to emergency situations using UC and social tools during this disaster.

How did IBM Japan staff communicate and behave on the day the earthquake occurred?

Mr. Kita had an appointment with a customer in the morning, and returned to his residence around 1 o'clock in the afternoon. When the earthquake occurred at 2.46 p.m., Mr. Kita was working at home, and so was able to avoid the difficulties getting home that many others had to face. In the week following the earthquake, Mr. Kita made the decision to continue to work from home to avoid the prevailing transport chaos, with the exception of Wednesday when he worked at a satellite office 30 minutes away from his house. In that week, Mr. Kita was able to perform his daily business duties almost completely unhindered, and without once commuting to the IBM headquarters in Hakozaki.

Mr. Kita was able to perform his daily duties without any obstacle because of IBM's regular practice of adaptable work styles. Other staff members were also able to respond to the disaster with this kind of flexibility.

First and foremost, IBM's flexible work styles are supported by the company's work-from-home system. As a company that focuses on diversity, IBM also recognizes the importance of diverse workplaces and work styles, and as such many staff members are proactive in their participation in the work-from-home system. Mr. Kita himself only ever goes to the company when it is absolutely necessary. Many other companies switched over to work-from-home systems at short notice when the earthquake occurred, but because IBM had already familiarized itself with this routine, the company was able to respond much more smoothly to the problem of getting people working again after the disaster.

The foundations laid for communications and collaboration that enable teamwork played an important role in overcoming the differences in workplace and work times that arose. Notably, one thing that was used with increased frequency during the disaster was the company's IBM Lotus Sametime UC solution. All face-to-face company meetings that had been planned were carried out online via UC instead, and about a month after the earthquake, the Lotus Business Division made it a rule that Sametime be enabled for communications whenever working from home.

Although telephone services were out for some time after the earthquake, staff members trapped in trains (which had also stopped running) were able to use the text chat functions in Sametime to communicate with colleagues, and the company's internal SNS product IBM Connections was also used more frequently.

Many people were working from home two weeks after the earthquake occurred, but these tools enabled staff to communicate about the recent event with each other and feel a sense of unity and solidarity.

As well as that, SNS tools greatly contributed to recovery efforts. After the earthquake, a volunteer community was established to discuss recovery efforts in the Tohoku region as well as IBM Japan's customers, and a number of the ideas born in this community were moved to the execution stage as part of IBM's recovery support policies. Volunteer communities in international IBM bases were also established to offer support to Japan.

As a company with businesses in 170 countries around the world, many IBM staffers were affected by the great earthquake, many staffers were able to lend their support to the recovery effort, and experienced people were able to offer a wide range of ideas and proposals. These were also some of the fruits of the One IBM policy.

Summary of the IBCS and IBM case

1. As a "workplace platform," office space, organizational structure and ICT system design are important factors that determine knowledge creation activities.
2. The design of office and ICT environments is a catalyst that generates a diverse range of *Ba*.
3. As the foundations on which project teams (knowledge communities) are formed, *Ba* formation is encouraged through the active and situational interaction of staff in organizational structures, in office spaces and in ICT environments.
4. Ultimately the design of organizational structures, office-space environments and ICT systems is up to managers and organizational heads, and it is these people who must always take the initiative to drive the formation of new *Ba* through flexible restructuring of organizations, and the use of ICT and office space.
5. It is also important for staff to trigger and develop new business through the formation of active *Ba* by purposely using ICT and office space to form flexible project teams (knowledge communities).
6. To realize IBM as a globally integrated corporation that includes IBCS, all staff members are encouraged to familiarize themselves with portal sites, e-mail/middleware, mobile devices, UC, company telephony and social networking services, and form knowledge communities both inside and outside of the company to create and share knowledge.

6.4 Sony's business transformation with video communication tools

Sony is well known around the world as a Japanese electronics corporation involved in the development and sales of audio devices (household and portable), video equipment (cameras, Blu-ray players/recorders, etc.), thin screen TVs, PCs, professional broadcast and audiovisual monitors, and other professional equipment. Sony also develops VCTs for business purposes, which it sells all over the world, and holds a top-class share of the market for these products.[7]

Sony is both a developer of VCTs and a large-scale user of them. As stated in Chapter 4, VCTs are ICT tools that enable "video collaboration," and Sony uses these tools to sustain business transformations within itself.

Merging the company's high-performance high-resolution video technology, high-quality audio technology and superior human interfaces, Sony's innovative videoconferencing systems enable a real-time video experience by "sharing time and space" across the IP (Internet Protocol) network.

With its overflowing sense of presence and previously impossible face-to-face dialogue and collaboration environment, videoconferencing is a revolutionary IP network solution that has redefined the way people interact globally.

Sony's headquarters in Minato ward in Tokyo is the network hub of Sony's bases all over the world, and features executive offices that double as videoconferencing rooms. As the company's most important decision-making body, Sony's top management hold meetings to decide on a great variety of issues in their executive rooms, which are equipped with videoconferencing systems, high-functionality audiovisual processing systems, high-resolution projectors, multiscreens, voice-tracking cameras and even simultaneous Japanese–English interpreter systems for bilingual communications, all of which bring together Sony's comprehensive technological capabilities.

The videoconferencing system and the executive rooms feature meeting space that is furnished with superior user interfaces fully customized to enable high-quality dialogue and discussion and prompt decision-making. This combination of meeting space and technology enables natural and effective communication and collaboration, because it is as if all participants are actually in the same room.

Another of Sony's unique executive meeting spaces features an oval meeting table and videoconferencing tools. Because the circular design of this room reduces the hierarchical nature of executives participating in meetings, it serves to flatten the relationships between participants, and the flattening of the hierarchies in human relationships with networked videoconferencing encourages open and creative dialogue among Sony's executives all over the world, and thus triggers the emergence of new ideas and business models.

The feeling of presence with these real-time face-to-face meetings creates a *Ba* across the IP network, and by dynamically sharing changing contexts, members are able to awaken and share their tacit knowledge, bring about concepts that can be expressed as new explicit knowledge, and set off the spiraling positive feedback loops of tacit and explicit knowledge. Thus, the use of these videoconferencing ICT tools promotes the creation and sharing of knowledge needed to bring about organizational capability.

Of course, time differences need to be considered, but Sony's videoconferencing rooms are in use all day long every day to maintain the company's global activities, because communications are in the morning for America, during lunchtime for China and in the evening for Europe. Moreover, videoconferencing is not just a privilege of top management, but are also tools that are actively used by middle management and staff in daily business.

Videoconferencing is proactively used in Sony's individual business divisions to share information and knowledge in the company, to speed up decision-making, and to improve productivity and profits.

Sony also uses videoconferencing routinely for all the individual meetings that take place right across the business chain leading to the creation of a new product (product planning and development through to manufacturing technologies, fabrication, sales and support) and to confirm progress at these various stages.

As well as that, Sony also takes advantage of the IP network for certain product development projects to enable real-time *Ba* sharing with 24-hour videoconferencing available to supervisors in various divisions (planning, design, manufacture, sales, etc.).

Sony's videoconferencing use has three main characteristics. Firstly, it achieves speed management. Because videoconferencing helps executives to gather information, it supports the quality and speed of decision-making. Furthermore, not only does videoconferencing enable bidirectional and direct sharing of information among all staff members such as the will and intent of supervisors in various business divisions, but is also a strategic tool that enables staff to announce information or share their knowledge and enable its use company-wide.

For instance, videoconferencing is a knowledge management tool that enables simultaneous, instant and deep sharing and use of information and knowledge with business people in other regions, because staff in various business divisions can convey the nuances of the spoken word even when delivering business results or progress reports.

Secondly, videoconferencing tools make business more efficient, and revolutionize existing business processes to bring about greater improvements in productivity. For instance, in a manufacturing company like Sony, much importance is placed on the processes of concurrent engineering and front-end loading in new product development (Khurana and Rosenthal, 1998), so the company must continually rethink its business processes. In the chain of business processes from product planning and design, through to development, manufacturing technologies, fabrication, sales and support, staff members who are separated by physical space are aided by videoconferencing as they share their ideas in real time to come up with solutions to individual specialized problems and issues. Notably, the combination of CAD (computer-aided design) and videoconferencing tools enables staff members in different areas of specialization to establish common knowledge among themselves—which demonstrates the role that these tools play in strengthening the linkages between different organizations by deepening the understanding of individual business processes.

Thirdly, these tools foster the imagination needed to drive the creation of new business models and innovations—a characteristic that can determine a company's competitiveness.

The cracking pace of technological convergence of recent years, the accompanying diversification of business models and the acceleration of network businesses is forcing organizations, companies and technological fields in the industry to become more specialized and fragmented. Therefore, an immediate challenge facing companies is to merge the wide-ranging knowledge that is dispersed both within and outside of companies, and to fuse the boundaries between organizations to a greater level of complexity (both in and out of the company). Because of this, staff must bring about strong organizational capabilities that are able to give birth to creative new technologies and products by comprehensively sharing information and knowledge, and making speedier decisions.

To drive this sort of creative business, the old-style vertically integrated departmental structures must be wiped away, and communications between departments must be invigorated.

The larger the corporation the more sectionalism there is between its product planning, development, manufacturing, sales and support businesses. However, organizational boundaries and the individual-knowledge boundaries that exist among people with different specializations are paradoxically both places of friction and conflict and breeding grounds for innovation (Leonard-Barton, 1995), and new ideas and innovations are easily born through creative dialogue between different areas of specialization along these boundaries. Therefore, videoconferencing tools offer a way to network staff members in different areas of skill in different departments and invigorate communications and collaboration. And just as achieved by Sony, videoconferencing tools gives staff the power to bring about creative management and spurn the emergence of new products and business models.

As shown, Sony is one company that has been successful with the implementation and use of videoconferencing tools—a success achieved through the diverse processes of trial and error and practice, leading to the accomplishment of the company's present-day ICT organizational capabilities.

As a part of the Sony group, the case example next illustrates the success achieved with videoconferencing tools through trial and error and organizational learning by Sony Marketing, the company charged with marketing and sales of Sony products in Japan.

In 2002, the President of Sony Marketing anticipated that the introduction of videoconferencing would firstly speed up decision-making in the company, secondly reduce costs (by reducing the amount of business trips, etc.) and thirdly invigorate communications in the company. The President decided on a plan, and ordered that the latest videoconferencing system be introduced into the general affairs department, an organization within the headquarters of the company.

The company deployed a multipoint videoconferencing system capable of holding four simultaneous meetings and simultaneously connecting up to 80 devices, with around ten bases in the headquarter building in Tokyo (about 40 devices), about 70 business centers nationwide (about 109 devices), for a total of about 80 centers (about 140 devices). The company also introduced an intranet-based system that enabled meetings to be booked and held over the Web—a top-down ICT investment decision made by the President to put the company among the top ranks of prominent global businesses.

However, when the system was first introduced (step 1), it was underutilized. The target of five meetings per day (25 per week) was nowhere near being met, with only 0.4 meetings per day (two per week)—in other words, only 7% of the operational capacity of the system. To solve this problem, the general affairs department at headquarters extracted a number of problems and issues that the staff had regarding videoconferencing, and embarked on measures to encourage the use of videoconferencing with staff in the business divisions as well. The company proactively held various study groups into videoconferencing use, and was able to eliminate many of the problems that staff had with the new system.

These study groups actually got the staff to look at video images. While staff viewed the video images, the study groups focused on the sensations created by usability and audiovisual quality by offering hands-on experience. The study groups also offered detailed explanations on how to operate videoconferencing and appealed to its usability in order to

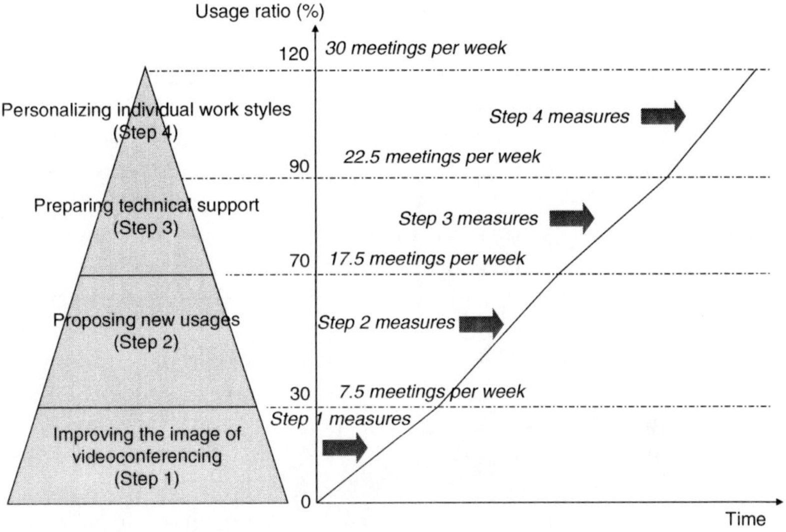

Figure 6.3 Increase in videoconferencing use at Sony Marketing
Source: Created from materials provided by Sony Marketing.

foster awareness among staff members of the good audiovisual quality and user-friendliness of videoconferencing. The actions that the company took at this step enhanced the opportunities for staff to "learn by doing" and gain valuable experience. After enacting these measures, the use of videoconferencing rose to 30% of the target (see Figure 6.3).

As the second step, the company proposed new meeting styles to staff in business divisions through the study groups. Specifically, these included suggestions for routine meetings such as the morning assembly, meetings to discuss the introduction of new products, supervisor meetings, policy meetings and regular departmental-head conferences, but as well as that the company proposed that the new videoconferencing system could be used for a range of meetings such as other morning meetings, meetings to discuss the introduction of new systems, environmental ISO meetings, occupational health and safety committee meetings and health consulting, which were originally held mainly by the high-end users in the company (the lead users). Through these actions, videoconferencing use increased to 70% of the target (see Figure 6.3).

Then as the third step, the company devised support platforms to help with technological aspects and further increase the usage rate. This included furnishing full-range technological backup systems and creating a more reliable and secure network to provide ICT support to staff. These measures included the establishment of a backup support center, and the distribution of easy-to-understand manuals to enable sharing of technical information about videoconferencing. The company set up a call center—just a phone call away—in case a problem occurred during a conference. This enabled staff to carry out video meetings with more peace of mind. After enacting these measures, the use of videoconferencing rose to 90% of the target (see Figure 6.3).

Then as the fourth step, the company introduced measures to enable staff members to develop their own work styles. One of these measures included developing tools that enabled staff to form independent videoconferencing communities. Specifically, this was a videoconference learning system that the company introduced called Web Study. With this measure, use was no longer limited to high-end users (the lead users), but now low-end users who had been hesitant about the system were successfully encouraged to use videoconferencing, and in addition staffers were encouraged to form videoconferencing communities among themselves (these are the communities of practice that encourage the smooth functioning of business, and the innovation communities mentioned in Chapter 2 that work together to come up with solutions). After enacting these measures, the use of videoconferencing rose to 120% of the target (see Figure 6.3).

The aforementioned steps describe how videoconferencing use rapidly increased. In this way, the three objectives of improving business process efficiency that top management had anticipated (speedier decision-making, cost reductions and invigorated company communications) were achieved, but in addition to that the creation of knowledge communities using videoconferencing that transcended organizational and specialist knowledge boundaries was also encouraged, which promoted the sparking off and creation of new knowledge.

Moreover, as staffers familiarized themselves with this cutting-edge Sony videoconferencing system, users were able to expand and accumulated knowledge, know-how and skills related to it, and thus fortify their ability to propose Sony's videoconferencing products to users outside the company (increasing the sales of Sony's videoconferencing products).

Thus, videoconferencing does not only increase business efficiency. It also contributes to enhancing the knowledge creativity needed to bring about new businesses.

As staff involved themselves in trial and error, the strategic actions that the company embarked upon resulted in the successful implementation of videoconferencing at Sony Marketing, and so Sony Marketing also advocates the strategic importance of video conferencing.

From the perspective of a unified ICT strategy, the actions taken by top management at Sony Marketing to pursue business efficiency through videoconferencing to bring about transformation in business by introducing videoconferencing into routine business processes achieved their aims, but the improved creativity needed to effect new marketing action and so on also became a major objective of the videoconferencing strategy.

The lesson learnt from Sony Marketing is that staff members use the physical videoconferencing resources to deepen interaction, and thus give rise to new meanings and contexts.

Based on the new videoconferencing idea of "learn-by-doing," the company was able to solve problems related to the system and induce productive interpretations and creative awareness in staff about videoconferencing as it embarked on the new videoconferencing challenge. This has brought about the effects of diverse communication and collaboration through the formation of new videoconferencing business networks (knowledge communities and networks knowledge communities), which have enabled not only the effective dissemination of information, but also creative dialogue and speedy high-quality decision-making.

As global and speedy management becomes more and more critical in the modern era, videoconferencing is becoming an important ICT tool that is accelerating deep and agile communications and collaboration both inside and outside of companies, and as shown in this case study, the real power of videoconferencing is demonstrated by its usability for communication and collaboration across a company's internal and external boundaries.

With the dramatically shifting circumstances of modern times, a wide range of businesses are grasping for new business models while consolidating their core competencies in order to survive and succeed. In particular, the diversification of business models and the convergence of different technologies places demands on companies to fuse a wide range of knowledge dispersed within and outside of themselves. This knowledge-integration process is one of the major challenges that companies face, as the acceleration of net businesses and increased specialization and fragmentation in organizations and technical fields are adding a new layer of complexity to the boundaries between organizations both within and outside of companies. Countering this, videoconferencing can greatly contribute to the bridging of the chasms between organizations, the communication of intent and the speeding up of decision-making processes.

Boundaries between organizations are paradoxically both places of conflict and friction and the breeding grounds of innovation. For this reason, invigorated communications along boundaries are a strong driver to bring about new creative technologies and products.

Sony is not the only company that uses videoconferencing tools. Many other companies actively use these tools in their marketing, development, manufacturing, sales and support operations to communicate closely across organizational boundaries and reinforce their ability to develop new products.

So what are the important points that need to be remembered for deploying and using videoconferencing?

The most important thing to remember is that business process transformations must also be accompanied by decisive action. This requires both top-down and bottom-up approaches. The top-down approach transforms the corporate culture. For instance, a company might introduce videoconferencing tools and ban business trips at the same time. This will have profound effects on speeding up decision-making and reducing transportation costs.

Beginning with the company president, it is important for managers to spread the use of videoconferencing in the company and give it momentum. This creates an atmosphere in which people feel the need to learn about ICT and VCTs in order to do their job, and so staff can be encouraged through company training. However, merely banning business trips may just result in staff backlash, but as the corporate culture is steered further and further toward ICT use, the justifications for business trips will naturally disappear, which enables a company to kill two birds with one stone by speeding up decision-making and reducing transportation costs.

On the other hand in the bottom-up approach, ideally staff members in various workplaces should form human networks that transcend organizational boundaries. This enables them to share common objectives and values, and create knowledge communities in the company as dynamic *Ba*. The formation of these knowledge communities as virtual teams that transcend physical space through the active use of videoconferencing enables a company to increase the creativity needed to bring about new products and new technologies, and thus reinforces its competitiveness.

Sony case summary

1. "Learning-by-doing" through human interactions with ICT promotes the spiraling of tacit and explicit knowledge and increases ICT organizational capability.
2. As a video collaboration tool, videoconferencing promotes the formation of knowledge communities as dynamic *Ba* in virtual space that transcend the knowledge and organizational boundaries in and out of companies.
3. Sustained use of videoconferencing does not only bring about speedier and higher-quality decision-making but also increases the human creativity needed to give rise to new products and technologies.

7
ICT Innovations in Health Care and Welfare

In recent years, societies all over the world have come to face similar health care challenges that stem from aging societies, rising medical costs, greater public awareness of health issues, medical treatment in emergencies and disasters, and the introduction of electronic medical records, telemedicine and remote care systems. Against this backdrop, as health care providers are searching for more and more ways to use these telemedicine systems, medical ICT solutions are advancing at a rapid pace to bring higher performance, quicker response and greater efficiency to the medical and welfare professions and reduce the burden on patients.

This chapter presents changes in product innovation in the medical ICT solutions field, and developments that have encouraged "user innovation" and "customers as innovators," and driven advances in user "ICT capability."

7.1 Movements in product innovation and customer value

Firstly, in ICT solutions in the medical field, there are the telemedicine systems linking hospitals via advanced medical information broadband networks that enable image diagnosis in the field of pathology, interpretations of radiograms and remote surgery support. Secondly, there are telemedicine systems joining large hospitals with local clinics to form district medical networks to provide medical support to remote areas. Thirdly, are the telemedicine systems that link medical institutions with patients in their homes to provide instruction in the use of respiration equipment, dosage advice and so forth. Fourthly, there are the systems linking medical institutions with healthy people—preventative medicine networks that provide access to health consultations (health checkups, home care support, and patient and family education).

The technological platforms that enable these telemedicine systems do not only involve information terminals for multimedia communications and exchange between cutting-edge medical equipment, but actually consist of the entire infrastructure, including optical fiber, DSL and mobile wireless broadband networks that link doctors with doctors, doctors with their patients, doctors with equipment and equipment with other equipment.

There has been an explosion of medical and welfare solutions all over the world thanks to the integration of smartphones and tablet PCs with cloud computing. No longer limited to DSL and optical fiber, wireless ICT telemedicine and medical information solution services on high-performance communications networks are becoming available everywhere with 3G and 3.5G mobile communications and wireless LAN infrastructure; and focusing on telemedicine and medical information transfer functionality, user terminals are rapidly shifting from specialized equipment such as videoconferencing systems as these functions become more and more accessible with general-purpose terminals such as PC, iPad and tablet PCs and smartphones running Android.

As illustrated by Figure 3.3 in Chapter 3, the focus of product architecture has moved from hardware architecture to software architecture, and from integral architecture to modular architecture. This is illustrated by the changes in user terminals from specialized devices to PCs, and then onto smartphones and tablet PCs.

7.1.1 Product innovations with modular architecture

When compared with integral architecture, modular architecture has the following advantages.

Firstly, modular architecture makes it quick and easy to create new functionality at lower cost, just by incorporating the right module for the job in the right place. Modules can be replaced individually if they malfunction, and there is no need for concern about affecting other modules. Or, if the module is a system bottleneck, then upgrading that module can improve the performance of the entire system. A typical example of this is replacing the MPU in a PC to increase the processing speed of the whole PC, without worrying about the other parts.

In many cases, advanced performance in modern smartphones and tablet PCs has been achieved by improving the CPU, memory, high-speed multimedia data application processors, wireless modems and so forth, and then combining all these into a single integrated and miniaturized high-performance module.

Secondly, diversified combinations of modules can respond to a wide range of customer demands. In modularized product systems, the modules themselves can be freely constructed, as long as they adhere to the interface design rules, and then new systems can be constructed by appropriately combining modules of various functions. This also means that individual modules can be mass produced, and if they can be assembled into a distinguishable combination, then in what is seemingly contradictory strategies can be achieved in which standardized, yet distinguishable, goods can be mass produced. This is nothing but the so-called mass customization strategy (e.g. Pine, 1993), and is also the thing that makes it possible to develop tablet PCs customized for medical and welfare applications.

Thirdly, individual modules can be independently developed in parallel product development, which accelerates the pace of technological innovation across entire systems.

Also in modularized product systems, because there is no need to consider how other modules will be affected as long as system design rules are obeyed, designers can focus their energies on the module they are developing. This means that to increase the memory capacity of a personal computer, one only has to focus on enlarging the HDD capacity, without considering how other parts in the computer might be affected. Similarly, wireless compatibility for smartphones and tablets can be achieved by independent development of wireless modem module chips.

These sorts of modularized products also affect the way labor is divided, depending on whether the design rules are open or closed. Put differently, whether to have open or closed design rules is really a question of whether to share the rules within the company only, or make them available beyond the company with partners or in society at large. Most modern PCs, smartphones and tablet computers have clearly been developed and produced in industries with this type of horizontal labor division.

This shift toward product development in horizontally integrated industries has encouraged the participation of a great number of vendors, has brought about cheaper products through the forces of competition, and has driven a huge market expansion.

7.1.2 Product innovations with software architecture

Software architecture too has advanced with the modularization of application sections controlled by users, core sections controlled by vendors and the establishment of software libraries (source code, executable code, library files, etc.).

Libraries are software tools consisting of various mathematical functions to control data input/output in terminals such as text display, key stroke reading, parameters and current icon positions, etc., and by freely combining these users can independently create unique screens to display information within their own original software applications. In short, this means that it is now possible for end users to add functionality of their own choosing.

For instance, applications for Android[1] smartphones are written in JavaScript, and so require a Java application development environment for their creation. As the originator of Android, Google enables users to set up the Android development environment by installing the Android software development kit (SDK) into a development environment called Eclipse, and the entire application programming interface (API) for Android has been released to third parties. Therefore, because developers can create whatever kind of applications they like, there are currently many developers all over the world who have released a wide variety of these applications.

As mentioned, libraries are usable collections of functions and so forth, while APIs are libraries for use with specific operating systems or programs—for example, the "Windows API." Libraries are an expansive idea. SDKs on the other hand, include APIs (the API libraries), and also include compilers and other utilities. So, rather than just say SDKs have APIs within them, the SDKs actually contain the things needed to use the APIs.

An example of SDK use is the recent Conceptboard whiteboard extension for Chrome created with the Google+ Hangouts API.[2] The Google+ Hangouts API (equivalent to an SDK) enables developers to offer end users the option of free applications (instead of paid applications) in a range of fields such as online video chat, pod casts, e-learning, games and so forth. Using the Hangouts API, developers can produce a range of creative applications. With this kind of open innovation method, Google entices developers to engage in new user innovation, which is why open innovation has the potential to greatly impact on existing SaaS and ASP businesses.

Because these simpler web conferencing systems offer an inexpensive alternative to dedicated TV conferencing systems (purchase costs, metered charges, etc.), open innovation strategies like Google's have the potential to destroy the existing video and web conferencing markets. As a disruptive innovation (discussed later), Hangouts is an element of Google's strategy to clearly distinguish Google+ from Facebook (e.g. Facebook can offer video chat with Skype, although it only supports one-to-one conversations, and cannot currently support group chat).

Many disruptive innovations like these have emerged in the high-tech product market of recent years. Even with PCs, mobile phones and gaming devices, technology and service trends have been moving from specialized to general purpose, hardware to software, dispersed to consolidated (the cloud) and from paid services (software, applications, contents) to free services (with paid options). Operating systems have been moving from closed to open source, games have shifted away from specialized devices to smartphone and game software packages and then on through to social games, PCs are shifting toward tablet computers, and mobile phones have advanced to become smartphones; while in the software field, there is also the potential for new disruptive technologies to emerge in digital appliance fields such as televisions and digital cameras. These trends are indicative of the modularization of software architecture as architecture becomes more advanced.

As mentioned in Chapter 2, high-tech companies (in their marketing, R&D, manufacture, sales and support innovation processes) are rapidly shifting away from the old doctrine of closed innovation toward open innovation.

Because open innovation offers a hidden potential to produce new disruptive innovation, companies must let go of their experiences of past success, free themselves from the chains of the old mental models, and forge organizational cultures and habits that constantly question everything. The open innovation approach is crucial for companies to establish strategic processes of democratic participation and seek out the varied thought processes and knowledge that spring from diverse fields of specialization, including those outside of the company, and build that knowledge into their formal strategic planning.

Just like the Google strategy, open innovation makes the most of core users and best partners all over the world, and ignites co-creation of new markets with partners and users and co-evolution among all the proximal industries involved. Open innovation establishes the advanced ICT platforms needed for co-creation and co-evolution, and raises the potential for new business ecosystems to be born.

7.1.3 Product innovation with "Customers as Innovators"

Following is a theoretical discussion of the SDKs that have been born through the advances in modularized software architecture.

As a leading researcher, Hippel (1998, 2002) showed that in certain industries (custom LSI and the CTI fields, etc.), developing toolkits for customers (SDKs) enables the work needed to customize products and applications solutions to shift toward customers as they use these toolkits. Custom LSI toolkits enable customers to develop, design and assess their own prototypes; and in the case of LSIs, devices that enable customers to create functions they desire by programming electronic circuits at the logical level (called field programmable gate arrays or FPGA) are equivalent to these, in the narrow sense of application-specific integrated circuits (ASICs)—rewritable programs enable the customers themselves to freely check the performance of prototypes.

Currently only enacted in a limited number of fields, the Customers as Innovators (CAI) approach shifts all innovation tasks related to needs information (prototype design and creation, simulations, assessments, etc.) to the customer, while the product developers and manufacturers (the company side) abandon their efforts to understand customer needs precisely or in any detail.

As a result, this toolkit approach can dramatically reduce costs related to transferring "sticky information,"[3] because product and service development tasks are divided into the two subtasks of needs information at the customer side, and solutions information at the company side, which enables the company to concentrate on routine business without having to understand the "highly sticky" details of customer needs, while the toolkit enables the customer to effectively achieve the precise functionality that they desire through trial and error.

Advances in software architecture like this have enabled users and vendors to operate independently and simultaneously to bring about new innovation as they work to develop application software and backbone software respectively.[4]

What are the factors that have come to define these kinds of software architecture advances?

There are big advantages for both vendors and users if software applications that have a high level of sticky needs information are developed directly by users. This has been enabled by software architecture advances in which the user application sections and the vendor development sections have been modularized. In other words, the encouraging of user innovation is a factor that has influenced the processes through which software architecture has evolved.

7.1.4 User innovation through software architecture

Who exactly is in charge of innovation?

Generally it is believed that vendors engaged in product development are the ones doing the innovating. In that case, user innovation is a

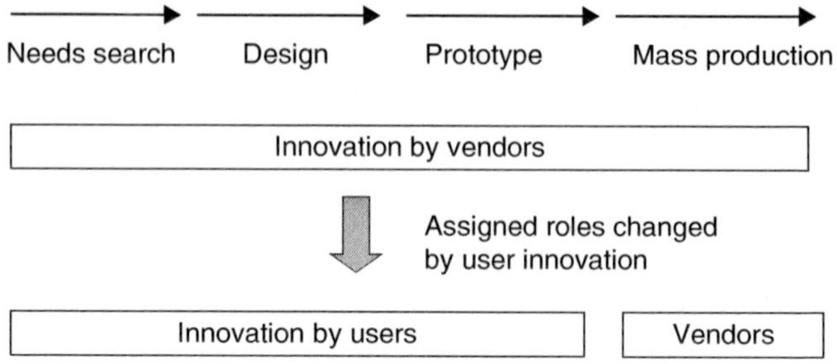

Figure 7.1 User innovation

phenomenon whereby the traditional consumers of innovation—that is, the users—have become the producers of innovation: users have become innovators as well. According to the research carried out by Hippel (1998, 2002), which first identified the user innovation phenomenon, there are cases where up to 67% of capital goods such as printed circuit board assembly equipment were innovated by users.

User innovation changes the roles played by users and vendors in the innovation process as follows.

In the general innovation process illustrated in Figure 7.1, the chain of processes begins with searching for user needs, which is followed by designing products to meet these needs, and through the development of prototypes finally arrives at mass production if all goes well. Traditionally, all of these processes were carried out by the vendor. However, in the case of user innovation, the only role played by the vendor is that of mass production, whereas the user performs the processes up to and including the development of prototypes. In this way, user involvement doesn't just simply stop at conveying needs information, but extends right through the development process.

How is it that users can be innovators?

One possible reason is the existence of "learning-by-using" processes. It was Rosenberg who pointed out that by actually using products and services, users are able acquire a deeper understanding of the characteristics and operability of a product, and as a result clarify knowledge and needs related to it. Rosenberg conceptualized the existence of these learning processes as "learning by using" (Rosenberg, 1982). With learning by using, knowledge can be acquired that only becomes clear for the first time through the experience of actually using something, which can result in reduced service costs when observed in terms of service costs indicators.

It follows that users who have deeper experience in the usage of a product will have valuable opinions about how the product can be improved or where it is defective.

Rapid prototyping in software development is also one way that learning by using is incorporated into product development. In this approach, software product prototypes are shipped as early as possible so that users will be able to actually start using the products early in the development stage, so that user demands can be reflected into the final product as soon as possible. User experience thus enables the acquisition of knowledge that is not available at the design stage, and that can be incorporated into the product design.

In other words, the process of "using" is not just simply consuming some product or service, but also contains a learning aspect. This is to say that there are cases where user knowledge and experience is superior to that of the vendor, and as such users have a hidden potential to become innovators. However, it goes without saying that users won't necessarily achieve innovation in every single instance—sometimes it happens and sometimes it doesn't.

How can we understand this difference?

Conceptually, this is related to the aforementioned stickiness of information—one that determines whether innovation happens at the vendor side or at the user side.

Using the SDKs provided by Google and Apple, users can freely develop all kinds of applications for smartphones and tablet PCs. Google and Apple have aimed for user innovation at the consumer level by releasing CAI toolkits to specific users, and then to the mass user.

7.1.5 Product innovation with video communication tools

In videoconferencing system hardware, the adopting of newer technological elements into products (e.g. Digital Signal Processors or DSPs, Micro Processor Units or MPUs) has resulted in new demands for modularization and design rules, and brought about advances in architecture.

One of the main factors that caused architecture to evolve was the incompatibility between conventional modular segmentation and the development of newer technical elements to make up product systems. Due to this incompatibility, modularized segments needed to be reconstructed so that they could fit with the advanced technological elements.

These advances have made it possible to include functions that were formally found across a range of components into a single component. A typical example of this is a single-system LSI that contains the functions of a number of different LSIs. Also, advanced high-density, high-precision surface mounting and 3D mounting technologies have made it possible to crowd many more functions into the same amount of space, which means it is now possible to include functions on a single printed circuit that used to be spread out over many circuit boards.

The ability to include more and more functions into single components in this way changes the mapping relationship between the functions and structure, and thus results in incompatibility with older module segmentation, which means new module segmentation must be found.

The outcome of this is fewer physical modules that comprise the system and simpler design rules that define the module interfaces, which simultaneously raises product quality, drives miniaturization and lowers costs.

Technological dynamism is also illustrated in the advances of hardware architecture, as shown in Figure 7.2. Hardware has evolved away from specialized teleconferencing terminals and TV phones (1) through to compact specialized terminals (2 and 3). Also, the trend of miniaturization through modularization has led to the developmental approach (4) of high-quality TV conferencing (telepresence, etc.) targeting high-end users and offering even greater functionality enabled by combinations of hi-tech modules; while on the software architecture side, more uniformity of programming languages[5] has helped to promote user innovation, and has had a huge impact on the pathway along which software architecture has advanced.

In particular, the more sophisticated programming languages of recent years have lowered the level of technical skill needed for application software programming and have made it easier for users to participate directly in innovation by developing applications for devices like smartphones and tablet PCs, and since more users can now program the threshold where user innovation is triggered is not as high as it used to be.

As is shown by the example of the smartphone, architecture adjusted so that vendors develop their section and users develop applications is one type of architecture that encourages user innovation. It is this direction that software architecture is heading (5 in Figure 7.2).

Typified by the smartphones and tablet PCs represented at (5) in Figure 7.2, the shift in product hardware and software architecture from integral to modularized has brought more compact products with lower costs and improved user interfaces, and has spurned an expansion into new customer bases from business users through to users in specific industries (e.g. health care, welfare, education, etc.) and mass users in general.

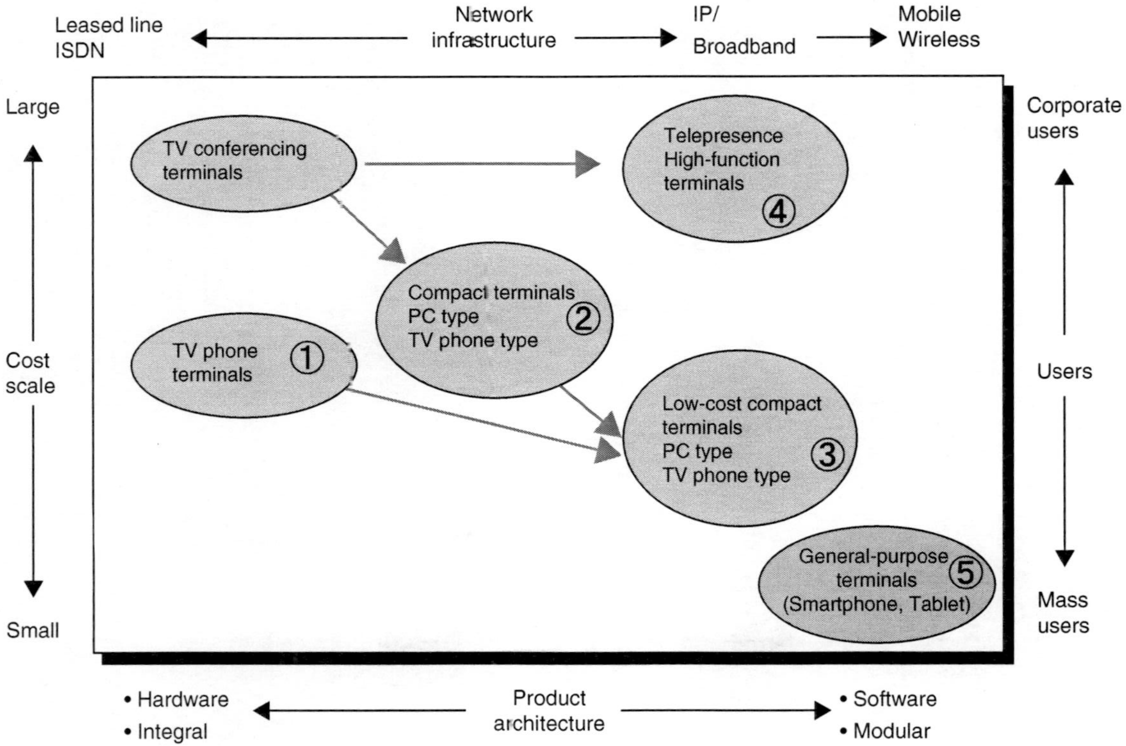

Figure 7.2 Technological innovations and advances in product architecture

As mentioned, with ICT solutions and the field of health care, the majority of terminals used are high-functionality specialized terminals shown at (4) for telemedicine between hospitals, compact PC and TV phone type terminals shown at (2) and (3) for telemedicine between large hospitals, local clinics and examination centers, specialized TV phones shown at (1), compact PC types (3) for telemedicine between medical institutions and patient residences, and the general-purpose smartphone and tablet terminals (5) for communications between healthy persons and medical institutions.

The product architecture of the smartphone and tablet PCs especially encourages the user innovation and CAI models mentioned, in which it is the users that raise the level of ICT application capability and ICT context architect capability (described later)—new elements of ICT capability.

Moreover, new application development and pioneering of usages enabled by the general-purpose terminals (5) are not only used for communications between healthy persons and medical institutions but are increasingly being used for communications between medical institutions and patients at their residence, large regional hospitals and local clinics and examination centers, and between hospitals (see Figure 7.3).

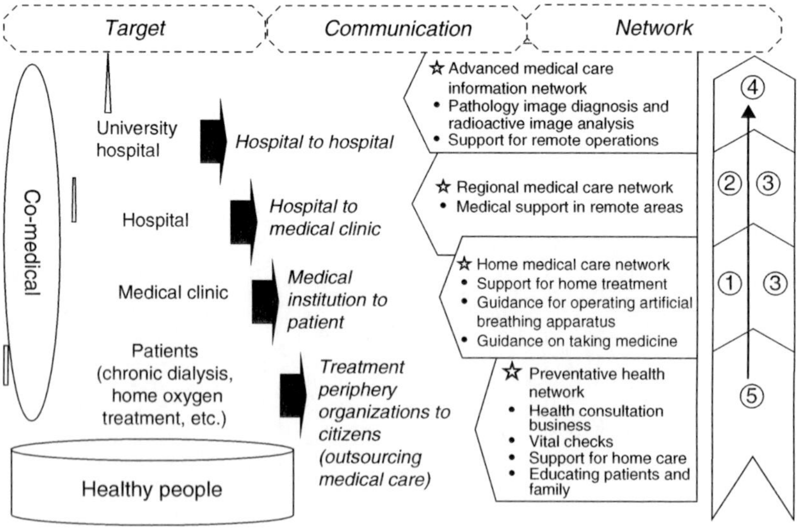

Figure 7.3 ICT solutions in medical care

7.2 Telemedicine and welfare cases

This section describes specific cases using various types of terminals that were developed as ICT solutions in the health care and welfare fields, enabled by the technological innovations and the changes in product architecture illustrated in Figure 7.2.

Firstly, we will look at the examples of telemedicine between medical institutions and patients in their homes using specialized TV phone terminals (1) and the PC and TV phone types (2) and (3) used to provide and home-care support and medical support to remote areas. Then we will look at actual cases of advanced health care support between health care workers and patients using the high-functionality terminals shown at (4). We will also look at usage in emergency situations. Finally, we take a look at a few cases of general-purpose terminal usage shown at (5), for communications within hospitals, between hospitals and between physicians and patients.

Important discoveries in these cases are the birth of new usages and mechanisms, and the development of new applications that arose by encouraging the process of "learning by using" among physician and patient users. These types of learning processes give rise to ICT application capability, new ways of using these systems and new mechanisms, while of special importance is the "ICT context architect capability" that creates new value and meaning.

7.2.1 Remote area and home-care medical support

As local government bodies all over the world aim to achieve societies with higher living standards, they are proactive in their approach to the wide-ranging challenges presented by education, health care, welfare, environment, business, tourism, public works, disaster response and so forth, and strive to develop a variety of measures aimed at solving these problems locally, while listening to the desires and complaints of citizens on a daily basis. Thus, there is an urgency to find comprehensive solutions to various individual problems in the education, health care and welfare fields.

Overcoming the barriers of distance and time in daily activities enables people to expand the domain of those activities and increase their potential, which is why ICT offers such a tremendous capability to respond to local problems and the needs of citizens, and raise the living standards of society as a whole. This section presents cases of remote medical support and home-care support, both of which are challenges of the present day.

7.2.1.1 Remote medical support

Especially in the medical, health and welfare fields, a serious twenty-first-century challenge for local societies is the achievement of "regional regeneration" through the effective use of ICT to create virtual communities and create new value within and between communities.

Created by a number of hospital and ICT businesses with active participation from the national and local government, the Multi Media Village Plan in Katsurao Village in Fukushima Prefecture in Japan is a grand technological project on a scale unlike any other (*The New York Times*, 1999) (see Figure 7.4).

To reduce the burden that patients and families must face by traveling to hospital, and to increase efficiencies related to home visits by doctors, Katsurao Village has a system of TV phones in place that enables remote home treatment and health consultation.

As general medical and welfare support, this system enables home helpers to see elderly patients on the TV phone screen and provide more thorough care with early discovery for faster response in case of emergency. The system also enables users to receive exercise lessons delivered to their home from the local welfare center. As well as that these TV phones provide sign language support for the hearing impaired, and information about insurance and welfare as video on demand (VOD) content viewable in residences in the village (see Figures 7.5 and 7.6).

The use of sensors and telemedicine to detect vital signs and medicine home delivery for patients with chronic illnesses after clinical examination via videophone (see Figure 7.7) were revolutionary developments in Japan: doctors can examine patients via videophone and prescribe medicines as required, and send prescriptions to a pharmacy via fax or e-mail and forward the prescription to the patient. The pharmacy then prepares the medicine according to the fax or e-mail prescription, then a staff member can go to the patient's residence with the medicine and match it with the original prescription. Then the patient can hand over the original prescription and the cost of the medicine, including the delivery fee, to receive the medicine.

Candidates eligible for home delivery are patients with chronic illnesses such as high blood pressure and rheumatism whose condition is stable (in April 1999, the Japanese Ministry of Health granted permission for home delivery of medicines following from examinations via videophone). Thus, beginning with Katsurao Village, the curtain was lifted on a brand new era of residence-centered multimedia systems that opened frontiers of exploration into the ways that these systems

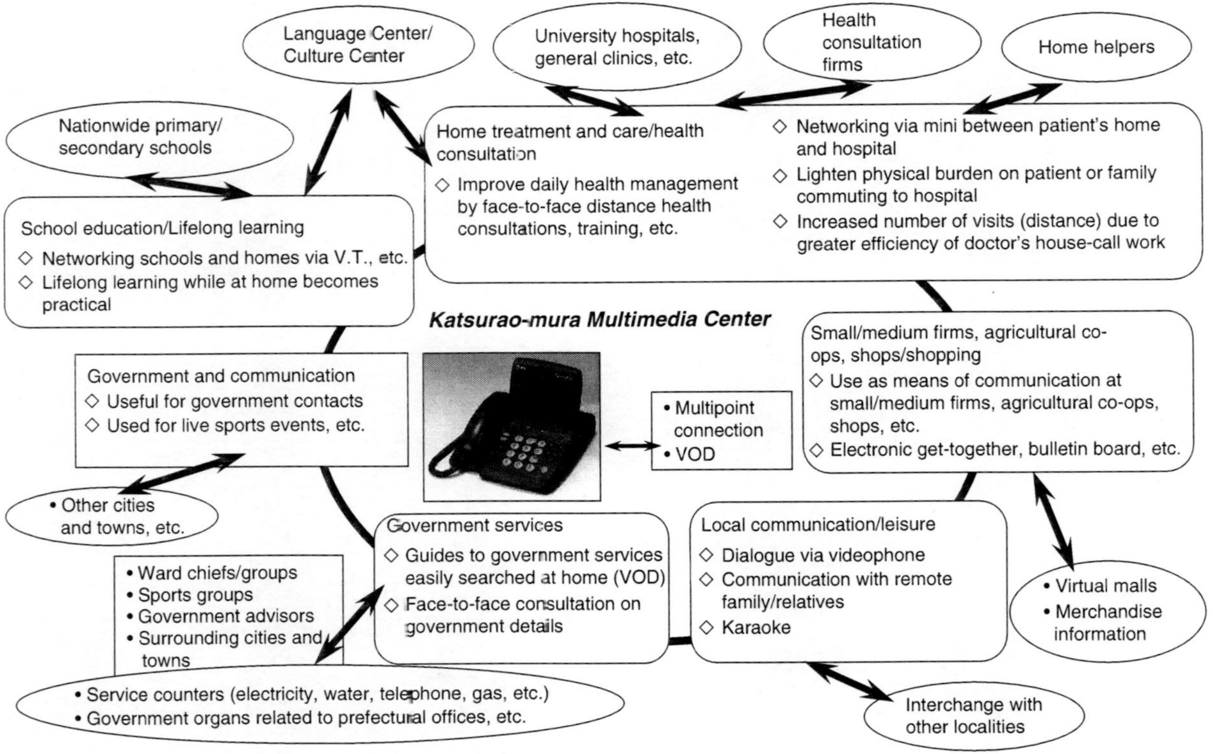

Figure 7.4 Multimedia village in Katsurao-mura encompassing treatment, education, government and leisure

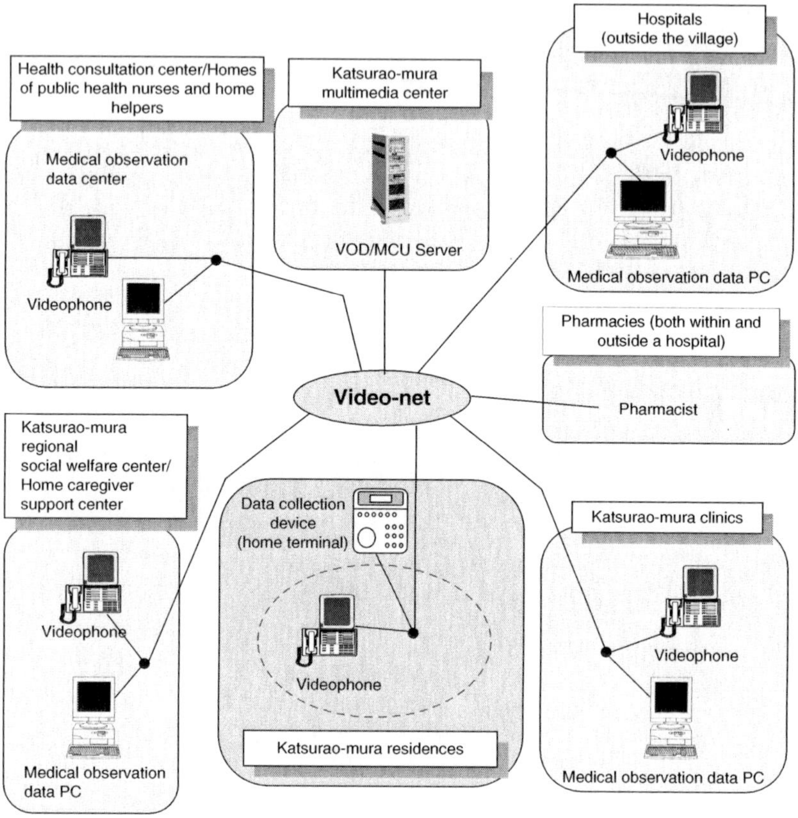

Figure 7.5 Medical care, health preservation and social welfare support video communication tools

can contribute to new transformations in healthcare, and in a range of other areas.

As developments like the Multimedia Village Plan stand poised to transfigure civilization and culture, they literally offer a new dawning of huge potentials to develop multimedia businesses. Consisting of villagers, hospitals and clinics, these face-to-face virtual medical communities engender trust between doctors and patients by enabling physicians to diagnose patients and give them appropriate advice through personalized contact, while the efficiency of medicine home delivery following from these videophone examinations can also be instrumental in building trust with chronic illnesses sufferers.

Videophone Application	Overview	Community Form
Health consultation	By using a videophone instead of a conventional telephone, the doctor can make his diagnosis while looking at the patient's image	Village residences and the health consultation center
Sign language assistance	Sign-language interpretation for the hearing impaired	Village residences and the health consultation center
Insurance, public welfare, and governmental consultation	Insurance and public welfare consultation by specialists at the town hall and remote calisthenics instruction	Village residences and the regional public welfare center
Comprehensive medical care and public welfare assistance	Support for the elderly and bedridden in their own homes, including contact, diagnosis, consultation and counseling	Patients and medical institutions outside the village, home-care assistance center, home helpers' homes
Insurance and public welfare information (VOD)	Searching of insurance and public welfare-related video information from each household and its application to home learning	Katsurao-mura multimedia center (VOD) and multiple village residences

Figure 7.6 Applications in medical care, health preservation and public welfare

As well as that virtual education communities that include children from the village and schools and universities and outside the village can encourage interactive communications between teachers and villagers for face-to-face learning with richer sharing of information, knowledge and wisdom; while in the relationships between villagers and government institutions, too, virtual communities can be created with the aim of improving local living standards.

The basic concept behind these ICT systems is the simple user interface of the videophone as it enables advanced linking between households, schools and the local community with multimedia services, regardless of the users level of skill. Multimedia projects like these hold great promise as we explore new and modern forms of local communication and cultural paradigms toward building the framework for a society with genuinely free communications.

ICT almost completely dissolves the sense of distance that exists between the town one lives in and other towns, between cities and between countries. As people use diverse and interactive face-to-face communications in wider domains and access a greater variety of video

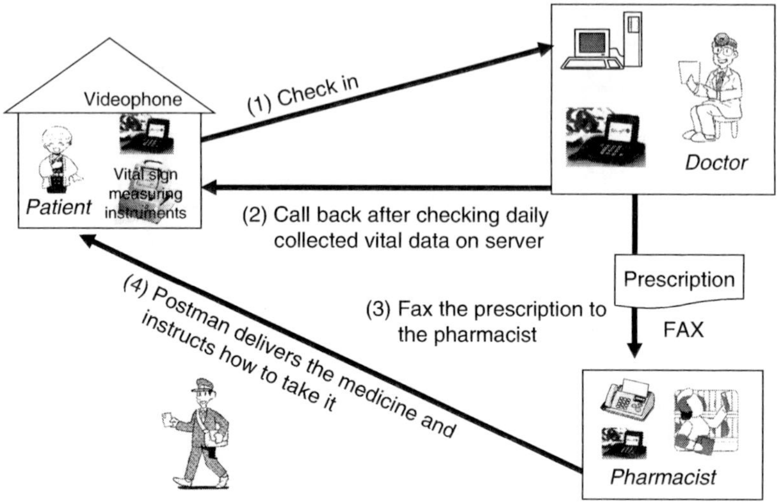

Figure 7.7 Medicine delivery service

content, more individuality can come to villagers and local communities alike, which can encourage information, knowledge and wisdom to be created and shared within and between these communities.

All over Japan in rural areas where depopulation and aging continue, systems are in place in which governments and the private sector work hand in hand to transform and invigorate living environments by deploying bidirectional voice and video ICT for multimedia communications using devices that are even easy for the elderly to operate, such as the videophone.

Following from the development in Katsurao Village in Fukushima Prefecture, the second multimedia village was established in Nosegawa Village in Nara Prefecture. Since then the multimedia village model has been adopted throughout Japan (in some 200 locations nationwide as of the end of FY 2011).

For genuine local regeneration to occur and new and unique local community value to be created, it is essential that each member of these societies have the opportunity to establish individuality and firmly define how they want to live. These established individuals can then use ICT to seamlessly and functionally connect with each other. In other words, as the individuals in local communities stimulate each other and grow together through ICT linking, they can create new information, knowledge and wisdom, and establish identities for regional regeneration.

These interactions are the driving force behind local development in the information era; and into the future the further creation of communities, including virtual ICT communities, in which human beings can meet directly with face-to-face contact will be an important factor that underpins the information society.

7.2.1.2 Telemedicine at home

In a shift away from expensive hospitalization, the number of elderly patients that elect to be treated in their homes has increased in recent years. The Ootsuka Clinic group, an affiliate of the Reimei-kai Medical Corporation, is a company that provides home-visit examination services to an aging society. Available in four wards of Tokyo (Toshima, Bunkyo, Kita and Itabashi), and some parts of Nerima and Taito wards, these services offer regular home-visit examination by doctors and nurses who travel by car, for a monthly fee of ¥2000.

The important thing about home care is that it enables regular confirmation of the patient's condition, and enables doctors to respond quickly and appropriately if the patient's condition suddenly changes. Thus videophone increases the doctor's ability to "visit regularly" and interview patients to determine their condition more quickly and respond more rapidly in times of emergency.

To this aim, a project team consisting of an ICT vendor of which Ootsuka clinic is a customer, and Ootsuka Clinic itself began to promote home telemedicine using a "home-visit examination support system" incorporating videophones, and has achieved the following.

As well as medical examinations conducted through videophones linked with Computer Telephone Integration (CTI) systems, patient databases can be accessed when an emergency occurs, which enables doctors to assess the patient's condition while looking at them and their medical history on-screen, and dispatch a medical professional or contact a supporting hospital as required (see Figure 7.8).

This videophone system also enables pharmacists to instruct patients in their homes about medicine they need to take, and enable patients to consult with the pharmacy about dosage if they do not understand.

In addition to regular visits, videophone interviews with patients increase opportunities for physicians and patients to communicate, which helps to improve trust. Also, in an emergency situation, videophone gives doctors a more thorough grasp of the patient's condition and enables more efficient dispatching of medical staff, which has led to an 80% reduction in emergency night-time visits, and greatly reduced the amount of time that staff need to be in transit, thus lowering overall costs.

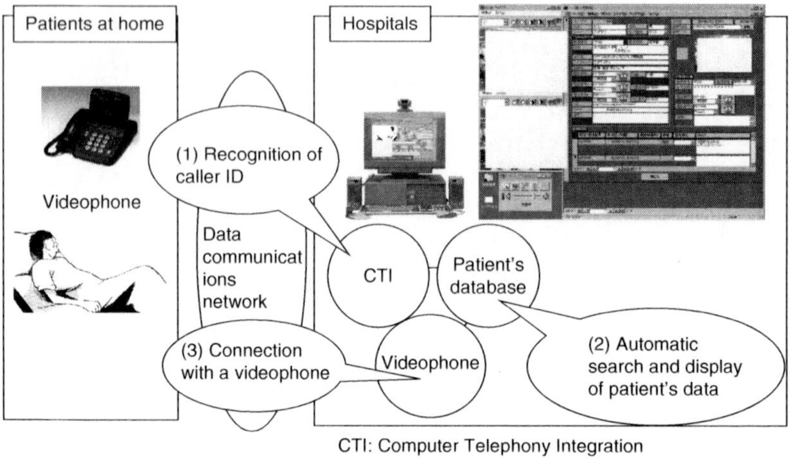

Figure 7.8 Image of CTI application with home medical care

Note: Another special feature of Ohtsuka's system is CTI or Computer Telephony Integration. Ohtsuka's home-care support system consists of a videoconferencing system, patient database and CTI application. When you call the clinic, the doctor can note who is calling and obtain patient data at the same time. This image is a displayed by Phoenix using the CTI system. It is useful in face-to-face communication, and when taking prompt emergency action.

Established by the joint Ootsuka Clinic-ICT vendor project team through the processes of fostering a customer base and learning with customers, this videophone home telemedicine business model has now been deployed in other hospitals, medical institutions and government bodies.

These businesses have grown from knowledge communities formed across the fields of remote medical treatment, paramedical services, health and pharmacological consultation, and their customers and patients.

Well-known IT vendors such as Microsoft and IBM have also developed even more efficient and cheaper unified communications cloud computing systems in recent years that offer seamlessly integrated and fused video/voice/data functions (see Figure 3.4 in Chapter 3) to hospitals and home treatment institutions, telemedicine and medical data management services, and these are being increasingly deployed in the health care field in developed countries.

As an example that exemplifies the character of remote home treatment, the insulin-dependent diabetes treatment team in a Pediatrics Department of the Faculty of Nursing at University Hospital (A) in

Japan uses videophone as part of the guidance they provide to diabetic patients. This involves providing (1) instruction into self-supervision and assessment (insulin dosage, diet—types of food and amounts—blood sugar levels, and actions to take in case of low blood sugar, and (2) life-consulting services for children and elementary school health staff, and management of and access to medical information (lifestyle guidance and dietary policy advice at the patient's home and school; see Figure 7.9).

7.2.2 The spread of high-functionality telemedicine and health care with advanced videoconferencing tools

7.2.2.1 Health care

American company Cisco Systems (Cisco hereinafter) announced the release of the company's Cisco HealthPresence™ Platform at the Healthcare Information and Management Systems Society (HIMSS) held in Atlanta. This advanced telemedicine technology platform gives patients access to doctors and medical examinations in ways never before seen.

Most conventional telemedicine approaches have focused on the issues of physical access to medical care; however, in addition to that, Cisco HealthPresence also offers solutions to the following four issues that face medical treatment: (1) medical care capability problems (lack of specialists and/or productivity), (2) collaboration problems (between one patient and many physicians, between multiple treatment facilities, and collaboration between multiple patients), (3) information exchange problems (participants ability to express and share important medical information) and (4) personalization problems (engaging more actively in patient examination).

As a new and simpler health care system created by the merging of Cisco TelePresence™ and Cisco® Unified Communications innovations, Cisco HealthPresence offers a high standard of care and can be applied in a wide range of treatment services. Featuring high-resolution video, clear audio, and interface capabilities with medical equipment, HealthPresence achieves a new dimension of support for collaboration and personalization previously almost impossible with conventional examination by interviewing patients. HealthPresence enables on-screen viewing of data during medical examinations from various diagnostic devices such as digital stethoscopes, and because of its superior audio capability, it enables full and clear understanding of diagnoses made by the physicians.

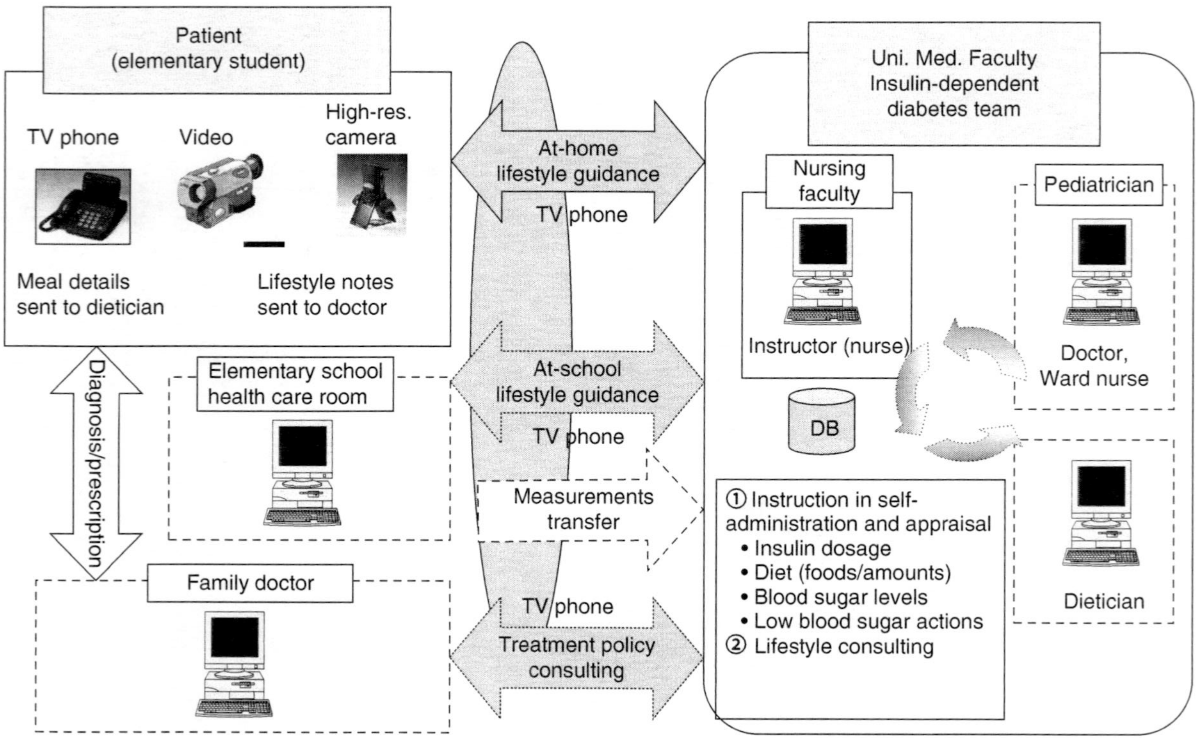

Figure 7.9 Guidance for diabetic patients

In the HealthPresence trials that began in 2008, patients who were examined expressed a tremendous degree of satisfaction with the presence of the video and the level of medical care achieved with real-time transmission of their physiological data, while physicians reported that HealthPresence enabled them to manage their patients much more efficiently.

Furthermore, the system enables many medical staff members to simultaneously participate in the examination of a single patient, and thus offers a new method of forming partnerships to care for patients. HealthPresence enables family doctors and medical specialists, care managers and rehabilitation providers, families and clinics to participate in treatment and care in a systemized fashion, and is a general-purpose point-to-point telemedicine solution that takes a massive step forward compared to the conventional direct interview-type examination.

The central role played by information and communications technology has enabled these new functionalities and raised the level and quality of health care availability, and at a reasonable price.

7.2.2.2 Advanced telemedicine

Cases of advanced telemedicine can also be found in medical institutions in almost all developed countries as remote pathology diagnosis support systems. As high-performance, high-definition TV conferencing broadband image transmission systems, these "interhospital videos systems" use camera-equipped microscopes to transfer images of samples (video and still) to pathologists, and enable pathologists to remotely adjust microscope magnification and switch samples (see Figure 7.10).

The following example also can be found in most medical institutions in developed countries, in use for remote surgery instruction in hospitals affiliated with university medical faculties. These hospitals are connected together by high-speed optical networks that enable surgeons to receive images from endoscopes and cameras used during surgery, and provide audiovisual capabilities that enable them to give advice to those in the operating theater (see Figure 7.11).

7.2.2.3 "Virtual doctors" via videoconferencing

ICT telemedicine services are available in a great many countries; however, they are only available in a few areas.

A recent example, coming from Pennsylvania in the United States of America, the country that leads the world in telemedicine, is the concept of "virtual doctors" via videoconferencing—a full-fledged application of ICT to provide on-site emergency medical support in the latest

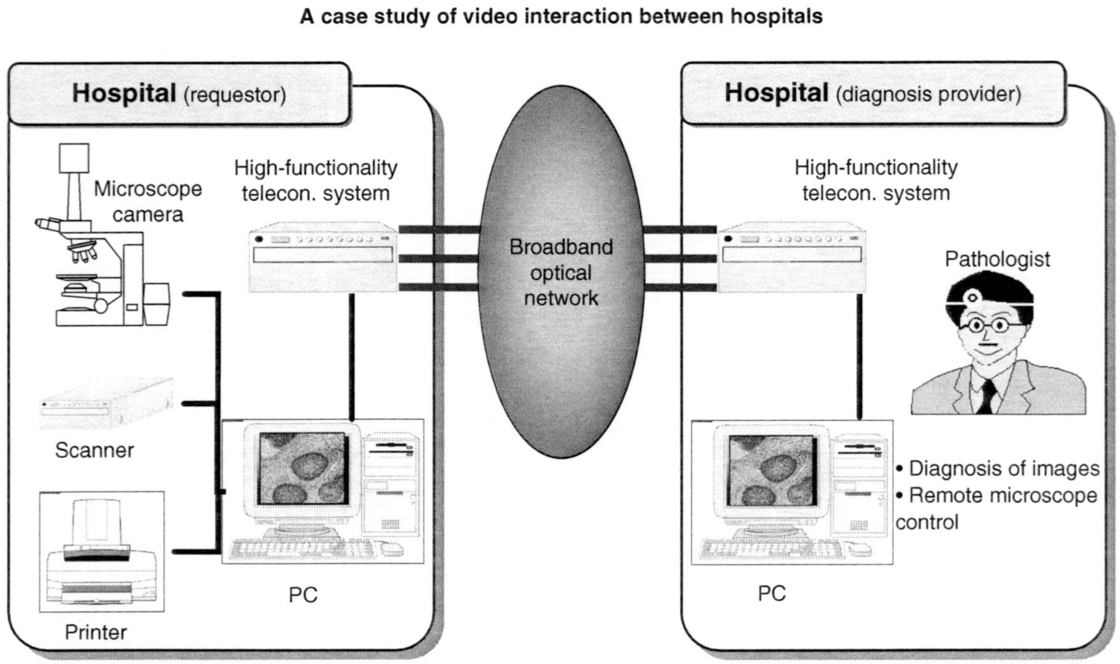

Figure 7.10 Remote pathology diagnosis support system

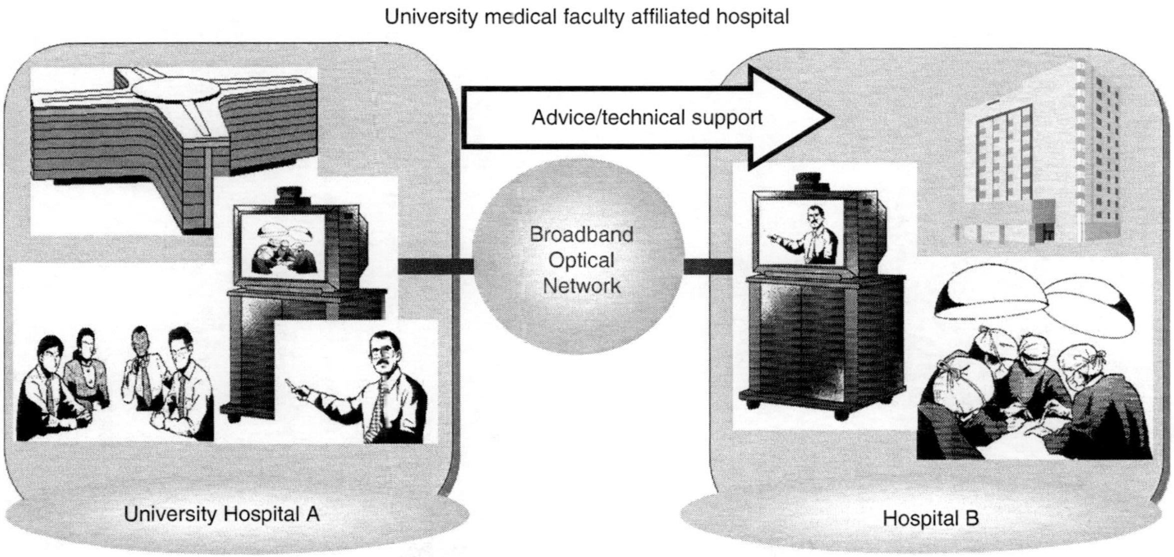

Figure 7.11 Remote surgery guidance

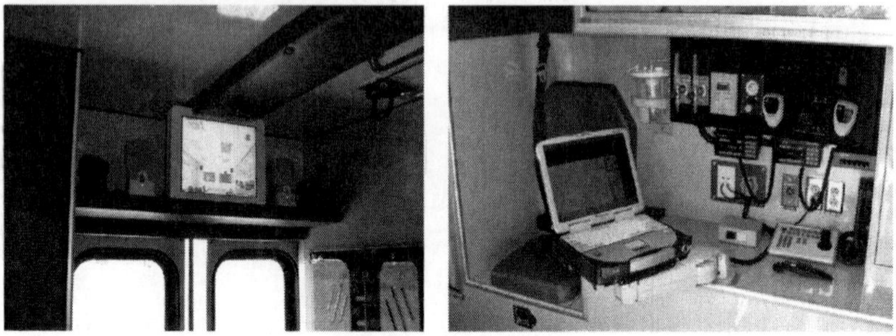

Figure 7.12 "Virtual doctors" via videoconferencing
Source: TeleSpan Inc.

ambulances. With six cameras, videoconferencing and telemedicine equipment installed, these high-tech ambulances use the Inmarsat satellite system for audiovisual communications and health monitoring equipment data transmission, and are capable of telemedicine traveling at speeds of up to 70 mph (see Figure 7.12).

7.2.3 The expanding general-purpose terminal health and welfare markets

Garnering attention in the health care and care fields of today are the smartphones and tablet PCs such as iPhone, iPad and Android terminals as they offer potential health care support. One example how these systems are used is the joint development, manufacture, sales and service of an imaging (color film, digital cameras, etc.) ICT solution (medical system, life science equipment, etc.) between Fujifilm and the Jikei University in Japan, that started as a project in July 2010 to "project to save even just one more life," and was commercialized June 2011.

Developed as a remote video medical diagnosis support system that runs on smartphones to provide comprehensive emergency medical assistance to stroke victims, this system has new functions that enable images of patients and their electrocardiograms to be checked from outside the hospital; and as diagnostic support for those working in the hospital, it also enables hospitals that have received emergency stroke[6] cases to send examination images of the patient and diagnostic data to a specialist outside the hospital who has a smartphone, thus enabling quicker and more efficient exchange of information about the treatment required.

This is a potentially life-saving system, because in on-site emergency treatment of stroke cases, time is of the essence—the speed at which treatment is administered can mean the difference between the patient living and dying, and can greatly affect how the patient recuperates. Early and precise diagnosis and prompt patient admission are crucial.

In developing this new remote diagnosis and treatment support system, the project aimed at creating a completely new medical information system that makes the opinions and diagnoses of multiple specialists and patient information readily available anywhere and at anytime both inside and outside of hospitals, via smartphones and tablet PCs, and provides the necessary imaging in a variety of modalities (CT, MRI, DSA, etc.) to be quickly and easily viewable in an emergency, through an easy-to-use and high-security system.

With high-speed image transmission and viewing in any situation, the system takes telemedicine one step further by including brand-new 3D image technology that enables viewers to freely manipulate images.

Not only does this system deliver video images but it also has functions to notify all medical staff members related to the treatment of a particular patient when the patient comes to the hospital. In stroke treatment, this is an important function that minimizes the amount of time it takes to call staff involved with the case and thus makes the most of teamwork.

These functions also display the time that the patient came to the hospital and the time that has elapsed, and because images and results of patient examination carried out can be known in real time (on a timeline display), all staff members involved with treating the stroke case can access the same information and respond more promptly.

Even if there is only one doctor on duty, this system enables doctors to get diagnoses from various other physicians and consult with them about the best way to treat a case, which gives unprecedented capabilities to on-site medical treatment. Because there are so many approaches to stroke treatment, this system has huge potential as it shifts the burden of judgment from doctors operating by themselves and entrusts it to the consensus of groups of specialists, because these specialists and attendant doctors can instantly view images of the patient, make observations and get information that is not possible with words only.

Also, because the system simultaneously sends medical data with the video, it enables doctors to make decisions when they are outside the hospital, it can run over networks between hospitals for medical consultation via video with other hospitals and patient referral, and it can be expanded so that the patient's medical data (BP, history, current medications, etc.) is stored on the patient's mobile phone.

These distinctive aspects mean that video or still images of the patient taken in the hospital with a smartphone can be viewed by specialists outside the hospital on their smartphones, along with streamed vital signs data such as ECG and blood pressure. Specialist doctors outside the hospital can also access information such as the patient's state of consciousness, external injuries and medical condition as if they were actually in the hospital, enabling them to get a more thorough understanding of the patient's condition and thus provide the most appropriate advice.

As well as those, functions that enable referencing of the patient's medical records and additional functions that send new medical data updates to hospital-external specialists' smartphones in real time make this system capable of meeting a wide range of detailed needs for on-site medical treatment, and since it is possible for specialists in all fields outside the hospital to access basic patient information for emergency treatment, not only does it have the potential to be applied as emergency support for stroke cases but can be applied in all other emergency cases as well.

This case exemplifies how ICT with smartphones and tablet PCs can provide wide-ranging and efficient support for on-site emergency treatment, raise the quality of health care, and contribute toward maintaining and improving overall human well-being.

The use of iPad in on-site medical treatment in the USA is also on the rise. Doctors working in the Johns Hopkins Hospital have been able to make more efficient use of their time by using iPad. If they didn't have iPad, they would have to go back to printing out images on paper and gathering them from here and there—finding an online computer and searching for medicine-related images—which is inefficient use of valuable time, but by taking iPad into the wards where patients are hospitalized, these doctors are able to examine patients and observe their reactions in previously unimaginable detail.

The pancreas clinic at the Johns Hopkins Hospital also lends iPads to patients which enables closer monitoring of the progress of treatment, while patients at the catheterization and angiographic examination facilities at Stanford University Hospital are able borrow an iPad in their waiting time (to watch movies, check e-mail, etc.). iPads are also used as a surgical support tool for accessing image data in operating theaters.

A diversity of large and small iPad projects like these have sprung up in hospitals all across the United States since its release in the spring of

2010. For instance, the Veterans Health Administration has introduced tablet terminals in 152 hospitals in its jurisdiction.

There are also countries that are working to build networks designed for smartphones and tablet PCs to enable access to welfare and care service information. In countries like the US, Sweden, Germany, Italy, France, Great Britain, Korea and Japan, the use of Internet-based bulletin boards for accessing information such as care advice, counseling and consultation within communities (among helpers, volunteers, carers, etc.) is on the rise (see Figure 7.13). This situation has brought with it an explosive broadening of general-purpose terminal uses across a broader range of areas such as communications support, as an aid in giving meaning to people's lives and social participation, as disability assistance, and as support tools for businesses involved in caring, health and treatment services. Figure 7.14 describes the common nature of the way these general-purpose terminals are applied in the US, Sweden, Germany, Italy, France, Great Britain, Korea and Japan.

The author's investigations indicate that in the process of using the smartphone and tablet PC general-purpose terminals in developed countries, networked usage has been promoted on networks initially established for particular functions—that is, welfare, education, business or government networks.

Following from that, the merging and integration of these individual functional networks has developed into the current infrastructure on which cloud computing and regional information distribution has come to be based, and there are indications that new local communities have formed through general-purpose terminals and cloud computing where there is established broadband and wireless ICT infrastructure available (see Figure 7.15).

Cloud computing and general-purpose terminal infrastructure is becoming more and more important as an ICT platform that promotes harmonization across the human-life support cycles from medical treatment through to welfare and health care, as it offers support for home treatment, provision of care and welfare, fitness and health promotion, and a range of social activities (see Figure 7.16).

7.3 Product architecture strategies and ICT innovation

The previous section describes usage cases that resulted from product architecture. An important observation of these examples is that advances in product architecture have had a profound influence on the way devices are used. As users engage in interactive learning with ICT,

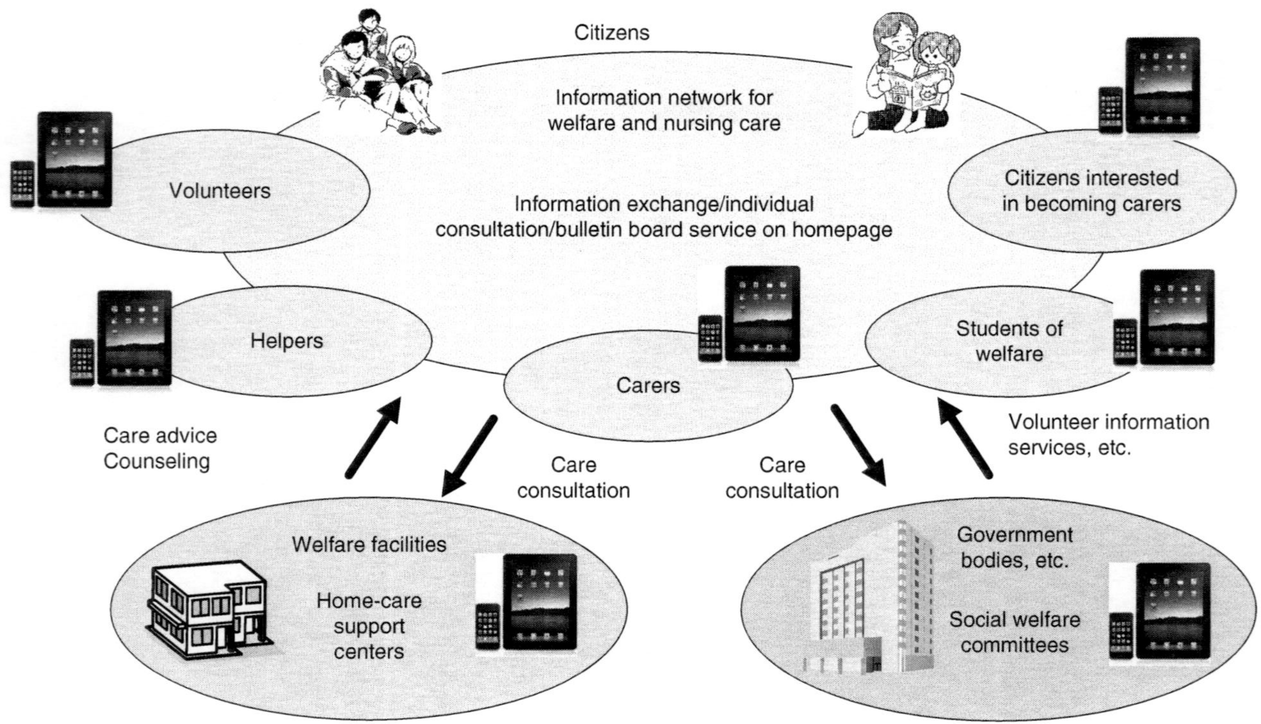

Figure 7.13 Care community example with general-purpose terminals ⑤

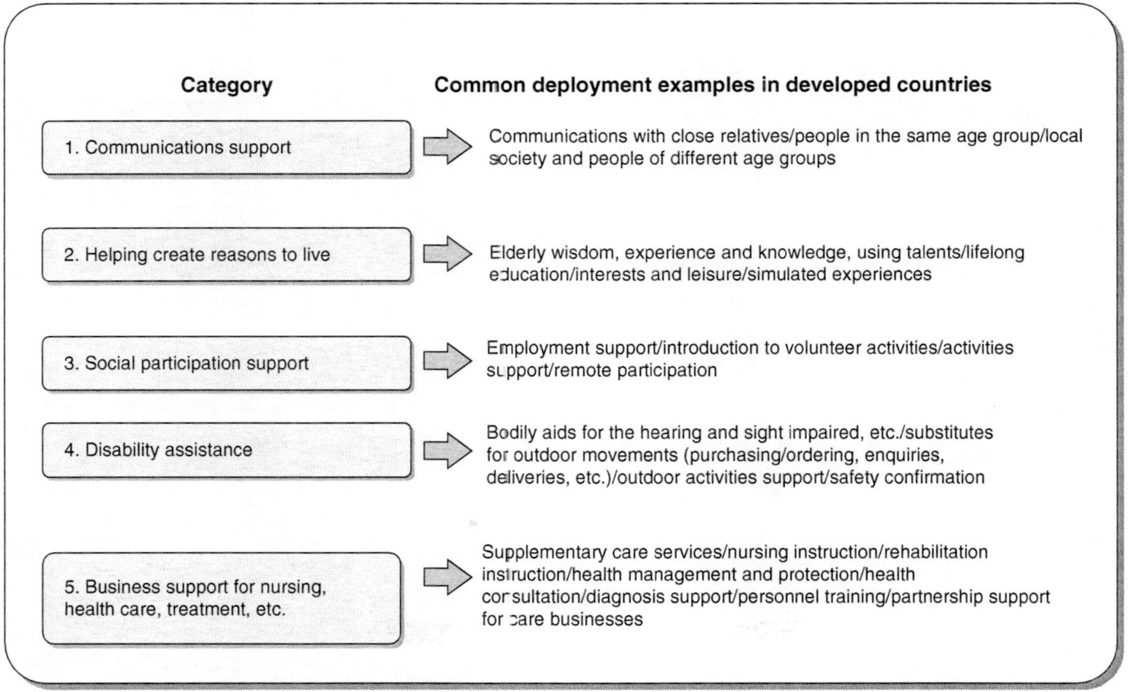

Figure 7.14 Usage examples with general-purpose terminals ⑤ (common examples from the US, Britain, Germany, France, Italy, Sweden, Korea, Japan)

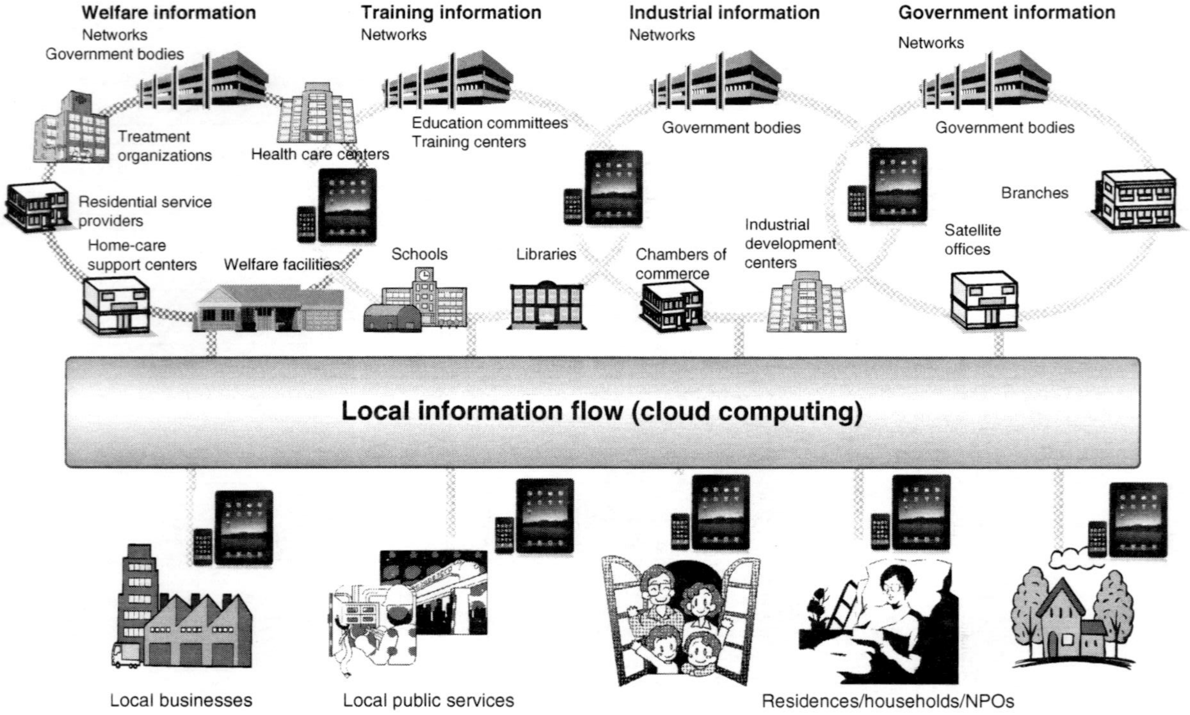

Figure 7.15 Creating new local communities: Virtual cloud communities using general-purpose terminals ⑤

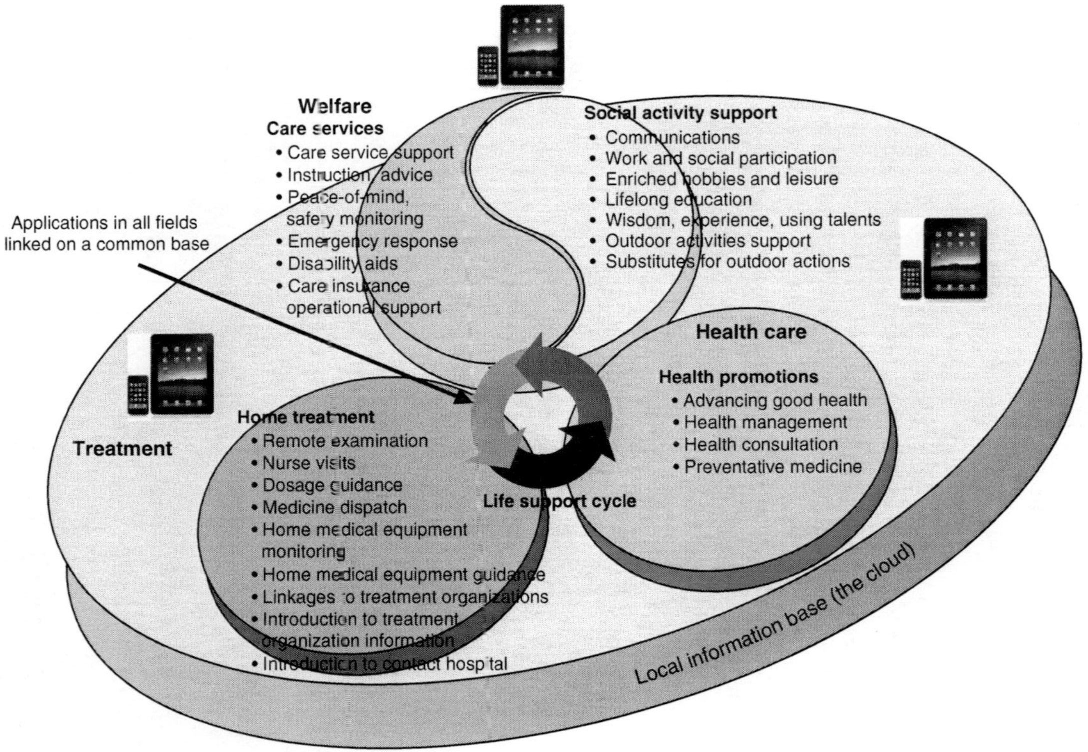

Figure 7.16 General-purpose terminals, cloud computing and related welfare fields

users have been able to increase their involvement in "user innovation," and bring about new "ICT application capability" and "ICT context architect capability."

7.3.1 Product architecture evolution and user innovation

7.3.1.1 Modular architecture, software architecture and architectural innovation

According to existing research, product architecture starts out as being integral, and then evolves to become modularized in any industry. However, this phenomenon is not uniform, in that the characteristics of a particular industry heavily influence the speed and the degree of modularization. For example, as electric vehicles are re-emerging in the automotive industry, there is progress toward modularization over the long term, although the speed of modularization is not the same as the electronics industry.[7]

Why do industries tend toward modularization? Existing research offers the following explanations.

Firstly, it is the design rationalization that modularization provides. As stated, modular architecture has many benefits and offers more rationalized designability than integrally designed products. Of course, modular architecture has its drawbacks, but on the whole it offers more advantages than integral design. This is why industries tend to put effort into design with modular architecture, although rationalizing design does not necessarily always match with business strategy rationalization—strategic business decisions could be made that select integral architecture over modular architecture.

Secondly, it is the argument that customer assessment criteria changes in response to product life cycles (Christensen, 1997). At the outset all new products are of low performance, and cannot satisfactorily meet customer demand levels for functionality and capability. In this situation, companies work to optimize product performance to meet the demand levels of customers, and as a result choose integral design for the product architecture. Just because modular architecture is defined by design rules, it does not necessarily follow that it can be applied in order to optimize performance.

In contrast, rapid advances in technology can overshoot customer demand levels for product performance, which in turn shifts customer assessment standards of product performance to a new level. Companies then choose modular architecture since it is superior in general, and it can offer product performance that satisfies the customer, and can satisfy other assessment standards by offering more rapid and flexible product development for example. Thus from the point of view of changes to customer assessment standards, products are integral when they first appear and accordingly shift to modularization.

Thirdly, it is the idea of more effective relationships with suppliers (Fine, 1998). In the current era of intense market and technological change, carefully managed outsourcing is required because it is near impossible for a single company to do all of the work needed to develop a product by itself. The most important objective here is to outsource tasks summarized into single packages that eliminate complex contractual interdependencies as much as possible, which in turn results in products becoming more modularized and their design becoming more open. Thus, the drive for more efficiency through rules applied to relationships with suppliers brings about product modularization. Recalling IBM's development of the PC, the company engaged in modularized and open development like this for efficiency and quick turnaround times through outsourcing.

As shown before and clarified by existing research, modularization of architecture in industry occurs because it is more rational. VCTs such as videoconference systems and videophones are no exception.

After the introduction of CPUs and DSPs into VCTs, video communication products consisted of the two different technologies of hardware and software, both of whose architectures have evolved in the direction of modularization.

One important aspect of complex technology products is that even if they move toward modularization, technical characteristics will evolve along different and particular paths. In VCTs architecture, too, the technological paths along which the hardware and software have evolved are profoundly different.

As mentioned, in the case of hardware, new demands for more modularization and design rules bring about architectural advances as newer technical elements are adopted into a product. Put differently, a major factor that has caused architecture to evolve is the incompatibility of conventional modular segmentation with advances in technical elements that make up product systems, and due to this incompatibility, module segments need to be revised so that they can accommodate the advanced technical elements.

Advances in technical elements have also made it possible to combine functions that were formally found across a range of components into a single component. A typical example of this is a single system LSI that contains the functions of a number of different LSIs. Also, surface and 3D mounting technologies have enabled high-density, high-precision mounting, which has made it possible to cram many more functions into the same space: it is now possible to include functions on a single printed circuit that used to be spread out across multiple circuit boards, and the size of circuit boards can also be dramatically reduced.

Including many functions in a single component in this way changes the mapping relationship between the functions and structure, and also results in incompatibility with older module segmentation, which means new module segmentation must be found, and as a result, the physical number of modules that comprise the system decreases, and the design rules that define the module interfaces become simpler, simultaneously raising the quality of a product while making it smaller and of lower cost. It's this dynamism of advancing technical elements that has brought about modern hardware architecture.

On the software architecture front, more uniformity in the way programming languages are described has encouraged more user innovation, which has had a huge impact on the pathway along which software architecture has advanced. In recent years in particular, programming languages have become much more sophisticated, and the technical knowledge level needed for applied software programming has fallen, making it much easier for users to develop applications and participate directly in innovation. This CAI approach is a trigger that gives rise to new user innovation as users develop their own unique applications, and because users can now program more easily, the threshold where user innovation is triggered is not as high as it used to be.

Software architecture in which the roles of vendor controlled and user controlled sections change is one type of architecture that promotes user innovation, and software architecture is being recreated in this direction.

Another important way of thinking about product architecture is "architectural innovation." Product architecture is the way that technical elements are assembled—in other words, the focus is on the way the technical elements are linked together and not on the technical elements themselves. Of course, in reality, assembly has a relationship with the technical elements and is not completely separate from them. However, it is important to understand this difference conceptually, because while everything can stay the same at the level of the elemental technology, changing the architecture has the potential to bring about highly competitive products. This type of innovation—radically changing the relationship between the structural elements in a product system—is called "architectural innovation" (Henderson and Clark, 1990).

Product miniaturization and advanced human interfaces are typical results of architectural innovation. Smartphones and tablet PCs such as iPhone and iPad are the results of changing the way the various components are assembled and repositioning them in a narrower space. In other words, the technical elements have not been changed very much, but the architecture has been dramatically altered, which has brought about miniaturization and the greatly improved human interfaces that are much easier to use. iPhone and iPad are cases of highly competitive products that have been developed along these lines.[8] Nintendo's Wii gaming devices are also examples of architectural innovation (Kodama, 2011a).

Architectural innovation has resulted in products that offer new and valuable experiences to customers. When combined with other ICT devices and software, advanced, compact and lightweight human interfaces have brought about new "user solutions" (such as the smartphone telemedicine systems), and are bringing forth new business processes and business models (such as "medicine pack", etc.).

As noted earlier, modularization in software architecture encourages users to develop their own application and contents, whereas architectural innovation pioneers new usages such as new business processes, user solutions and business models. Innovation in product architecture encourages user innovation through the process of learning with ICT, and brings about new uses for ICT and enables users to acquire ICT application capability, the ability to use ICT itself, and ICT context architect capability, in which users themselves bring forth new meaning and significance to the use of ICT. These two capabilities are important factors that comprise ICT capability (see Figure 7.17).

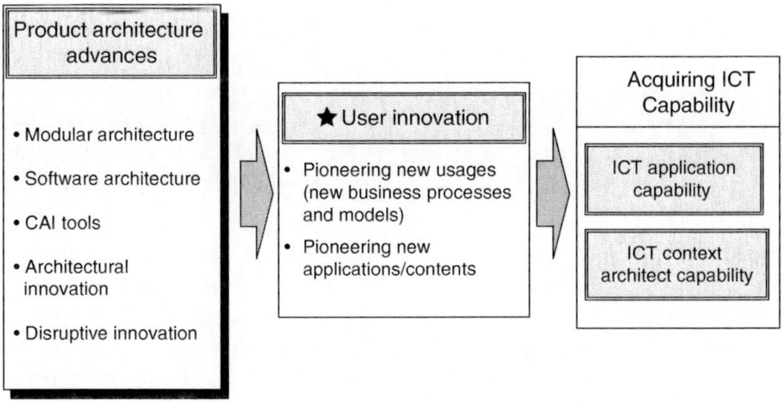

Figure 7.17 Product architecture advances and ICT capability

7.3.2 Disruptive innovation and sustaining innovation

Products that have encouraged user innovation through software and modular architecture often start out with inferior performance to traditional hardware and integral architecture products, and are often confined to the low-end user market. The product architectures of these products are examples of disruptive technology or disruptive innovation.

Why do blue chip companies with their extensive business resources fail at technological innovation? Christensen (1998) classifies innovation as two types—sustaining or disruptive—where the former is beneficial for existing companies, while the latter disadvantages them. Christensen argues that it is disruptive innovation that has caused many established companies to fail with technological innovation.

Christensen (1998) clarified this principle with a detailed investigation into the HDD industry. According to this research, after IBM developed the first HDD in the 1950s, there were 116 technological innovations up to 1990 of which 111 were sustaining innovation, with the remaining five being disruptive; and of these 111 cases of sustaining innovation, all were driven by established blue chip companies, whereas the remaining five disruptive innovations were the achievements of start-ups. What's more, not one of those established companies was able to maintain its existing market share after the advent of the disruptive innovation.

At this point we should take a quick look at the problem of product value, because disruptive innovation has an intrinsic relationship with the problem of value that is offered by a product.

Products and services are not offered in one single value dimension, but through a multiplicity of them. For instance, the value of a thin screen television has multiple dimensions such as image quality, screen size, depth, service life, power consumption and price, any of which the customer could consider when making a decision whether to buy one of these devices. However, not all of these dimensions always carry the same importance—the importance of a dimension changes over time according to what is important in the mainstream, what is important in the market and so forth. In the case of the thin screen television, image quality was important in the early stages of the product, which forced companies to increase image quality until it reached an acceptable standard, at which point the value focus shifted to screens that were larger and even thinner. Similarly, the increases in awareness of environmental problems raised the value of energy-saving models. These transformations illustrate how the value of products and services consists of multiple dimensions, and how the importance given to each dimension can change.

Considered in terms of the dynamic nature of value dimensions, sustaining innovation is innovation that raises product value to an even higher level in line with the current mainstream value dimension of the product. For example, HDD memory capacity was the most important value dimension early on. This meant that the technological innovations to bring increases to memory capacity were sustaining innovations in which the established company had demonstrated strength.

Conversely, disruptive innovations may temporarily have value dimensions that are lower than the mainstream, but at the same time they are innovations that offer new value dimensions. In the case of the HDD, the smaller versions were lower than the mainstream value in terms of memory capacity, but they were disruptive innovations that offered the new value dimension of compactness. Established companies have a strong tendency toward failure in dealing with this type of innovation (see Figure 7.18).

Why do established companies fail with disruptive innovation? According to Christensen (1998), blue chip companies became blue chip companies by carefully listening to the opinions of their customers, but ironically, it is this very laudable business practice itself that causes them to fail when challenged with a disruptive innovation.

How can listening to your customers' opinions be a cause of failure? The answer lies in the concept of a value network.

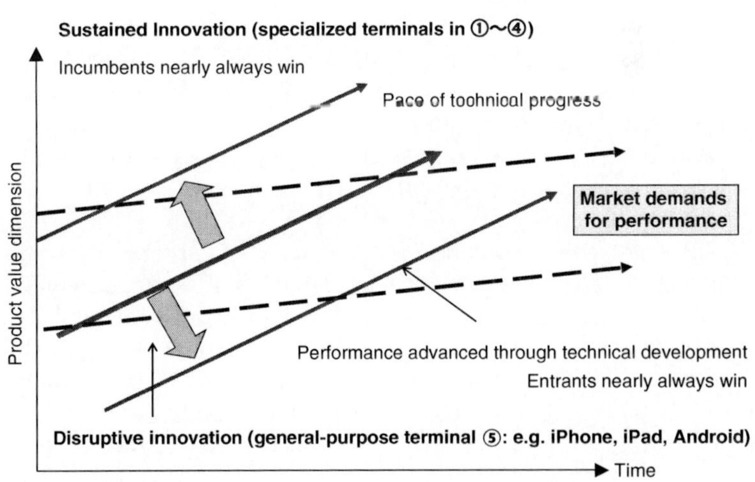

Figure 7.18 Disruptive innovation and sustained innovation
Source: Christensen (1997).

As mentioned, products offer a variety of different values, which can be described as values in a number of dimensions, although it is not always self-evident which of these dimensions is important to the customer.

In this context, companies and customers form a value network that focuses on a particular value dimension, which can be viewed as a constraint, because it prevents the company from being able to accurately assess the value dimensions offered by new products or services. Taking the example of the HDD, its manufacturers who were active in value networks that focused on memory capacity and processing speed were not in a position to easily assess the value of HDD devices that had superior reliability and energy-saving characteristics. This is because customers and markets in such a value network, with its focus on memory capacity and processing speed, can only give a low appraisal of a new HDD device despite its superior power-saving features.

What happens to business decisions in blue chip companies as a result? Because the established company listened intently to the desires of its customers, management refused to allow the development of a new HDD with better power consumption because the memory capacity and processing speed wasn't good enough. As far as management knew, existing customers only wanted HDD devices with large memory capacity and fast processing speed—there was a reluctance to invest business resources in the disruptive innovation, even though it was dismantling the current mainstream value dimension.

Rapidly advancing technologies began to meet the level of demands of existing customers, and by the time the existing company had realized there had been a shift in value dimension, it was already too late.

This illustrates how the mechanism for failure when challenged with a disruptive innovation is built into management itself—management that is paradoxically commendable for listening closely to its customers' opinions. Christensen (1998) called this mechanism "the innovator's dilemma."

Recently, Polycom,[9] a well-known American TV conferencing system vendor, developed and released HD (high-definition) videoconferencing software for iPad 2 and Android tablets. The videoconferencing systems industry has also advanced with product development strategies shifting from hardware architecture to software architecture. As described in Figure 7.2, videoconferencing system product architecture (including multipoint control units or MCUs) has progressed in stages over the last 20 years.

In conjunction with the shift from switching circuits to IP broadband network architecture, videoconferencing hardware and software architecture has evolved into systems that are both high quality and low cost. Compared with older videoconferencing systems that used leased lines and ISDN, IP-based videoconferencing is a disruptive innovation that has outstripped switching circuit videoconferencing both in terms of image quality and cost (see Chapter 3, Figure 3.2). And as disruptive innovations with TV phone and TV conferencing functions, the general-purpose smartphone and tablet PC devices are still lower in performance than the existing specialized teleconferencing terminals that have been developed through sustaining innovation; but with improvements to hardware performance, better CPUs, advances in software technologies and so forth, these devices will see dramatic improvements in video transfer capability.

No longer limited to business users like conventional teleconferencing, general-purpose devices such as iPhone and iPad have the lurking potential to relegate the specialized teleconferencing equipment that has dominated the health care, welfare and education market to the scrap heap of history. These are the sorts of disruptive innovations that will be born into the world of IP broadband in the future.

More recent cases illustrating the "innovator's dilemma" can be found by comparing the "specialized game device + packaged game software" business models pursued by Nintendo and Sony with simple game software offered by social game vendors that runs on general-purpose smartphone platforms.

Smartphone- and tablet-based social games are disruptive innovations that are encroaching on the business domains of Nintendo and Sony. Compared to gaming devices that were created through sustaining innovation such as PlayStation 3 (PS3), Nintendo's Wii was a disruptive innovation that branched off from the semiconductor miniaturization technology roadmap, and created a new game market (a "blue ocean" market) that was different to PS3 (Kodama, 2011a).

However, the new disruptive technologies of present day smartphones and social games have created a light user market, and are beginning to eat away at the existing layers of game users that Nintendo and Sony have dominated, because as we move into the future, advances in smartphone and tablet PC core processors will bring even more social game functionality, which will be even closer to the functionality of specialized gaming devices. When this happens, which game software will the end user choose? Specialized gaming device based or smartphone/tablet PC based? Will Nintendo be able to meet the competition by maintaining its current strategic position, or will the company move on to some other new strategic position?

Shifting strategies from old to new like this present difficult managerial problems, and remains as an important area of research in strategic business and innovation theories (Kodama, 2011a).

Ideally, companies need to find a strategic position that has a high degree of uniqueness and then fight to achieve supremacy in that position. Thus, discovering and establishing a new position is a critical strategic objective. Moreover, companies need management that can maintain both the old and new positions simultaneously, in what has been called "ambidextrous management" (Kodama, 2011a), and then pour their efforts into rapidly shifting to the new position from the old with different products and services or new technologies. This kind of dynamic strategic sense can give companies a sustainable competitive edge. Ambidextrous management, then, presents an important strategic challenge for both teleconferencing systems vendors and specialized gaming device manufacturers.

8

ICT Capability and Knowledge Integration

On March 11, 2011 Japan was struck by a magnitude 9 earthquake, now known as The Great East Japan Earthquake. The Japanese media reported that nobody thought of connecting the television conferencing system in the Prime Minister's official residence when the accompanying nuclear accident happened.[1]

As mentioned in Chapter 5, the intensity and style of video communication tools' (VCTs') usage is dependent on risk, uncertainty and speed of change. In the situation right after the earthquake, there was a greatly elevated level of uncertainty and risk associated with taking new actions, as well as increased urgency due to rapid changes in the external environment. Accordingly, when the levels of uncertainty, risk and urgency all rise at the same time, content and context change dynamically, and the knowledge that emerges anew in these situations transcends individual knowledge, and the knowledge domain of organizations. This is why ICT tools with higher levels of media richness that give individuals and organizations greater information-processing capabilities are selected and used to overcome the differences between existing knowledge and emergent knowledge, and for these reasons, videoconferencing systems, with their superior real-time functionality, are used in situations where there is a need to solve difficult problems and issues and take swift actions.

In short, people and organizations use ICT tools appropriately and consciously (or unconsciously) in response to circumstantial change. So what was really going through the minds of those charged with safety and security at the Prime Minister's residence, and those information systems supervisors who were faced with that unprecedented emergency?

The Chief Cabinet Secretary commented: "Safety officers were crammed into the official residence working the phones and fax machines, and

I don't really know why the videoconferencing system wasn't used—whether it was because it wasn't needed or because there wasn't time." Low levels of uncertainty, risk, emergency and speed of change are characteristic of routine business (e.g. product development for existing products and so forth), as presented in Chapter 5. In these cases, the main ICT tools used for information transfer are telephone and e-mail. In other words, in the case of the Great East Japan Earthquake, the usage patterns at the Prime Minister's residence were completely opposite to those predicted by the results described in Chapter 5. How can these results be interpreted?

These results highlight the fact that it isn't possible to use ICT tools effectively in an emergency situation if the capabilities to network different people and organizations while sharing and transferring dynamically changing contexts don't exist. Just simply supplying people or organizations with the physical ICT resources themselves is not enough—the significance and meaning must be sufficiently understood, and regular learning through dialogue must be pursued and experience accumulated.

As the title of this chapter suggests, ICT capability can be seen as having an intrinsic relationship with the intangible assets of practical knowledge that stems from the experiences of people and organizations.

In light of the theoretical and empirical research presented in Chapter 4, and the case research presented in Chapters 5 to 7, this chapter analyses and discusses the factors of ICT capabilities founded in the practical knowledge held by individuals and organizations that enable the simultaneous pursuance of speed business, efficiency management and creative business through the flexible use of ICT tools in response to changing circumstances.

There are two main concepts that form the core of this chapter:

- The first is the idea is that there are four components of ICT capabilities that promote the formation of knowledge networks and accelerate innovation.
- The second idea is that organizational ICT capabilities encourage the formation of knowledge communities as "small-world networks."

8.1 Knowledge boundaries and ICT tools

As discussed in Box 5.1 in Chapter 5, there are three boundaries that exist in the conveyance of information between humans with regards to how information is interpreted and the way that actions are taken (Shannon and Weaver, 1949; Jantsch, 1980; Carlile, 2002, 2004).

Practitioners recognize these diverse boundaries and carry out regular business along these. However, depending on the way that practitioners overcome the boundaries between themselves, the results of their practical actions vary.

Regular routine activities in daily business are examples of syntactic boundaries. These syntactic boundaries are constantly generated through the course of day-to-day business routines. The accumulation of practice on syntactic boundaries is one of the foundations of a corporation, and can also trigger innovative change.

Routine best practice to improve and upgrade products and services (organizational learning) gives rise to new meanings among practitioners, which they also share. Orr (1996), who researched copy machine maintenance, found that the daily activities of service men observed represent a typical case.

The creation of new meaning like this, and the spurning of practitioners toward new actions illustrate the characteristics of semantic boundaries. It is on semantic boundaries where the first steps toward advancing creativity are taken.

As routines have transformed from past to present, there have been incremental and radical advances. However, in managing change, practical actions along these critical semantic boundaries must embrace novelty, urgency, risk and uncertainty, new ways of looking at things, and new understandings.

With radical transformation in particular, practitioners must face elevated levels of novelty, risk and uncertainty. Thus with innovation, where high levels of novelty, risk and uncertainty emerge on pragmatic boundaries, there are demands for new knowledge creation that transcends organizational learning, and thus transformation of existing knowledge and new meaning on semantic boundaries.

Wide-ranging problems and issues are brought forth on these pragmatic boundaries, and practitioners must face the challenge of solving them and creating new knowledge. Practitioners working on pragmatic boundaries are required to engage in creative conflict (e.g. Leonard-Barton, 1992) at a more practical level, and even participate in political negotiations (e.g. Brown and Duguid, 2001). To deal with new issues that have never existed, and achieve objectives, practitioners work through conflict and friction, and even political power in their activities to transform existing knowledge.

Actions and considerations about "things" that stem from dissimilar viewpoints affect the individual thought worlds (Dougherty, 1992) and mental models (Spender, 1990; Grinyer and McKiernan, 1994) of practitioners. Pragmatic boundaries that go beyond the mental models of individuals raise the amount and diversity of knowledge and experience that practitioners must assimilate all at once (see Figure 8.1).

These three-tiered boundaries are interdependent, and fluctuate dramatically (syntactic boundary → semantic boundary → pragmatic boundary) with the intents and interests of practitioners, and the speed of circumstantial change (customer needs, competitive environment, etc.). In achieving innovation or corporate reform in particular, the boundaries among practitioners shift toward the pragmatic (syntactic boundary → semantic boundary → pragmatic boundary) when there are strong changes in circumstances or movements in the intentions of actors.

As mentioned in Chapter 5, strategic communities (SCs) are teams or communities formed of practitioners with diverse knowledge, or of diverse formal organizations, whose boundaries have the characteristics of pragmatic boundaries with a basic semantic boundary nature, but without question, it is ultimately the dependence on the routine syntactic boundaries of business activities that form the foundations of SCs, whereas communities of practice (CoPs) are formed for ordinary routine improvement and upgrading activities with semantic boundary characteristics based in the syntactic boundaries.

Practitioners engage in organizational activities on these three types of boundaries—(1) routines, (2) improvements and upgrades (learning, incremental) and (3) innovation (radical change)—and as presented in Chapter 5, the usage of VCTs increases in SCs, in addition to the use of telephone, e-mail, and telephone and data conferencing. In contrast, VCTs are not used as often in CoPs, but there is more usage of basic ICT such as telephone, e-mail and telephone and data conferencing (see Figure 8.1).

As shown in the case research presented in Chapter 5, companies that successfully and frequently engage in innovation activities use VCTs with dexterity and ingenuity. One example is P&G in the US—a company that deployed cutting-edge videoconferencing systems in a number of its bases in 2009. This company quickly went on to expand its deployment to 43 locations worldwide, and now uses VCTs in more than 80 of its global facilities. Not only was P&G able to save $4 in transportation costs for every dollar invested on the system, but the company has also been able to achieve innovation by enabling much closer partnering of its product development staff, who are scattered all over the world.

In other words not only do VCTs offer more business efficiency in terms of cost reductions, but they also encourage the creativity needed to bring about innovation in business.

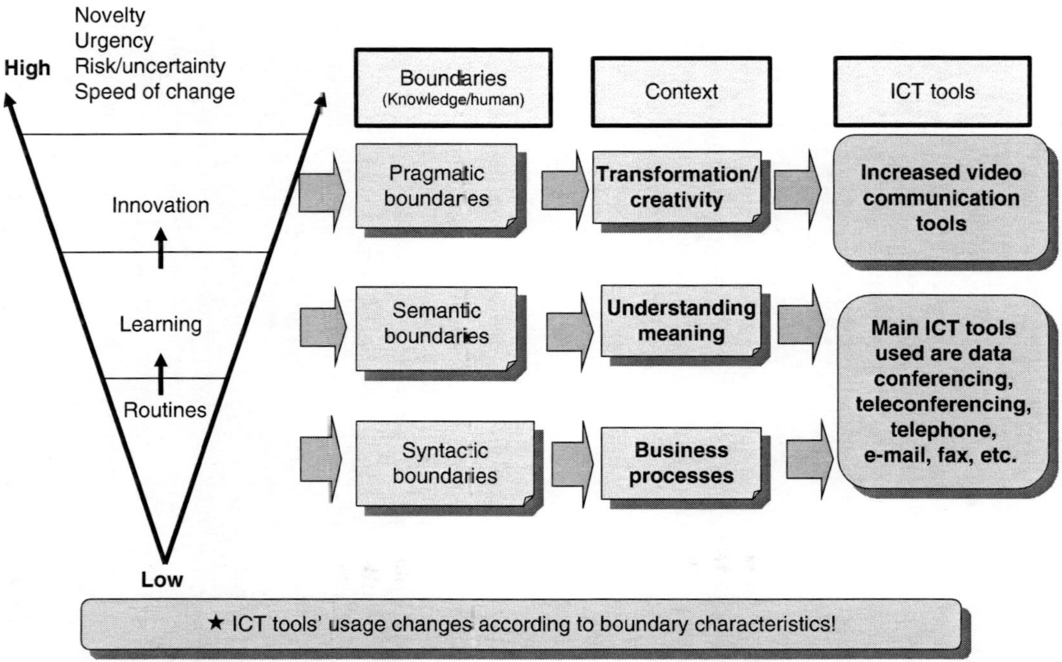

Figure 8.1 Business activity and ICT tools

Japanese stationery specialist Kokuyo also forms virtual, real-time *Ba* through VCTs that are always on, connecting its geographically dispersed product development facilities. By creating these virtual *Ba*, the company is able to constantly share its dynamically changing contexts.

However, there are some companies that almost never use VCTs or only use them a few times a month, in spite of the fact these companies have the equipment. These companies do not often engage in new product development (e.g. their R&D investments are a lot lower than the companies mentioned earlier). Therefore, it is crucial that individuals and organizations acquire "ICT capability" in order to demonstrate the synergies of ICT use with the practical actions of businesspeople.

By using VCTs, business people are able to intentionally (or as a result of their use) formulate networked CoPs and SCs as "knowledge communities" that transcend organizational and knowledge boundaries, and create new contexts and knowledge, and as organizational and knowledge boundaries are overcome, business people are able to dynamically create new contexts with the ICT capability induced into them through the new perspectives they gain. These new contexts in turn give business people the "knowledge community building capability" needed to create new networks. In this way, ICT capability is one of the core competences companies need to achieve the "speed business," "business efficiency" and "creative business" mentioned in Chapter 4.

VCTs complement the ICT capability of business people. As a positive feedback effect, the use of VCTs promotes ICT capability, which in turn encourages even more use of VCTs. The new perspectives gained through the proactive use of VCTs induce new understanding and awareness. As these tools raise the level of ICT capability, they also improve knowledge community-building capability, through the new contexts brought about by the dynamic strategic and organizational contextual synergies that emerge inside and outside of companies, and then the synergistic effects between ICT and knowledge community-building capability drive even more use of video communications, and thus raise a businessperson's ICT capability to new heights.

However, ICT capability does not just mean high levels of media richness, skill or know-how. Improving the level of media richness is just one thing that needs to be done to raise ICT capability. The essence of ICT capability lies in the creative awareness and productive interpretation of businesspeople that springs from their new perspectives (Wiseman, 1988). The components of ICT capability are analyzed and discussed in light of the material presented in Chapters 5 to 7, and the other discussions throughout this book.

8.2 ICT capability—theoretical concept

Top management in leading companies throughout the world recognize the importance of acquiring competitiveness through the proactive use of VCTs.

The author has extensive business experience of VCTs in the processes of VCTs marketing, product development, deployment and customer consulting; and through formal and informal dialogue with VCTs' developers in a number of companies and promoters of ICT deployment, the author has gained a number of important insights about the ICT capability of companies that produce competitiveness through the use of VCTs.

During the course of the long-term field research from which the findings presented in this book were extracted, it was clear that ICT capability emerges from the dynamic and synergistic relationships in the daily practice of actors, strategic and organizational contexts, the context of the circumstances surrounding a corporation, and the new perspectives, interpretations and awareness that actors gain.

Practitioners from a number of companies interviewed about their VCTs' use for the case studies presented in Chapters 5 to 7 dynamically combine and supplement real-space business activity with business activities in virtual space, to bring forth new value and meaning to the planning, development, and deployment of VCTs, and create new knowledge. The following points are crucial for a company to instill ICT capability in actors using VCTs in this way.

The first point is forming linkages that give actors the ability to dynamically approach business processes in real space, and enable synergistic effects with business activities in virtual space (ICT) and real space (face-to-face). The second point is the quality of dialogue between people. Thirdly, the ability to formulate strategies to achieve goals lies in the capabilities of actors to form new contexts and meanings through the synergies between real and virtual spaces. The fourth point is the capability of actors to create new knowledge with a high level of added value based on these new contexts and meanings. Actors must be able to bridge the organizational and knowledge boundaries through the dynamic synergies between virtual and real spaces (Kodama, 2007a, 2007b) to solve problems and succeeding with new challenges.

8.2.1 ICT capability as a source of competitive superiority

The true significance of broadband in the ICT era lies in its potential for management and innovation of virtual businesses through sharing *Ba*

(Nonaka, Toyama and Konno, 2000; Kodama, 2005), which result from an overwhelming sense of realism that transcends time and distance. In the broadband environment, however, the usage patterns of many corporate ICT collaboration tools such as VCTs and their management effects have often been unclear. In particular, very few academic studies have addressed the relationship between companies (organizations) and VCTs.

A small amount of literature,[2] which discusses the relationship between VCTs and corporate management, claims that VCTs, in contrast to e-mail and groupware, not only promote the sharing and utilization of knowledge and competences within and among organizations but they are also strategic network tools for rapid decision-making.

However, this literature does not clarify how organizations or their actors master the use of ICT, or what components constitute an actor's capability (or even organizational capability).

On the other hand, there is a certain amount of existing literature on the relationship of ICT and organizational capability. In this literature review, the author reviews existing research regarding the organizational capability of companies using ICT, and presents the results and practical significance of new research topics.

Recent studies have reported the practical business insight that ICT has already become commoditized and cannot be the source of a company's competitiveness (Carr, 2003, 2004). In the field of academic research, meanwhile, from the strategy research foci of positioning-based and resource-based views, scholars have indicated that while ICT has the potential to raise operational efficiency by itself, the fact that it is easy to copy means that ICT alone cannot become a source of competitiveness, and is unlikely to produce differentiation among rivals. It cannot, therefore, sustain competitiveness (Clemons and Row, 1991; Porter, 1991, 2001; Mata, Fuerst and Barney, 1995; Barney, Wright and Ketchen Jr., 2001).

Moreover, scholars researching the relationship between organizational capability and firm performance through ICT point out various factors involved in gaining a high-value, copy-resistant ICT organizational capability. One aspect is that ICT organizational capability can be acquired through the interaction of the three resources of physical ICT infrastructure (hardware and software), human resources possessing ICT skills and intangible assets enabling ICT (Bharadwai, 2000). A second aspect is the need to acquire ICT organizational capability to build trust, coordinate and negotiate through communication and collaboration among in-house ICT and business unit managers (Ross, Beath and Goodfue, 1996).

As a third aspect, these scholars point out that the relationship between an organization and ICT, and the effects of integration of human resources, ICT and business activities involving redesigning business processes offers the potential to create ICT organizational capability with a sustained competitive edge (Powell and Dent-Micallef, 1997). They also suggest that organizational learning (Huber, 1991) can be grasped as a process developed by companies' new knowledge and competences, and that ICT organizational capabilities that enhance company performance are enabled through the experience-based study in organizational learning processes within a company (Tippens and Sohi, 2003).

In this way, acquiring and sustaining ICT capability can be thought of as not simply a matter of the resources of the ICT infrastructure itself and skilled ICT administrators. Rather, ICT capability enables resources (such as people and organizations) to more effectively interact and cooperate with one other, and with company-held contexts (such as changing environments, strategy formulation and implementation processes, and corporate cultures) inside and outside the company, thus enhancing company performance.

Generally speaking, the strategic context (strategy formulation and implementation) and organizational context (including business and decision-making processes, organizational structure, in-house political power and corporate culture) differ from company to company. This creates the potential for copy-resistant organizational capability and sustained competitive edge that differentiates the company from its rivals (Clemons, 1991a, 1991b; Clemons and Row, 1991; Weill and Broadbent, 1998; Weill and Ross, 2004), because as ICT is embedded in a company, it leads to mutual benefits gained through ICT interaction with the company's inherent strategic and organizational contexts.

Meanwhile, systematic research into ICT and productivity by Brynjolfsson and Hitt (1995, 1996) indicated that supplementary investment in intangible assets, such as organizational resources within a company, must take place simultaneously with business process innovation in order to enhance productivity through ICT. The research also suggested that ICT investment enables companies to demonstrate the effects of productivity by linking it with investments in personal and organizational intangible assets. It became clear that the same cost of ICT investment can bring about high productivity gains in one company and low gains in another (Brynjolfsson, 2000).

Accordingly, from the previous discussion, it can be said that the linking of the intangible assets of human resources and human competency with ICT-related resources raises the quality of ICT organizational capability, and contributes to improving company performance and competitive advantage. The aforementioned research presents new implications, on the academic side, regarding the practical business insight (Carr, 2003, 2004) that ICT infrastructure alone cannot become a source of a company's competitiveness.

Much of the findings of past academic research on ICT organizational capability are the results of statistical analysis of large-scale sampling of the connection between ICT organizational capability and company performance. This researches centers on experimental study analyzing the structural elements of ICT organizational capability in a static competitive environment, and thus much of it does not ascertain the formulation and implementation of ever-changing ICT strategies in a dynamic, competitive environment on a real-time axis, nor does it analyze ICT organizational capability. In other words, this research lacks a dynamic analysis.[3]

However, a large number of talented businesspeople face a range of problems and issues on a daily basis. They ask such questions as "How can we structure ICT organizational capability to create a competitive edge?" "How can we reconstruct existing business processes, and use ICT to raise operational efficiency and productivity?" or "How come other companies have had success with adopting this ICT system, and we haven't?"

The viewpoint of strategic management as practice (Kodama, 2007b) implementing the "who," "what," "why," "when," "to whom" and "how" approach with regard to these many issues and ICT strategies are important concerns of many businesspeople. For this reason, the author believes that the construction of a dynamic theory, which the author refers to as "ICT capability" in this book, embracing planning, development, installation, operation and results, will become an important theme in future academic research, and furthermore the pursuit of this "ICT capability" may have beneficial managerial implications for businesspeople.

Therefore, in this chapter the author will first identify the components of "ICT capability" possessed by (or should be possessed by) actors and organizations using VCTs that underscore the insights previously mentioned, and will continue by observing and analyzing the interaction of these components.

8.2.2 Enacting new business structures with video communication tools

Usage examples of VCTs based on findings obtained through interviews and questionnaire surveys of users in various industries and types of operations are shown in Figure 3.9 in Chapter 3. In the future, it is clear that the use of these tools will expand well beyond simple videoconferencing. In addition to interpersonal communication in such areas as education, training and discussion, they will be actively used for other forms of image transmission, such as monitoring and exchange between people, machines and products, and further expansion into ubiquitous image networking among machines is also conceivable.

A look at matters from an agency perspective (Barley, 1986; Robey and Sahay, 1996; Orlikowski, 2000; Orlikowski and Barley, 2001) shows that actors belonging to different companies and industry types will have different strategic and organizational contexts, and thus usage will differ even with the same type of VCTs. The result is that the enacted structures (such as business activities and forms that emerge as a result of actors' training in video communication and ICT tool applications) will also differ (Orlikowski, 2000).

Actors are improving the functions of VCTs in response to market environments and social demand, and creating a wide range of differentiated usage patterns and business models. Put another way, if the structuration theory (Giddens, 1984) and agency theory (Emirbayer and Mische, 1998) were combined, while limiting the definition of human agency to the physical structure of ICT, the human agency will transform its own thoughts and actions while interacting with ICT (the physical functions and applications) and create new structures, including usage patterns, routines and business models.

The author believes that the introduction and use of VCTs is triggered by the formation of CoPs, networked CoPs and SCs as knowledge communities (see Figure 8.2).

Firstly, business communities form with the goal of sharing a range of knowledge and information. This does not just mean business meetings within a company, but also communities of entrepreneurs, industry-specific community groups, franchisee communities and other CoPs such as nonprofit organizations and volunteer groups. Secondly, governmental communities are formed such as CoPs that enable public and welfare-related information to be shared flexibly within municipalities and so on. Thirdly, CoPs also include knowledge businesses in the private sector offering new value to customers as medical, welfare and education services, etc. (knowledge-based businesses) (Kodama, 2001c), and VCTs play an important supporting role in contributing toward the building of trust and shared values in these CoPs and in SCs.

As presented in Figure 5.7 in Chapter 5, in knowledge-creating activities in a company, e-mail, groupware and databases are powerful tools used

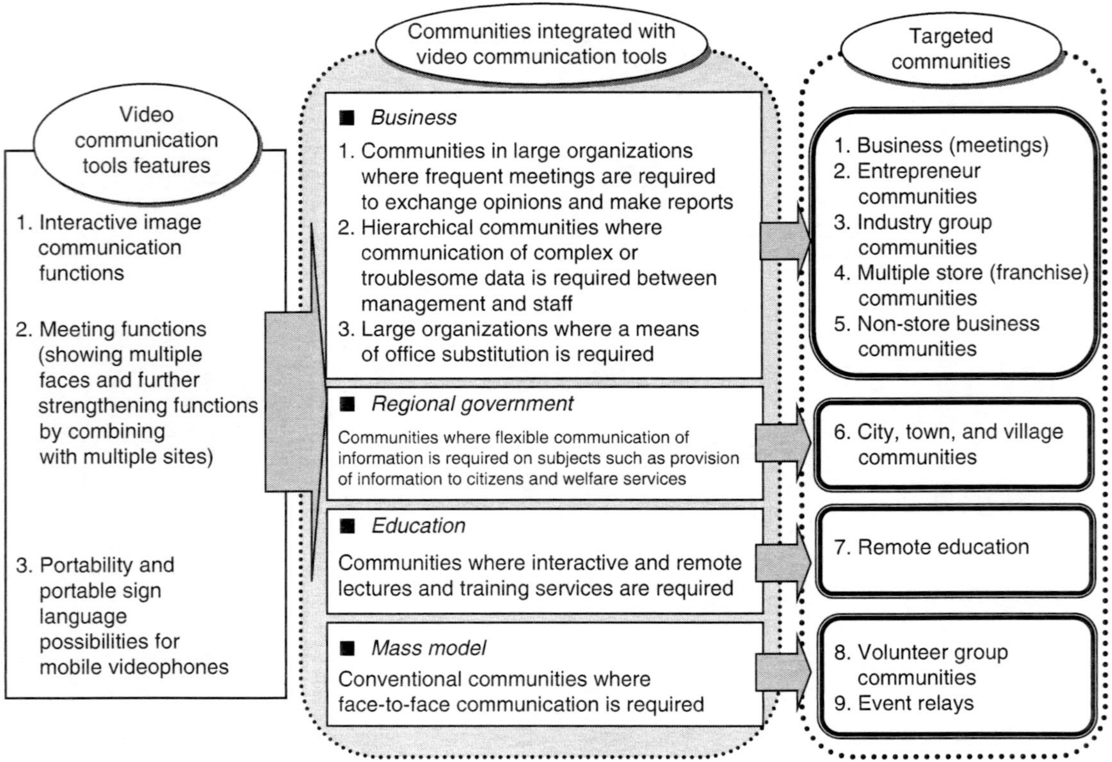

Figure 8.2 Creating knowledge communities with video communication tools

to link up and bring efficiency to explicit knowledge (i.e. knowledge that has already been documented). In contrast, through real- and virtual-space convergence, VCTs offer the potential to trigger new concepts, imagination, perception and emotions in human beings as they operate at the tacit knowledge level (the level of knowledge that cannot be very easily verbalized—human beliefs, thoughts, etc.) in the dialogue and collaboration in corporate activities, and the social lives of people. In the area of business in particular, this capability will bring about the work styles of the future in the form of virtual teams and virtual corporations using VCTs; and the activities therein that enable actors to ignite, create and share new knowledge by transcending space–time will be crucial for developing best practice and the emergent thinking needed for innovation.

High-performance video communication environments (e.g. broadband high-presence communications, communications for translation or communications using the five senses) could bring about an age of "creation" in which the unevenly distributed and diverse knowledge around the world is collected and merged to create new knowledge and value (in which rich tacit knowledge emerges, and tacit knowledge is transformed into explicit knowledge), because VCTs have potential to support human thought and activities in the area of tacit knowledge.

Importantly, VCTs will dynamically transform individual and entire organizational cultures through the introduction of information networks based on these tools. Thus, for companies that use VCTs, it is important to promote dynamic business activities through the synergies of face-to-face, real-space and virtual-space communications.

8.2.3 Designing new business networks (CoPs, networked CoPs, SCs) and promoting knowledge activities

The dominant stereotypical idea among managers and leaders that VCTs are just a "substitute for business trips" is just not true. At their core, VCTs offer new forms of communication, and new styles of participation that can be found nowhere else, which emerge as people engage in meetings via these tools: in meetings held via VCTs, participant are able to remark and contribute in ways that are not possible in other situations, even in meetings held by the same people in real space.

The formation of CoPs and SCs are important as the starting point for *Ba* (Nonaka and Konno, 1998) in which information can be drawn out and shared using VCTs to a level that is not possible with face-to-face or group meetings.

Active VCTs users recognize that VCTs themselves are not just a substitute for real-life meetings. They also recognize the emergence or establishment of CoPs and SCs as new types of forums that are not possible with other ICT tools such as groupware or e-mail. VCTs have enabled actors to move to new activities through the flow of new knowledge and information among themselves, by starting up close-knit and previously nonexistent groups as *Ba* or CoPs once VCTs are deployed.

Moreover, as mentioned in Chapter 4, VCTs conversely increase the frequency of meetings. These extra meetings are of great significance because in the past, even though a meeting may have been required, it wasn't possible without this new form of communication.

Thus, video communications have caused a shift toward a flow of new information that begins in these new and previously unknown meeting forms. They offer more opportunities for actors to meet up. However, they are also significant in that they also provide opportunities for new types of communication and collaboration for which there was previously no realistic method available, even though there has been a need for these interactions.

It's the combination of video, voice and data—modified real-time communications and collaboration functions—that enable effective information transfer and decision-making that is not entirely possible in real space. This comes back to even more practical activities, because VCTs enable communication and collaboration without the participants having to physically go to a meeting location, they remove the usual restrictions placed on communications, and they enable the design of new business networks (knowledge communities), by providing an environment or *Ba* for sharing dynamic contexts. Video offers a way to transfer information that is difficult to express with text or spoken words, and thus leads to new tacit knowledge, and promotes practical activities that are linked with the creation of new knowledge through the emergence of new contexts.

From the surveys conducted, it was clear that the expansion of knowledge communities (CoPs and SCs) did not happen at once with the introduction of VCTs, but was born through the accumulation of long-term organizational learning with ICT.

As mentioned in Chapter 6, Sony was one company that formed a number of knowledge communities through the use of VCTs. However, the formation of these diverse knowledge communities required an organizational learning process with VCTs that took several months.

This organizational learning process raised the ICT application capabilities of actors, and brought about a wide range of usages in which the actors used VCTs to enact new business structures (see Section 8.2.2).

There are four components of the organizational capabilities of actors that lead to the formation of these diverse knowledge communities with these wide-ranging usage patterns, as described further. These four components of organizational capability using VCTs promote the formation of knowledge communities and are thus enablers that give rise to new knowledge.

The research also examined "strategic innovation capability" needed to dialectically manage the diversity of business activities described in the Chapter 5 capability map (domains I and II—exploration for new product development and new business activities; and domains III and IV—exploitation for existing product and business improvement and upgrading).

The data explicitly showed that the use of high-media richness VCTs increases with higher levels of risk and uncertainty, or as the pace of change increases (see Figure 5.5 in Chapter 5). Furthermore, the greater the weight placed on tacit knowledge in strategic, organizational or business contexts, or the higher the conversion level in SECI processes (used to index knowledge creating activities), the more the use of VCTs (see Figure 5.7 in Chapter 5). In short, this means that the way practitioners use ICT and the types of ICT that are used varies according to the levels of risk, uncertainty, urgency or pace of change.

In light of the results presented in Chapter 5, and given the fact that personal and organizational capabilities change in response to changing situations, it is clear that the concept of ICT capability is also inherently dependent upon fluctuations in circumstances. The following observations can be made about the components of dynamically changing ICT capability with respect to the concepts illustrated by Figures 5.5 and 5.7.

8.3 Strategic innovation capability and ICT capability

Figure 8.3 describes the capability map in Chapter 5 with discussions of each domain (I to IV) and "strategic innovation capability."

In domains I and II there are great changes brought about to organizational contexts and strategy due to uncertainty, risk and urgency between practitioners, within organizations and between organizations. For example, dissimilar contexts emerge as practitioners and organizations face and share problems and issues, and work to solve these and achieve goals. These new contexts are shared among practitioners and between organizations. These are examples of *Ba* (Nonaka and Takeuchi, 1995) in which the level of sharing and integration of dissimilar knowledge is raised. However, dialogue among practitioners is crucial to raise

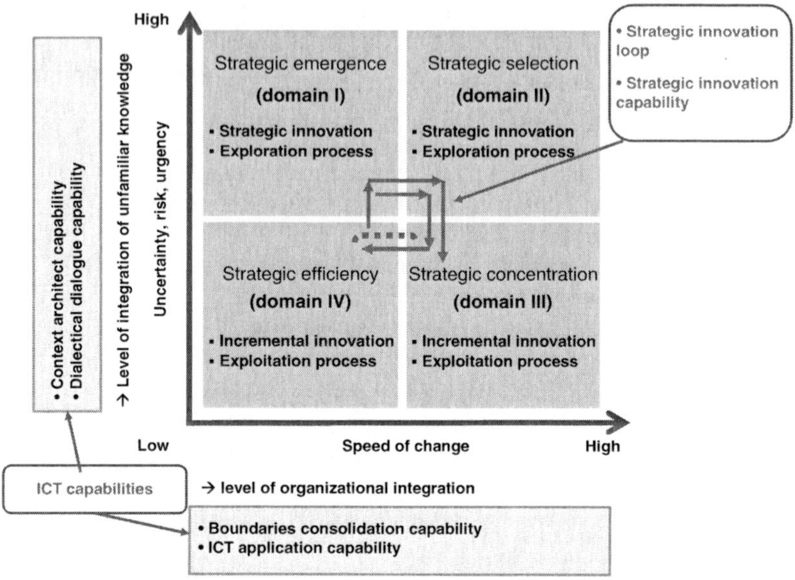

Figure 8.3 Strategic innovation capability map and ICT capabilities

the level of integration of dissimilar knowledge in the *Ba* once it is formed.

In business domains I and II, where the demands for creativity are extremely high, the key method to achieve knowledge creation is the dialectic. The dialectic can be taken as a logical way to solve problems that characteristically unifies both intuitive and analytical methods. Generally, in the process of problem-solving, "thesis," "antithesis" and "synthesis" can be seen—in other words affirmation (thesis), negation (antithesis) and negating the negative (synthesis).

The dialectic is characterized by replacement by a new logical space that includes the logical space of thesis and synthesis in the forward process from thesis to antithesis to synthesis. However, this logic is not formal logic but the logic of meaning, and so it can be said that "logical space" here is actually "meaning space," because in formal logic, syllogisms cannot produce new propositions or meanings.

Hegel named the creation of new logical space as *aufheben* (sublation) in which the acts of negation and retention are simultaneously carried out. To clarify, even if a proposition can be judged to be true or false, for every proposition (thesis) there is always an opposite one (antithesis) to replace it.

Solving problems in situations where the affirmative and the negative conflict is not a matter of selecting either–or to eliminate one or the other, rather it is the synthesis (sublation) and retention of the advantages of both that produces new propositions of higher dimensions (new meaning spaces). However, because the dialectic process involves thesis, antithesis and synthesis, once a synthesis is achieved a new antithesis can be derived, for which new synthesis is required—the process can go on forever.

However, the qualitative aspect of the dialectic brings forth "mutual transformation of quantitative and qualitative change," "unification and conflict of opposites" and "denying the denial" (Kodama, 2004). This process enables dichotomies to be overcome and new diverse meaning and knowledge to be brought forth.

In contrast with Hegel's Western dialectic that seeks to logically eliminate contradiction, practicing this process of thesis, antithesis and synthesis in business or management situations is thought to be more like an Eastern style of dialectic (Nisbett, 2003) where contradictions are allowed to flow naturally and balance is sought while ambiguities are tolerated. In this so-called soft dialectic, things are not taken to be absolute truths, an abstract concept in itself, but are understood as having a relationship to an entire context, and emerge dynamically as moderation points that go beyond compromise.

The SECI model presented in Figure 5.7 in Chapter 5 can also be thought of as a dialectical process, but the dynamic model put forth by Nonaka and Takeuchi (1995) is characterized by the conceptualization of the knowledge-creation process from an ideal position of pragmatism in which meaning of truth, goodness and beauty based in human ontology and epistemology is pursued alongside the dialectic practice of tacit (subjective and bodily knowledge) and explicit (objective and verbal knowledge). The dialectic process is mostly actualized as "dialectical dialogue capabilities" (dialectics of thinking) and "dialectical practice capabilities" (the dialectics of actions).

When talking about dichotomies such as company versus environment or creativity versus efficiency in terms of the SECI model, dynamic contexts are shared at all times, and clashes occur in dialogue and practice between tacit and explicit knowledge, the subjective and the objective and the emergent and intended. There is no path other than to relentlessly pursue the truth through repetition of the practical and dialogue dialectics.

Accordingly, thinking about organizational capability in terms of the dialectic, in domains I and II where uncertainty, risk and urgency cause large strategic and organizational contextual change, the need for dialectical dialogue and practice capabilities is increased. These capabilities are required by practitioners who use ICT tools, even in routine business. This chapter refers to "dialectical dialogue capability" as described previously.

To achieve new knowledge-creating activities in domains I and II, the integration of dissimilar knowledge is required of practitioners, but in order to be successful "context architect capability" is required to transform existing contexts, and bring forth new strategic and organizational contexts. The use of ICT tools (ICT application capabilities of actors) invigorates existing knowledge communities, and creates formal and informal human networks as new knowledge communities. Then the formation of these networks creates new dynamic contexts (or converts existing ones). These transformative contexts and knowledge give rise to new meaning for the actors in knowledge communities, and spurn the creation of the new knowledge needed to reach common strategic goals.

In contrast, in domains II and III where the speed of change is great, there is a need for congruence (Kodama, 2009b) between changes in a company and changes in external circumstances. In particular, it is important to raise the level of organizational integration, share and use knowledge, context and information between organizations, and engage in the "boundaries synchronization" discussed in Chapter 5. Accordingly, practitioners in each organization have to raise the level of linkages between dissimilar organizations, which means they especially need ICT application capabilities to maximize their learning, application and use of ICT. While at the same time, practitioners also require "boundaries consolidation capabilities" to raise the level of interorganizational integration through boundaries synchronization both in real space and with ICT in virtual space.

Human networks formed as knowledge communities are not just places for formal and informal meetings using VCTs. Even in temporary knowledge communities such as cross-functional, task or project teams, new contexts and knowledge are created through the dynamic synergies that emerge in and between real and virtual spaces through the use of VCTs.

By using VCTs, practitioners are able to intentionally (or as a result of their use) transcend organizational and knowledge boundaries, create new contexts, and formulate knowledge communities as human networks; and when organizational and knowledge boundaries are conquered by practitioners, the new perspectives gained induce practitioners to bring forth new contexts among themselves through their context architect capability. Then the new context gives practitioners the boundaries consolidation capability needed to form new human networks.

As described, the four capabilities—"direct dialogue," "context architect," "ICT application" and "boundaries consolidation"—are required by practitioners and organizations in each individual domain to deal with uncertainty, risk, urgency and rapid change. Moreover, because the significance of each of these individual factors also dynamically shifts, practitioners and organizations have to adjust and integrate the four ICT capability factors to suit changing circumstances.

As stated in Chapter 5, leading corporations have the strategic innovation capability that enables them to make use of both the processes of exploration found in domains I and II, and exploration found in domains III and IV. Driving this strategic innovation capability means demonstrating ICT capabilities that adjust and merge dialectical dialogue, context architect, ICT application and boundaries consolidation capabilities to respond to circumstances of uncertainty, risk, urgency and rapid change—strategic innovation capability and ICT capability are always in a mutually complimentary relationship.

8.4 The four components of ICT capability

Practitioners strengthen their dialectical dialogue capability through their ICT application capability. It is dialectical dialogue capability that enables practitioners to raise the level of their context architect and boundaries consolidation capabilities.

VCTs encourage the context architect and boundaries consolidation capabilities of practitioners, which in turn encourage practitioners to use VCTs more often. Then the new perspectives that managers and leaders gain about ICT bring forth new interpretations and awareness about proactive ICT use that promotes creative abrasion among practitioners and induces dialectical dialogue capability, and brings the context architect capability that enables the birth of new contexts through dynamic synergies of strategic and organizational contexts, and thus raises the level of boundaries consolidation capabilities that practitioners need to form human networks. The synergies of context architect and boundaries consolidation capabilities further promote the use of VCTs and raise the level of practitioners ICT application capability.

As mentioned in Chapter 5, ICT application capability is not merely a matter of high levels of media richness. A high level of media richness is just one aspect of raising ICT application capability—the essence

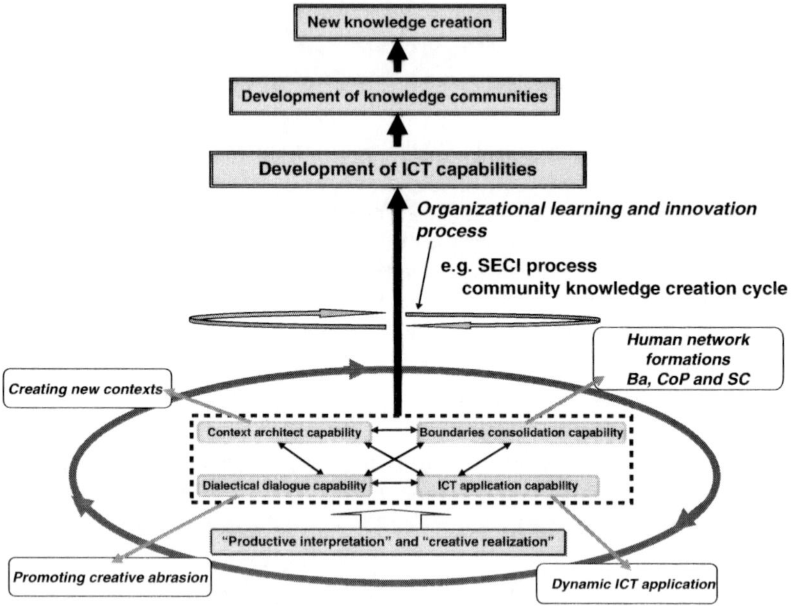

Figure 8.4 Four ICT capability elements

of ICT application capability lies in practitioners' creative awareness, productive interpretation and creative realization that springs from their new perspectives (Wiseman, 1988).

While the four components of ICT capabilities—ICT application, dialectical dialogue, context architect, boundaries consolidation capabilities—interact with each other, new knowledge emerges through the organizational learning and innovation processes (the community knowledge creating cycle; Kodama, 2007b), and through the SECI process (Nonaka and Takeuchi, 1995) mentioned in Chapter 5.

The four components interact to bring forth organizational capabilities using ICT (referred to as ICT capability in this chapter), and promote creative abrasion through the use of VCTs to give rise to the dynamic loop of human network and context formation as illustrated in Figure 8.4. The following examines these four components.

8.4.1 ICT application capability

The meaning of ICT application capability is not restricted to the technological functions of ICT itself or the skills of actors operating ICT. While ICT is certainly a tool for actors to implement daily organizational activities and business processes, a more important aspect is that actors also use it to create new meaning and context relating to daily activities while interacting with the strategic and organizational contexts of their companies. It is important for actors to improve and transform their organizational practice of ICT activities to create new business processes and product ideas, and to implement new forms of ICT use and business improvements from improvised learning (Orlikowski, 1996) at the worksite. Transformation of this kind of organizational practice is enacted not just through the technical functions of ICT but also through actors' ICT dynamic activity. In other words, the ICT resource itself does not determine organizational transformation. The ICT activity patterns are determined by the planning and judgments of human agents (actors), and transformation comes about as new structures are formed through actors' trial and error (Orlikowski, 2000).

Put another way, ICT activity as a result of specific thinking and behavior through actors' recursive practices revolutionizes routine and habit, and creates structures as new social systems (Orlikowski, 2000). The resonance of values (Kodama, 2007b) among actors rooted in a company's or organization's vision and mission provides meaning, power and motivation, and transforms actors. Actors deliberately or emergently exploit ICT, and go on to repeat and create (production) routine change and new business innovations (creation of new structures).

From the viewpoint of agency perspective (Barley, 1986; Robey and Sahay, 1996; Orlikowski, 2000; Orlikowski and Barley, 2001), ICT activity is socially constructed. ICT is created from new, diverse social meaning among actors, and becomes an "interpretatively flexible" entity supporting actors' business actions (Orlikowski, 1992, 2000). An organization's most effective processes for using ICT tools is highly dependent on the environment surrounding actors and its strategic and organizational contexts—that is, the effective introduction of ICT depends greatly on the context of the organization, and installation and results differ from organization to organization (Barley, 1986; Fuller, 2001), because the ICT learning processes differ among organizations, even among actors using the same technologies.

It follows that different organizational settings lead to the enactment of different structural changes, even when the same ICT systems have been adopted. Put another way, the efficacy of ICT activities (its structures) created from the content of actors' thinking and behavior also differs among individual actors (and organizations).

Looking at the VCTs' usage method in Figure 3.9 in Chapter 3, the method differs according to a company's industry and circumstances (whether it be involved in education, medical care, welfare, consulting, security or broadcasting) and even these companies are using VCTs with the same functions. Actors' usage habits and business structures also change according to intention and strategic objectives.

The introduction of ICT can also produce results different from the intentions of the original system designers as a result of an organization's strategic and organizational context (DeSanctice and Poole, 1994). Even though an organization may possess high-level ICT, positive, business-efficient results will not occur if actors use the technology inappropriately. Structuration theory (Giddens, 1979, 1984) argues that structures cannot be enacted as the "technology-in-practice" (Orlikowski, 2000) of rules and resources. The capability to use ICT also involves the specific thinking and behavior of actors who can enact new technologies-in-practice.

This kind of ICT application capability can be thought of as being constructed through organizational learning (Robey, Boudreau and Rose, 2000) as a result of actors' trial and error with ITC. The mechanism of this construction process is described by the human-agency perspective, Giddens' structuration theory (Orlikowski and Robey, 1991; Orlikowski, 1992, 2000) and the actor network theory (Walsham, 1997; Jones, 1999), but the basic thinking is that its essence lies in the organizational learning process through the interaction of human agencies and institutions mediated by ICT.

As previously mentioned, actors' minds, or specifically, actors' "productive interpretation" and "creative realization" with regard to ICT can be considered important practical factors for enhancing ICT application capability. While the acquisition of ICT capability can be considered separate from the strategic or organizational context surrounding actors, an improvised learning process of reinvention (Boudreau and Robey, 2005) arising, for example, from actors' ICT inertia can lead to productive interpretation or creative realization with regard to ICT.

The thought and behavior of actors attempting to embed ICT within a company's strategic and organizational context is an important element of their productive interpretation. Moreover, inspiring new knowledge from virtual-space interactions of actors from different specialist fields is an important element of actors' creative realization. The significant elements existing in the background of this productive interpretation and creative realization rely on the new perspectives that management gains with regard to ICT.

Management has to consider matters from a variety of viewpoints. They must do more than weigh up the benefits and disadvantages of

ICT investment costs and technological features. They also have to consider a large number of elements, such as the impact of ICT on the company and society as a whole, the integration of in-house business processes, and opposition from the organizational culture. Next they have to accurately and objectively make an overall judgment of the pros and cons of ICT by analyzing the gap between current ICT strategies and future scenarios. They must be wary, however, on settling for a logically analyzed compromise.

From the viewpoint of the agency perspective mentioned previously, the actors' dialectical action in regard to ICT creates a new perspective to be grasped constructively and productively. The new perspectives gained by management then bring forth productive interpretation and creative realization in actors in the company, including the leaders themselves.

This kind of productive interpretation and creative realization is born of actors' dialectical dialogue capability, new context architect and boundary consolidation capabilities, as described further.

To respond to dynamic changes in the environment or to create change in themselves, actors promote the interaction of practice (through ICT activity resulting from induced productive interpretations and creative realizations) and a company's constantly changing strategic and organizational contexts.

8.4.2 Dialectical dialogue capability

This productive interpretation and creative realization transform discussion among the actors to a productive and constructive context. These two factors trigger creativity and imagination as new ideas and concepts among actors in the organization. Therefore, not only do they pursue efficiency through the utilization of ITC but also simultaneously pursue creativity, and this promotes creative dialogue among actors in knowledge communities. At the same time, dialectical dialogue among actors induces them to create new productive interpretations and creative realizations.

Dialectical dialogue enables the sharing of deep thoughts and feelings among actors. In the space and time in which creative dialogue occurs, the issue to be considered is not whether one "has or does not have" but rather, the process of "how to create." In other words, creative dialogue delves into content (meaning), and makes use of "negative productivity." Therefore, open cogitation among staff members, including leaders, is important, and takes place in an environment of both self-assertiveness and humility, where it is crucial that people are aware that mistakes are made while realizing a desire to advance through the mediation of conflict with others.

In this way the actors' productive interpretation and creative realization of ICT form their dialectical dialogue capability. Furthermore, while the dialectical dialogue within knowledge communities creates new ICT value among actors, it also builds mutual trust, which transcends knowledge and organizational boundaries and is an important factor in developing collaboration in new knowledge communities. The dependence of business performance on mutual trust in virtual ICT-based teams has already been reported in a significant amount of existing research (O'Hara-Devereaux and Johansen, 1994; Odenwald, 1996; Lipnack and Stamps, 1997; Jarvaenpaa and Leidner, 1999; Duarte and Tennant Snyder, 2000; Zigurs, 2003).

8.4.3 Context architect capability

An important element of the third focal point of ICT capability is actors dynamically creating new contexts through interaction with ICT. Actors transform existing contexts and create new contexts through ICT activities (or through ICT media). This is how actors engage in business context architecture. In this book, the author calls this an actor's "context architect capability", and gives examples of context architect capability through empirical studies of new product development processes.

Figure 8.5 shows the chronological process of a joint development between a Japanese manufacturer and an Israeli manufacturer. In step 1, discussions about the technical specifications of the joint product development are carried out in Tokyo, and opinions are aligned on the meaning of the development, technical specifications and development schedules. In step 2, the Japanese and Israeli sides separate, activate VCTs, and proceed with discussions on more detailed specifications. In step 3, the actors meet in Tokyo to finalize the specifications for the development. In step 4, prototype software tests are carried out through international telecommunications networks to confirm development targets. The various developmental themes up to this point are focused upon, and actions at the Japanese and Israeli ends of the business are taken to solve problems. In step 5, field tests begin on the commercialized product with conditions established in Tokyo, and more software-related problems emerge. After this, software debugging is carried out remotely from Israel over a broadband network to bring the product to completion.

With this example, complex problems and issues emerged at each step. Actors used VCTs effectively to closely share information and context,

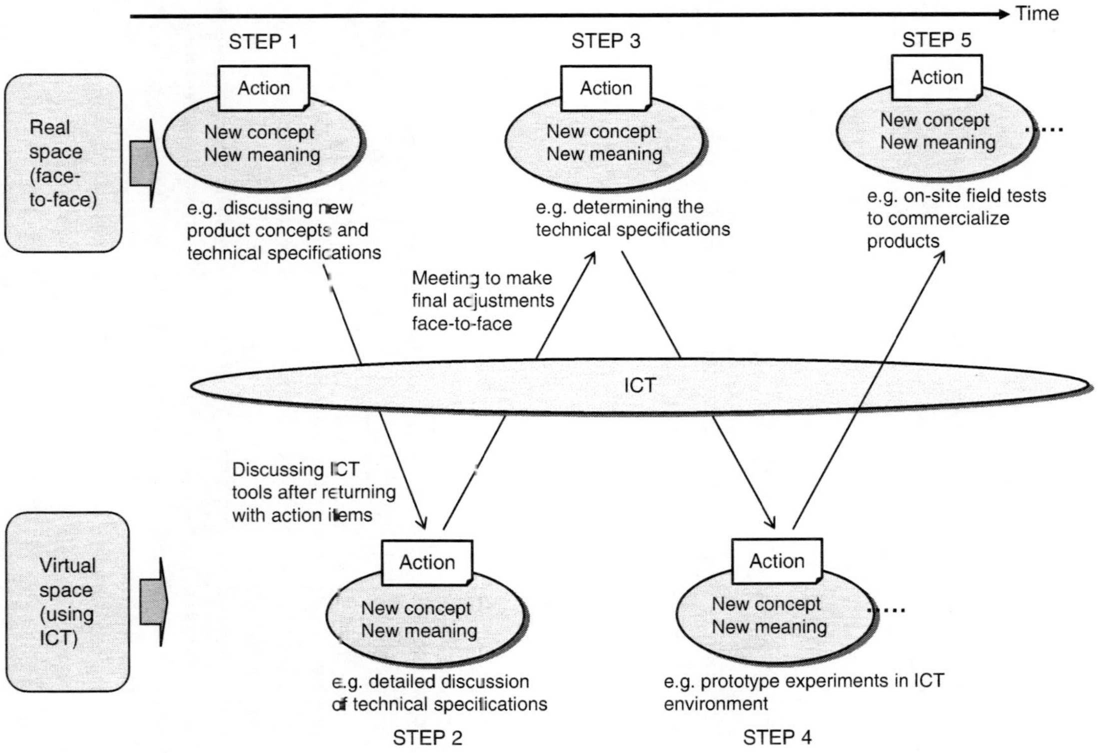

Figure 8.5 Interaction between real and virtual spaces: Case of new product development

and were able to create new contexts and link these with specific actions. Various uncertainties in driving the product development and solving knotty problems required strong motivation for what is, for the actors, the creation of new context and knowledge in a major situation.

In this case, the combination of face-to-face interaction in real space and in virtual space using VCTs transcended company boundaries and raised the performance of the joint development project. Some hold the view that this is also consistent with past research that shows that a combination of media including face-to-face contact outperformed media without face-to-face contact (Ocker et al., 1998). Moreover, DeSanctis and Jackson (1994) reported that the benefits from using more complex communications technology increased as the task became more complex.

In this case too, the use of VCTs as an advanced communications technology (Hinds and Kiesler, 1995) to promote real-time collaboration in place of non-real-time e-mail and voicemail and execute complex tasks conferred considerable benefits (sharing of dynamically changing information, contexts and knowledge) to actors. In this way, the actors were able to create new contexts and meaning through the traffic in real space and in virtual space using VCTs. This is the "context architect capability" as an ICT capability.

8.4.4 Boundaries consolidation capability

The forth component of "ICT capability" is actors' boundaries consolidation capability.

As mentioned previously, with the processes of new product development described by the empirical studies shown in Figure 8.5, the new product development mission was deeply shared among project members. Actors faced the important decision of whether to develop under the guidance of their own company or jointly through a strategic alliance. The actors' decision to opt for joint development with the world's most advanced partners created new meaning and context and temporarily built an intercorporate network for the joint development that crossed corporate boundaries.

The new meanings and contexts created improvised action in the actors (Kodama, 2005), and these improvised actions led to communication and collaboration with actors in companies holding dissimilar values.

Although communication with actors belonging to different organizations (companies) and possessing knowledge from different specializations naturally gives rise to abrasion and conflict, it also enables the creation of new knowledge through actors' dialectical thought and action (Kodama, 2005). In this case, the combination of face-to-face interaction in real space and interaction using VCTs in virtual space enhanced the performance of the joint development project, by enabling actors to transcend dissimilar knowledge, corporate and organizational boundaries.

Other cases also demonstrate boundaries consolidation capability in which practitioners maximize use of ICT application capability and achieve knowledge integration across different industries.

This has a relationship with the phenomenon of convergence illustrated in Figure 2.5 in Chapter 2. In recent years differing technologies, including ICT, have been integrated to create new product and technological developments, and achieve business models based on new rules that span dissimilar industries, and with convergence behind these developments, new layers of complexity have been added to competition between companies.

Convergence has accelerated M&A and strategic partnering between corporations, including customers, and has triggered dramatic changes to existing company boundaries. For this reason, innovation through partnerships formed among dissimilar industries that transcend the older style competitive frontiers between businesses is becoming more and more important as a core driver for corporate strategy. Modern corporations face the challenge of quickly shifting to innovation through joint developments across a range of industries (or companies), including customers, as competitiveness between companies within an industry or between industries moves out of the focus of strategy.

This means that where ICT is concerned, productive interpretation and creative realization will bring forth new applications across differing fields, and the boundaries consolidation capability of practitioners will give rise to new business models that cut across different industries.

The remote medical support mentioned in Section 7.2.1 in Chapter 7 is a case of ICT in a joint industry–government–academic collaborative venture in Japan that typifies convergence of the medical, welfare and insurance fields, and is an example of boundaries consolidation capability. In this case, virtual district communities were achieved through ICT application and boundaries consolidation capabilities.

The aforementioned four components of ICT application, dialectical dialogue, context architect and boundaries consolidation capabilities form the core framework of ICT capability. These four elements have an interdependent relationship. Actors' context architect capability enhances their boundaries consolidation capability. Boundaries consolidation capability in turn creates new meaning and context, and further enhances context architect capability. This is a relationship of dialectical, recursive interplay.

Moreover, as actors are spurred toward productive interpretation and creative realization regarding ICT, their ICT application capability and dialectical dialogue capability is enhanced, which gives them new meaning and context, and simultaneously enhances context architect and boundaries consolidation capabilities as organizational learning and innovation processes moving between real space and virtual space, as shown in Figure 8.4.

These high-level context architecture and boundaries consolidation capabilities create meaning and context about new ICT usages, thus further enhancing ICT application capability and dialectical dialogue capability. By interacting with dynamic strategic and organizational contexts, actors engage in a spiralling of organizational learning and innovation processes, and are therefore able to simultaneously enhance the four capabilities in response to circumstantial change, while creating ICT capability as an organization. The result is the creation of new businesses and the achievement of new business processes (see Figure 8.4).

High-level ICT capability enhances corporate operational efficiencies and productivity ("knowledge efficiency" or "knowledge productivity") as new business processes are established. This capability also enhances a company's creativity ("knowledge creativity" in this book) and gives the company the potential to achieve a unique and copy-resistant competitive edge with its new product and service developments and new business models (see Figure 8.4).

8.5 Knowledge boundaries and ICT capability

Practitioners possess their own unique thought worlds and mental models. Having only personal experiences of society and unique worldviews, practitioners have practical knowledge rooted in tacit knowledge born from professional experience across a range of job functions embedded within themselves. Therefore, as the level of novelty and uncertainty increases with strategies aimed at achieving certain objectives, practitioners are mutually faced with greater levels of knowledge diversification and disparity, which can easily give rise to friction and conflict along pragmatic boundaries.

There are demands to convert practitioners' existing knowledge at pragmatic boundaries because in particular, in the innovation of new and different products, or the creation of new businesses that are completely different to the conventional, there is a potential for the deeply embedded existing knowledge of individual practitioners to be challenged and, as in the innovators dilemma (Christensen, 1997), their actions might become stagnated.

To achieve success with a new business development, practitioners forming SCs on pragmatic boundaries must first of all reach mutual understanding to generate new meaning through profound dialectical dialogue. This is characteristic of actions taken in virtual space using VCTs.

Dialectical dialogue is an enabler that promotes understanding and sharing of meaning among practitioners who face new challenges. However, while there may be general agreement, comments such as "There are problems with the details!" or "This lacks concrete theory!" can be heard in discussions among practitioners in the workplace. Discussions such as "We know what needs to be done, but specifically who is going to do it and when, and how is it supposed to be done? And do we have the resources?" emerge. This kind of friction and discord in organizations is unavoidable.

However, the friction and discord that arises in facing the challenge of new issues and current problems is also an opportunity for innovation. Practitioners—management at all levels, including top management—must proactively and diligently engaged in deep dialogue that asks, "Where is the friction and discord?" "What are the problems, and what are the solutions?" It is no good to try reaching easy compromises in disputes with external partners either, because this will nip new corporate growth in the bud. Panasonic CEO Kunio Nakamura describes this by saying, "To make innovative changes, we cannot be afraid of friction within the company."

To turn friction and discord into a growth driver for a corporation, business persons need to establish shared values and find common and mutual viewpoints that clarify specific actions (e.g. common interests between organizations) (Kodama, 2007c), motivate partners and build win–win relationships with all stakeholders. In the internal context of a company, decision-making processes and rules about current and future priorities—what must be done now, and what needs to be invested—must also be clarified and disclosed fairly to all members of staff. If these issues are not addressed, trust and unity will not arise through the dialectical dialogue of practitioners.

By forming SCs and sharing common values, practitioners establish a common foundation (Bechky, 2003) in which they transform the conflicts and frictions among themselves into "creative abrasion" (Leonard-Barton, 1995) and "productive friction" (Hagel III and Brown, 2005), which in turn leads to mutual trust that can promote collaboration across the boundaries between dissimilar knowledge.

Harvard Business School's Professor Rosabeth Moss Kanter states that it is important to push conflict in the direction of creativity—it should not be thought of as something that leads to confusion and should therefore be avoided (Kanter, 2001, p. 231).

As the component of ICT capability that enables common ground to be established, dialectical dialogue capability raises practitioners' awareness of dissimilar contexts and knowledge, while at the same time promotes creative collaboration across different fields of specialization and between different genres; and as the level of mutual understanding and awareness of different contexts and knowledge about strategy, organizations, technologies and operations is raised among practitioners, congruence is promoted between these areas of business. In short, encouraging dialectical dialogue expands practitioners' dynamic range (called "the dynamic range of knowledge boundaries" in this book) about changing knowledge boundaries where there is interaction between formal organizations and SCs (or networked CoPs).

Practitioners use these ICT capability components—dialectical dialogue, context architect, ICT application and boundaries consolidation capabilities—to expand their "dynamic range of thoughts and actions" to raise their awareness of dissimilar knowledge (in business processes in domains I, II and III), while on the other hand, by sharing knowledge in formal organizations (mainly CoPs in domain IV) executing daily business—the practitioner's business territory—they also raise awareness of similar knowledge (see Figure 8.6).

To succeed with new innovation through the processes from domain III or IV back through to domains I → II → III, practitioners need to form new organizations to bring about new knowledge integration and achieve congruence with strategy.

This means creating new organizational cultures that do not exist in traditional organizations as SCs consisting of practitioners with backgrounds in dissimilar specializations and a variety of different capabilities (projects, cross functional teams, small-scale independent organizations, venture teams within companies, etc.—most important in domains I and II). It is also important to assimilate personnel with different ideas from both within and outside the company (see Chapter 5). This blows new winds across both existing organizations and teams formed from members with dissimilar backgrounds, and stimulates and inspires

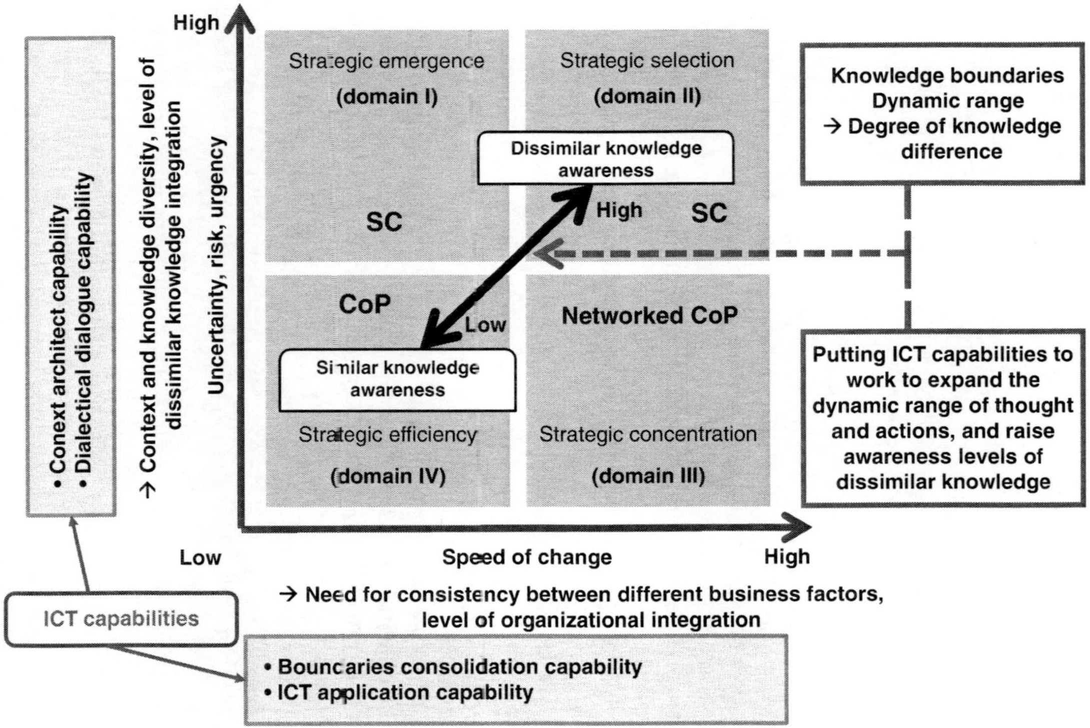

Figure 8.6 Dynamic range of knowledge boundaries and ICT capabilities

practitioners as they work toward strategic objectives to achieve breakthroughs, transformation, creativity and innovation (and of course involves conflict and friction).

Innovation arises in SCs where practitioners from different specialist areas and dissimilar cultures interact—and it is the proactive use of VCTs that enables practitioners to raise the quality of their ICT capability, and strengthen the forming, maintenance and development of SCs. The key to this is the continued support from top management to furnish and maintain the ICT and organizational environments required to enable dialectical dialogue between SCs and existing organizations and nurture close-knit collaboration.

8.6 Practical processes as collaborative organizations

As mentioned earlier, the dynamic range of knowledge boundaries describes the extent of changing knowledge and contexts, while at the same time it also describes the depth of awareness that practitioners have of a variety of values and diversification. Practitioners in corporations where VCTs are proactively used all possess a wide dynamic range of knowledge boundaries.

The width of the dynamic range of knowledge boundaries reinforces practitioners ICT capability to change boundaries as circumstances change, and expands the dynamic range of personal thoughts and actions (see Figure 8.6).

In real and virtual spaces, dialectical dialogue widens the dynamic range of thoughts of practitioners, enabling more recognition of diverse contexts and knowledge in SCs (and networked CoPs) and creates a common foundation built upon shared meanings and values among members. The expansion of this dynamic range of knowledge boundaries enables practitioners to share and resonate values with each other and build trust (Kodama, 2007b), foment commitment and promote creative collaboration.

Creative collaboration through dialectical dialogue in organically constructed SC organizations merges and integrates wide ranging contexts and knowledge, and as practitioners work toward achieving the objectives of challenging new strategies, they bring congruence to all business areas as they solve urgent problems and issues in organizations, technologies and operations.

It is important for innovation companies to enact unified strategies that enable them to make use of both incremental innovation adapted for circumstantial change (domains III and IV in Figure 8.3) and radical innovation that creates new circumstances through previously nonexistent new businesses (domains I and II in Figure 8.3).[4] The author calls this organizational capability to leverage both radical and incremental innovation the "strategic innovation capability" of a company (see Chapter 5).

Through their exchanges in real and virtual spaces, practitioners have to use their ICT capability to respond to changes across a diversity of boundaries and raise their awareness of different contexts and knowledge; and the way that these organizations are optimized for, adapting to the thoughts and actions of practitioners is crucial.

Corporations that have practitioners with high awareness of dissimilar contexts and knowledge form collaborative organizations. These collaborative organizations are characterized by the dynamic practical processes that bring about new knowledge and contexts by reassembling networked human relationships through interactions in real and virtual spaces in response to the dynamic formation and disappearance of ever-changing contexts.

The basic formative elements of collaborative organizations are practitioners in formal organizations working on decentralized networks as SCs (including networked CoPs) (see Figure 8.7).

SCs encourage dialectical dialogue among practitioners along knowledge boundaries, and are organizational forms that bring about new knowledge and foster the practical processes needed to deal with new challenges. The practitioners in SCs are chiefly concerned with decision-making as top management teams to establish important strategies, consolidating company-wide awareness of strategy in middle management at the practical business level and solving problems and generating new ideas.

In formulating important strategies, it is without question that top and middle management carry out thorough coordination and suitably nurture a unified awareness of objectives or contexts of interest.[5]

Furthermore, in the context of establishing strategies, task teams formed from ordinary staff members more deeply involved at the practical business level or dealing with specific problems and issues also need to seek out solutions and optimal directions through discussion and dialogue (see Figure 8.7). To do this, these practitioners engage in interactions in real and virtual spaces using a range of ICT tools, including video communications.

As organizational platforms, SCs expand the dynamic range of knowledge boundaries of practitioners, raise the awareness of dissimilar contexts and knowledge, and through the interactions in real and virtual

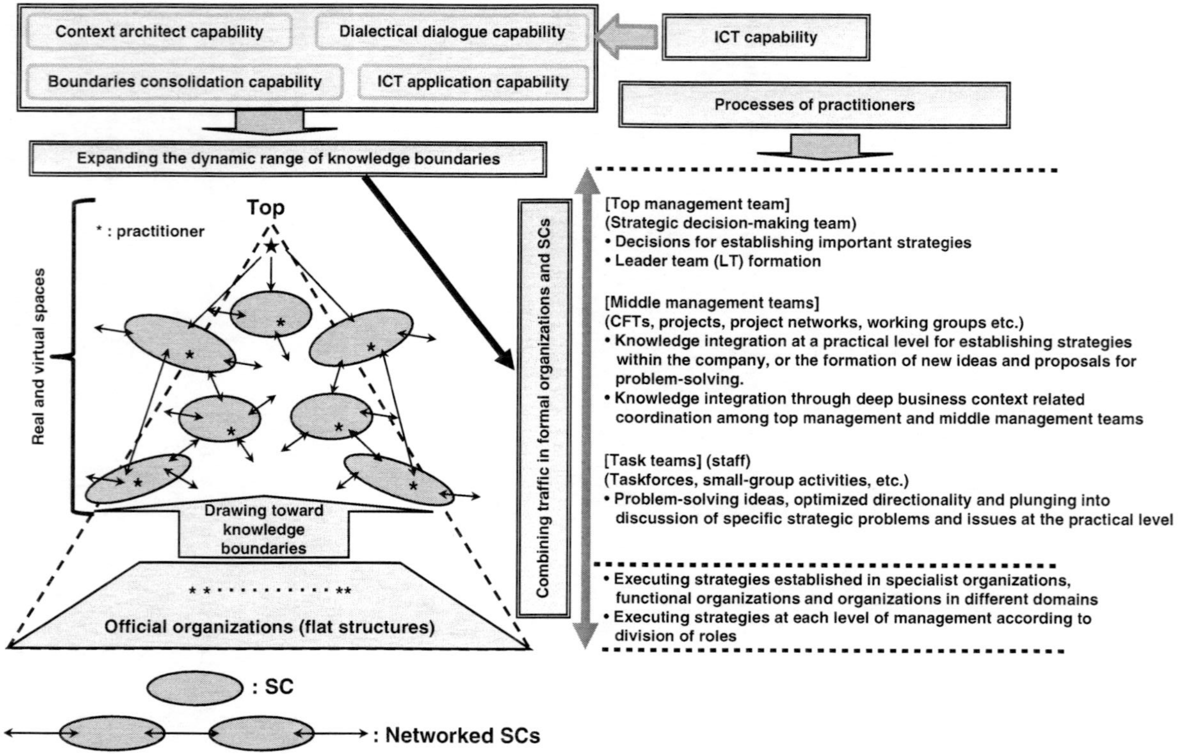

Figure 8.7 Practical processes in collaboration organizations

spaces SC practitioners are able to dynamically and mutually interlock these different boundaries and find solutions to problems when facing new challenges.

As formal organizations, however, collaborative organizations are not the same as the outdated hierarchical and bureaucratic organizations of the past. In contrast, collaborative organizations are formal organizations with horizontal hierarchies that enable rapid delegation of authority and decision-making, and as described by Figure 4.4 in Chapter 4, organizations in corporations that actively use VCTs generally have these flatter hierarchies.

These flat, formal organizations are made up of a number of different business units, and the critical mission of practitioners in formal organizations is to carry out the specific business strategies within the confines of their business units to achieve the strategic objectives established by decision-making in SCs (or in networked CoPs).

At the same time, CoPs that exist in formal organizations or between formal organizations in the same area of specialty or job functions must work to improve and upgrade existing business routines and bring more efficiency to operations, and on top of that practitioners from these business units also form autonomous and dispersed SCs while they collaborate with practitioners in other business units in response to contextual changes. SCs can also include external partners and certain customers as required, and thus through the formation of SCs and the exchanges in real and virtual spaces, top-class practitioners bring about new knowledge through interactions with their external partners and with customers.

Knowledge is intrinsically linked with context, for context consists of situations, conditions and spaces. To create, acquire and share knowledge, practitioners must share dynamically changing contexts. But practitioners cannot share these things unless they participate in certain SCs when a particular context has been established at a particular time and space, because it is through the medium of these shared dynamic contexts that the sharing and integration of knowledge is achieved.

In particular, for practitioners to link together dissimilar contexts and create new contexts from them, they need to voluntarily create SCs in real and virtual spaces as new knowledge boundaries into which practitioners are drawn as stakeholders. The author describes this phenomenon as "the pull of knowledge boundaries" (see Figure 8.7).

It is the context architect capability, a component of ICT capability, which achieves the pull of knowledge boundaries. When SCs are formed, certain practitioners must be included in them as required, in order for top-class practitioners to bring about new and high-quality knowledge; and as practitioners interact in real and virtual spaces, they voluntarily create or participate in multiple and different SCs; and through the flow of knowledge and context between different SCs, practitioners behave in ways that cause contexts and knowledge to be ignited and shared among themselves. This is the boundaries consolidation capability of practitioners, which they use to network diverse SCs as they move in and out of real and virtual spaces.

These context architect and boundaries consolidation capabilities bring forth the imagination, new ideas and solutions needed to carry out measures to achieve strategic objectives, and also give rise to the dynamic practical processes of business persons as they move in and between formal organizations and SCs (see Figure 8.7).

8.7 Combining interactions on dual networks

SCs (or networked CoPs) are not in opposition to formal organizations. In fact, as collaborative organizations, SCs and formal organizations complement each other, because as they manage their own business territory, practitioners in formal organizations also embrace the SC management methods that promote the sharing of dissimilar contexts and knowledge needed to solve problems and issues, and generate ideas that lead to achieving new business development.

The processes of practitioners in collaborative organizations are performed through the interactions in the centralized networks of formal organizations, and the SC decentralized networks in real and virtual spaces. In other words, practitioners achieve strategic objectives through the dynamic interactions between the formal organizations and SCs, in the space–time of knowledge and contexts that span knowledge boundaries.

Practitioners in collaborative organizations do not only adhere to the basic rules of CoPs and formal organizations within the company but also manage the autonomous, dispersed and challenging organizational activities of SCs, while developing, expanding and coordinating those SCs; and the four components of businesspersons' ICT capabilities—dialectical dialogue, context architect, ICT application and boundaries consolidation capabilities—expand the dynamic range of knowledge boundaries for businesspersons, and bring about the creation of dual networks with the differing characteristics of both centralized networks and decentralized networks (see Figure 8.8).

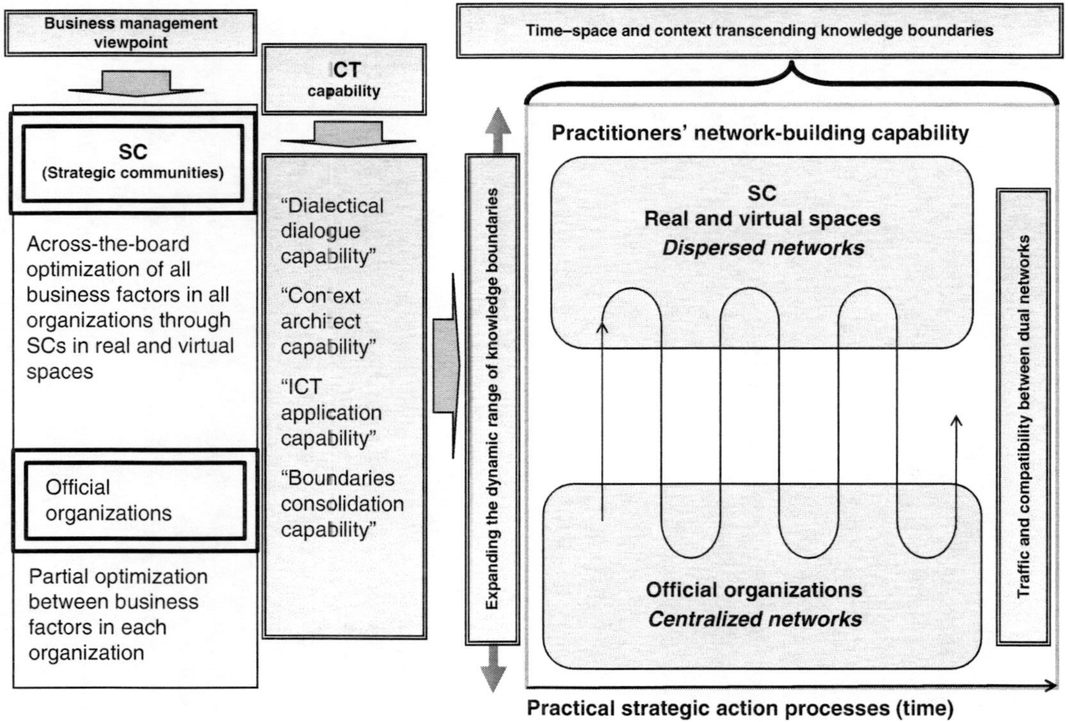

Figure 8.8 Traffic and compatibility between dual networks

From the point of view of corporate management, the interactions between, and combination of these dual networks is significant for the following two reasons:

- Firstly, in the centralized networks of formal organizations, there is partial optimization of managerial factors (strategy, organization, technological and operations) in individual organizations. While thoroughly integrating awareness in management at all levels, and organizations linked in SCs, practitioners promote optimization of all business elements in their own organization to achieve congruence between all business elements within the corporation.
- Secondly, as practitioners seek congruence among business elements within their own organizations, they check and adjust all business elements for overall optimization by forming SCs that span a range of formal organizations.

Through these dual network interactions and combinations, practitioners are able to merge and integrate diverse contexts and knowledge both in and outside of their organizations, which contributes to the creation of an optimized management system throughout the whole company.

In terms of organizational management from the SC perspective, practitioners are released from the mental models of conventional formal organizations, because completely new management models are important for practitioners. In other words, this is a management model that executes strategies dynamically by flexibly reconfiguring SCs to suit strategic objectives as the interaction of these dual networks aligns itself with dynamically changing contexts.

Moreover, when there is a high level of complexity involved with developing new business for new business models, or there are an increased number of difficult problems and issues to be overcome, SCs need to be simultaneously both dispersed and integrated (networked).

SCs can be organizational forms on missions to achieve targets, or solve problems—also the organizational forms such as product teams or cross functional teams in real and virtual spaces. Multiple projects also give rise to project networks (also called project convergence) (Kodama, 2007c).

The organizational activity in these SCs is also an example of creating new business models as participants in different projects collaborate with each other. In collaborative organizations, business people reconfigure SCs in response to circumstantial change, while at the same time they dynamically generate new knowledge by raising the level of interaction between dual networks.

Looking at the strategic activities of collaborative organizations on a time axis, practitioners engage in business activities to effect strategies within their own business territory in their formal organizations on centralized networks (business improvement and upgrading), while at the same time they engage in SC-based business activities to solve difficult problems and issues through traffic in real and virtual spaces across dispersed networks, and embark on the challenge of achieving high-quality business by creating new products, services or even new businesses themselves.

This means that collaborative organizations simultaneously promote incremental innovation to achieve sustained growth and greater efficiency in existing business (domains III and IV in Figure 8.3), and promote radical innovation to produce long-term businesses (domains I and II in Figure 8.3).

Because strategic objectives in collaborative organizations adjust to dynamically changing circumstances, collaborative organizations are also the best organizational form for independently creating the right circumstances in which practitioners can create and deploy new businesses.

8.8 Small-world networks and ICT capability

The following describes practitioners' ICT use and the characteristics of SCs that span formal organizations from the viewpoint of network theory (Barabasi, 2002; Watts, 2003).

The complimentary relationships of people at the micro level, groups and organizational networks with formal corporate organizations is an important platform that promotes knowledge management and knowledge-integration processes, and thus the form of these interactions has a profound influence on the transfer of knowledge and information,[6] and for a company to acquire and maintain its organizational capability, it is essential that it can dynamically configure networks (Kodama, 2007b, 2007c), and it must be able to dynamically reconfigure networks in real and virtual spaces to respond to changing circumstances and strategic actions.

Network theory provides valuable insights into the relationship between practitioners' actions and between practitioners both in and between companies, and the creation of human networks reinforces the ICT capability of practitioners, and is an important trigger in the knowledge-integration process.

Broadly speaking, network forms can be classified as centralized or decentralized. Centralized networks are most appropriate for processing information and passing knowledge in a routine fashion (knowledge and information is passed from a central node to peripheral nodes) (e.g. Tushman, 1979; Albert and Barabasi, 2000). Therefore, the layered configurations of formal organizations are examples of centralized networks.

In contrast, decentralized networks are characterized by a simultaneous joining of localized clusters (the close relationships between practitioners) with dissimilar clusters to create shortcuts between practitioners from different backgrounds and network them together. This networked topology has been called "small-world networks" (Watts and Strogatz, 1998), and in terms of network theory this enables a node to connect to another node via several other nodes. Thus networks like this are characterized by the connections between the nodes on the network, even though they may not be neighboring nodes.

Technically, the average path length[7] is short and the number of clusters is high,[8] and in a typical small-world network adjacent nodes (the joining points—e.g. individuals in a company) are connected according to rules, while nodes that are far apart on the network can be linked by random shortcuts or bypasses.

The small-world network—a decentralized network—is the most appropriate network form when directly faced with the challenges of uncertainty and risk, facing new issues, seeking urgent solutions to problems or when circumstances are rapidly changing (Watts, 2003).

In small-world networks, while there is adjacent networking of individuals who are closely connected—for example, practitioners in the same formal organizations—these networks are also places in which practitioners who are organizationally dispersed are able to access each other via the shortcuts available, expand the boundaries of individual knowledge, and use resources (knowledge) more efficiently across entire organizations.

Small-world networks are robust networks that offer organizations resilience against information overload or bottlenecks within organizations, sudden circumstantial changes such as unexpected problems and accidents, or destruction (Shah, 2000; Newman, 2004).

From the point of view of social network theory, SCs are examples of clusters formed from the smallest nodes—the individual—and "creeks."[9] Creeks are formed from the interchange and sharing of information, knowledge and context in groups of closely linked practitioners, while in SCs information is not exchanged in simple groups but rather in collectives characterized by pragmatic boundaries formed from a matrix of semantic boundaries in which teams create new knowledge and context by dynamically responding to contextual change.

Furthermore, business people with wide-ranging professional skills in SCs also use ICT to solve pressing problems and achieve new creative strategies as they coordinate and merge the four ICT capability factors—dialectical dialogue, context architect, ICT application and boundaries consolidation capabilities. These are groups that promote the formation of organizational small-world networks as they work to achieve new innovation.

With this in mind, the SC and networked CoP organizational forms in domains I, II and III in Figure 8.3 are configured from a mix of creeks and a multitude of shortcuts between practitioners in decentralized networks and a range of clusters of centralized networks in formal organizations. This entire network is an example of a small-world network (see Figure 8.9).

The author places particular focus on SCs as dynamically changing and dispersed networks, whose network forms are examples of group-interlocked networks (Watts, 2003).

Duncan Watts (2003) said that given that practitioners have a relationship with a particular context, business people proactively form groups (or SCs) within a particular context in the real business world

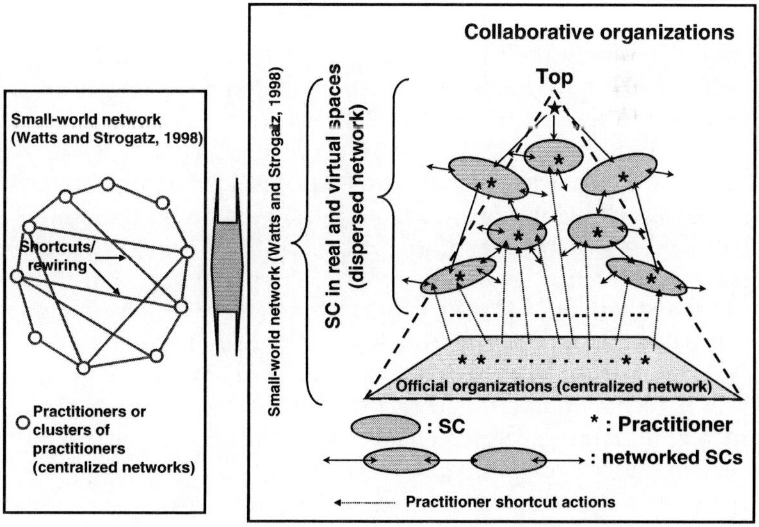

Figure 8.9 Small-world networks and collaborative organizations

while bringing in certain practitioners (in other words links are created with other practitioners—the pull of knowledge boundaries mentioned earlier). Accordingly, SCs change dynamically in response to context, and networked SCs are also formed from SCs dynamically.

Practitioners dynamically reconfigure SCs in real and virtual spaces as part of their daily activities. Multiple practitioners participate in multiple SCs to share knowledge and information, and practitioners who also participate in other SCs transfer knowledge and information and share it with those practitioners. This is the process through which SCs are formed as group-interlocked networks mentioned earlier.

In the context of the group-interlocked network, SCs are examples of either nodes or hubs.[10] Practitioners who belong to hub or node SCs inside or outside of companies create networks among the SCs by dynamically bridging multiple and different SCs, and new contexts and knowledge are created in these networks of multiple SCs.

Practitioners use their ICT capabilities to intentionally network multiple SCs both in and out of companies, and deeply integrate these SCs to create new product developments and new business processes.

8.9 ICT and collaborative organizations

Achieving a collaborative organization is not just a simple matter of deploying ICT such as VCTs for practitioners to use to create new knowledge.

Cisco Systems in the United States is a company that believes only companies that have the word "collaboration" written into their DNA will be able to succeed (Chambers, 2007). This is because it is not possible to grasp and respond quickly to the undercurrents in diverse market places if integrative capability (ICT capability) is not applied across the company, if matters are left up to a select few leaders. Thus, rather than charging management alone with tasks, Cisco forms collaborative organizations that cross over different departments and cut through the range of managerial layers within the company to solve important problems (Cisco calls these "councils" and "boards").

Councils are formed when there is the prospect of business opportunities on the $10 billion scale, whereas boards are formed when the scale is $1 billion, and from these boards and councils working groups are formed to take strategic initiatives.

These organizations are examples of SCs and networked CoPs, and they give staff at Cisco ability to engage in constructive discussion, understand their partnerships and make decisions swiftly. Collaboration enables these organizations to get the best opinions as swiftly as possible, and enables teams to work together to solve a wide range of problems; and as Cisco forms SCs and networked CoPs in real and virtual spaces for thorough collaboration between staff, ICT use in the company is characterized by its central role as a place of staff activity and corporate culture change.

The ICT environment that supports the activities of Cisco's council, board and working-group organizations is the companies "TelePresence" VCTs system—a system that provides huge time savings, business efficiencies as savings in transportation costs and contributes to speedy decision-making.

With decision-making for important proposals, it is important to have the ability to sense obscurity in diverse information sources. When difficult decisions have to be made, such as when facing challenging negotiations with tough customers, it is critical to be able to read expressions and body language. TelePresence enables users to instantly see the widening of the customer's pupils, how they are folding their arms and so on—clues that cannot be expressed with words—and thus change the flow of discussions.

The Cisco case is a good example of how dialectical dialogue and context architect capabilities are demonstrated through discussions in real and virtual spaces as organizations are formed as councils, boards and working groups by the boundaries consolidation capability rooted in the ICT application capability of the company's practitioners.

CEO Buckman of Buckman Laboratories, a paper-manufacturing company that farms out research and development with virtual-space collaborative organizations consisting of 1,300 staff members in research and business facilities in 21 countries, had the following to say:

> This does help, at least initially, by causing knowledge that has been written down to be organized and made available to the organization. Useful as that step is, however, we've found that it is not sufficient to achieve success. It can deal with no more than a small fraction of knowledge in the company—perhaps about 10% of the total. The dynamics of a company don't change when it organizes its explicit knowledge.
>
> We found that the vast bulk of the knowledge in Buckman Labs was in the heads of our people—and it was changing every minute of every day. It was not written down. Therefore, if we wanted to achieve success in the fast-changing environment confronting us, we had to learn how to engage people and arouse their interest

> and trust, making them willing to move their knowledge across the organization to where it was needed, when it was needed.
>
> Buckman (2003, p. 20)

Basically, ICT is a method of promoting the sharing and access to explicit knowledge, but it cannot give company competitiveness by itself. Corporate heads and management leaders have to stoke the interests of practitioners, and practitioners have to share values and build trust, and they have to create knowledge communities. Then, as practitioners actively use ICT in knowledge communities, they promote the processes of inspiring and sharing knowledge, which is an important factor in creating and accumulating knowledge.

A characteristic of Buckman Laboratories is the unique way that the company's staff works. When an idea for a new product arrives at the research stage, there is one page that the staff always access on their computers. This is a place on the net called Techforum.

Techforum is a network forum for sharing tacit knowledge and inspiring and creating knowledge. Staff members from all countries access Techforum to call together other staffers with similar knowledge and interests.

Regardless of international borders, specialties, sections, organizations and so forth, if enough staff members agrees on Techforum, they set up an independent project, and staffers go about their research and development jobs while engaging in discussions and bringing their own knowledge to these net-born projects.

Buckman Laboratories produces more than 20 new technologies every year through these forum-based projects, including technologies in their main paper manufacturing area.

Through the knowledge-creation process in the Techforum knowledge community, staff members proactively inspire and share tacit knowledge through their dialogue and thoughts, and perpetually produce new knowledge as new product developments. The Buckman Laboratories case is a good example of fostering context architect capability in practitioners to give rise to new contexts through dialectical dialogue capability rooted in ICT application capability, through discussions in virtual space, and demonstrates boundaries consolidation capability across business units in various locations.

The Buckman Laboratories and Cisco Systems cases described previously illustrate the strong tendency for new knowledge to be created—in other words innovation, along the boundaries between disciplines and specializations (Leonard-Barton, 1995).

Corporations are segmented into a range of job functions and specializations, and there are many visible and invisible boundaries that exist therein (e.g. geographic boundaries as globalization, industry boundaries as strategy, organizational boundaries as corporate theory and human cognition as bounded rationality).

In today's world of tough competition and wildly fluctuating circumstances, actors in many corporations must transcend these numerous boundaries both in and between companies, including customers, and implement strategies to integrate knowledge to create new knowledge and bring about innovation.

Most certainly, knowledge is the wellspring of corporate competitiveness (Kogut and Zander, 1992; Leonard-Barton, 1995; Nonaka and Takeuchi, 1995); however, not only do knowledge boundaries exist as organizational boundaries as sectionalism between practitioners in companies but they also exist as boundaries between practitioners' values, backgrounds and specializations (Brown and Duguid, 2001). This means that the mental models of practitioners (Spender, 1990; Grinyer and McKiernan, 1994) or path-dependent knowledge can present barriers to innovation (Carlile, 2002).

So, how can actors manage knowledge to create new knowledge by transcending organizational and knowledge boundaries? There needs to be a mechanism in place that will induce productive interpretation and creative awareness of business in practitioners as they share a common mission, because this enables practitioners to resonate values and build mutual trust through dialectical dialogue and deep collaboration, and through their ICT capabilities, form and network knowledge communities; and as described in Figure 8.8, practitioners need management strategies using ICT capability to combine the dynamic synergies of SCs and formal organizations that emerge from dual network interaction in real and virtual spaces to bring forth new contexts and knowledge. It is not only a deep understanding of ICT held by practitioners that is required but also the nurturing of staff unity in community-based organizations and, moreover, mutual understanding of individual practitioner's thoughts and values that companies must pursue.

These knowledge communities (SCs and networked CoPs) are not in conflict with formal organizations. These are in fact two aspects of collaborative organizations that complement each other.

Practitioners who participate in SC knowledge communities (or networked CoPs) pursue exploratory activities as new business (domains I, II and III). Dispersed and autonomous knowledge communities have features of both passively arising with circumstantial change and the active aspect of taking up the challenge of facing the unknown and building new businesses. In contrast, while CoPs in formal organizations engage in exploitative activities for existing business (domain IV), it is also important that the tasks undertaken by formal organizations with flat hierarchies are not just concerned with executing existing business, but are also concerned with rationalizing and planning the new businesses brought about through the knowledge communities (SCs).

Accordingly, a paradoxical collaborative organization management style is required for both flat-hierarchy, formal organizations that focus on rational and principled deliberate strategies, and autonomous and dispersed SC or networked CoP knowledge communities (organic organizations) that focus on creativity and improvisation.

The important focus of collaborative organizations is, in terms of new knowledge creation for companies and new customer value, the promotion of optimized flat formal organizations streamlined throughout entire companies and the constant reconfiguration of dynamic knowledge communities.

Practitioners must be the architects of these knowledge communities, and these architect capabilities are a key factor for a company in bringing about continued innovation and sustaining a competitive edge.

9
Implications and Conclusion: Convergence and ICT Capability

9.1 New business models and "ICT capability": Convergence and collaboration

In the knowledge economy of the twenty-first century, diverse human knowledge will become a source of new and valuable products, services and business models that creates competitiveness. Many corporations must seek out new business as they bid farewell to mass-production/mass-consumption businesses that flourished in the twentieth century.

However, with the business efficiencies brought about by the implementation of ICT such as cost reductions, outsourcing and off-shoring, and management techniques such as human resources rationalization, it is no longer possible for companies to turn a profit just by simply developing and producing products and services and offering them to customers. Moreover, corporations face the new challenge of sustaining competitiveness in the economies of developed countries where there is already an oversupply of goods and services, a rapidly developing Asia, and in economies that are more intensely globalized.

The ICT and Internet revolution has not only transformed the way that corporations must act but has also had a dramatic impact on consumer behavior. For this reason, companies are forced to continually bring forth innovative and competitive products, services and business models, and constantly offer new value to consumers. And the more large corporations are involved in global markets the more they need to combine innovation with business efficiency to simultaneously pursue economies of scale, economies of scope and business speed.

As discussed in Section 2.2 in Chapter 2, the phenomenon of convergence has triggered the creation of new industries and business models, while the technological advances and diversification of recent years, and the rapid advances of ICT, have made it even more complicated for companies to come up with effective business models: the necessity to merge differing technologies and services, and develop products and services across dissimilar industries to produce new business models is becoming more and more pronounced.

Until now, technological innovation has been developed through the pursuit of specialized knowledge in a particular field; however, there are now many cases of new products and services that have been developed with new and unconventional ideas that converge technologies from one area with those of another. This means that companies must not only fuse and integrate the knowledge that exists in the different specializations within themselves, but they must also integrate dissimilar knowledge found across the boundaries between companies.

Centered on ICT, the convergence across industries and technologies of recent years has accelerated the formation of new business networks and increased the pace of innovation in e-services such as welfare, health care and education, telematics in the automotive industry, and has advanced energy and environmental technologies such as the smart grid and smart cities concepts for the next-generation urban environments.

Into the future, the increasing pace of convergence between all kinds of different businesses and industries will bring about new business models and new value chains, and the key business driver in this new world will be innovation management (see Figure 9.1) through collaboration, co-creation and co-evolution (the 3Cs) that transcends and spans different companies and industries through convergence and ICT capability, as mentioned in Chapter 2.

With the convergence of recent years, the reason that ICT capability is important is because integration through ICT across dissimilar fields has become essential for creating new products, services and business models.

The phenomenon of convergence has added new layers of complexity to the traditional model of corporate competitiveness. Convergence has accelerated M&A and strategic partnering between corporations, includes customers, and has triggered dramatic changes to existing company boundaries. This means that the knowledge-integration process (Kodama, 2011a), in which simple competition between different businesses is transcended and collaboration between businesses is encouraged, is becoming increasingly important as a core driver of corporate strategy.

Modern corporations face the challenge of quickly shifting to collaborative strategies with a range of industries (or companies) and customers,

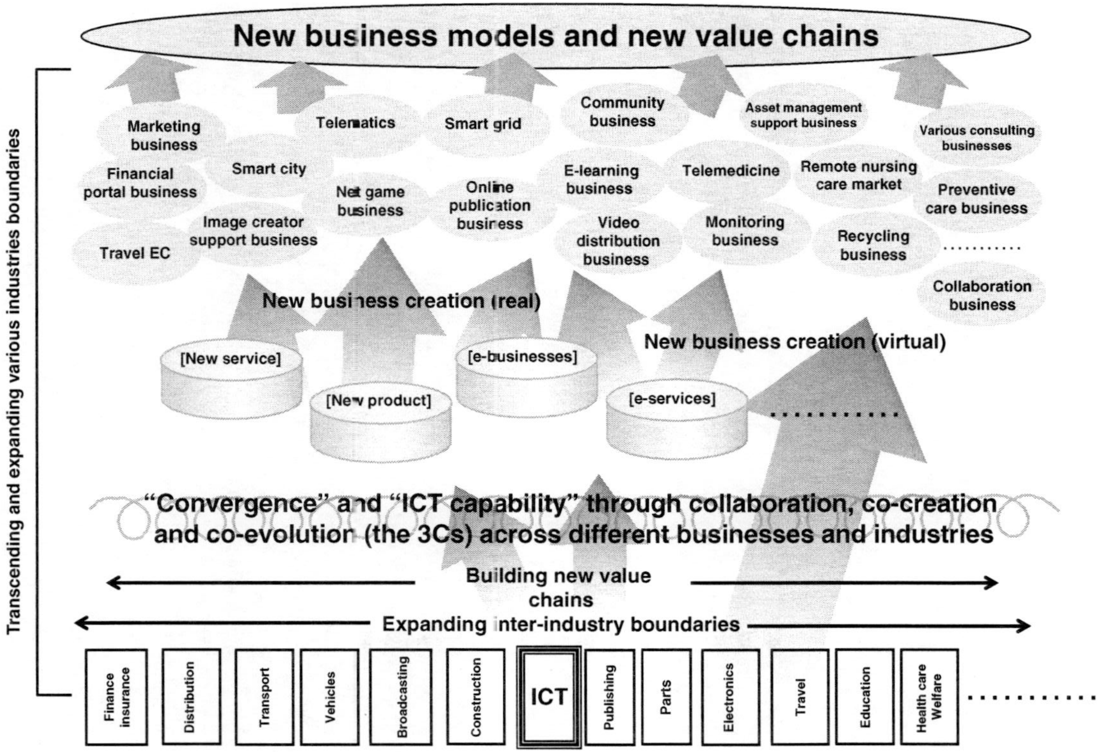

Figure 9.1 Innovation through collaboration, co-creation and co-evolution (the 3Cs)

as the simpler idea of competitiveness between companies within an industry or between industries moves out of the focus of strategy. This means there is an ongoing expansion of diversity of knowledge as dissimilar industries are integrated and converged, and thus the knowledge-integration process is a major issue facing many corporations, leading to the necessity for new innovation management through the 3Cs (see Figure 2.1) with customers and external partners, as described in Chapter 2. To achieve this innovation management, the organizational capability required by companies is ICT capability. However, although the convergence phenomenon has been continuing for some years now, it remains as an underdeveloped area of business management or information systems research.

As illustrated by the case studies presented in Chapter 7, the convergence of the ICT industry with health care, nursing, insurance and the pharmaceutical industry has given rise to the new business processes and business models called "life innovations" such as telemedicine, remote nursing, tele-health care, medical information management systems, dispersed pharmaceutical development projects, and pharmaceutical and health care information support services.

Satoshi Miura, President of leading Japanese ICT company, NTT, was quoted in the *Nikkei Shimbun* as follows (Miura, 2012):

> Have you heard the word "convergence?" Simply put, it means fusion. It may sound ambiguous, a word that we are not used to, but in fact there are many different ways that convergence has already become infused into our society. Many new and useful areas of study have become established in today's world—for example, the merging of finance with mathematics to create financial engineering, or the merging of biology, medicine and science to create biotechnologies and genetic engineering.
>
> No longer confined to particular areas of specialization, industries fuse with one another and new industries bloom. In particular, as we live in an era of wide-ranging digitalized information and networking, new services are emerging as advanced ICT technologies are converged with the energy, environmental, automotive and housing industries. Naturally, this also includes the merging of human resources and is creating new forms of employment.
>
> An example of particular interest to me is the convergence of ICT with the health care field that is continuing in Hinoemata—a village in a remote mountainous area of Fukushima Prefecture.

> As this village faces a shrinking and aging population, the NTT group has teamed up with health care organizations to provide remote health services to the village, which we began providing last summer. This health care service is provided across optical fiber networks linking medical institutions in the prefecture with houses, clinics and community halls in the village. We have created a system to provide care to all residents of the village by linking this community with health care organizations through ICT ... [W]e no longer live in an era in which services and industries can be established by single companies operating independently. Opening up to the outside and integrating opens the door to the creation of value, and just as the word co-creation suggests, this is not just simply a matter of mixing things together—co-creation means bringing forth new synergies to give birth to new innovations, and as Japanese society seeks to create new value and dynamism, ICT is playing a useful role as an accelerant.

In promoting innovation management to respond to convergence, conventional closed innovation is not enough. Not only do companies need to integrate diverse knowledge across different organizations and specializations within themselves, they must also face the ultimate challenge of creating global networks with best partners and converging the high-quality knowledge dispersed around the world with the knowledge within themselves (Kodama, 2011b).

A key ingredient of this organizational management is the "collaboration strategy"—which aims to create knowledge communities on collaboration networks with stakeholders both within and between companies, and the main ICT tools that support the formation, maintenance and development of these knowledge communities are the video communication tools discussed in this book.

Put differently, ICT capability using ICT such as VCTs encourages convergence, and has the potential to bring forth new knowledge creation as new models for innovation.

In the modern smartphone and automotive industries, for instance, new products and services are being brought to the market as the boundaries between businesses, industries and organizations are transcended and dissimilar knowledge is integrated, and new value chains are being created as new strategic frameworks.

To achieve the products and services of the future, mobile phone carriers are also proactively developing strategic partnerships with a wide range of businesses such as smartphone makers, computer manufacturers, communications equipment manufacturers, semiconductor vendors, content providers, international communications carriers, financial institutions and automotive businesses. This is exemplified by the iPhone, iPad and Android-based business ecosystems that have emerged through convergence with the new innovations of Apple and Google instead of developing under the control of the telecommunications carriers alone.

More specifically, the modern business strategies of leading global telecommunications carriers are designed to achieve services integrated with smartphones and other products and services (see Figure 9.2). Providing consumers with environments that enable smooth usage in mobile, fixed, broadcasting and home networks enables the telcos to provide convenient and easy-to-use services with smartphones linked to not only networked appliances, vehicles and broadcast devices but also to health care, welfare and education services that can be tailored to the usage patterns and needs of users. Linking smartphones in this way with a range of lifestyle tools and services to provide converged services is the strategic objective of telecommunications carriers.

In its pursuit of computerization, improved safety and environmental measures, the automotive industry is also engaging in wide-ranging strategic partnerships with businesses in the ICT, electronics, semiconductor, software, computer, iron and steel, and science industries to develop new vehicles and services, and provide the even more comfortable and convenient automobiles of the twenty-first century.

In particular, automobile makers are directly faced with the challenge of meeting more stringent safety and environmental demands. With the stricter environmental regulations and skyrocketing oil prices of recent times, automotive makers have begun commercializing economical and "green" automobiles such as hybrid and electric vehicles, and as demand for hybrid vehicles is set to expand into the future, forming collaborative partnerships with electronics companies while strengthening partnerships with their existing parts manufacturers will be indispensable for automobile manufacturers.

These companies are also under pressure to develop high-functionality automotive semiconductors (microcomputers and system LSI) to meet these demands for safety, environmental performance and computerization, as well as develop higher-capacity batteries. On top of that, carmakers are also promoting strategic alliances with diverse materials manufacturers (e.g. GE and DuPont—companies that develop plastic and aluminum materials and so forth) and steelmakers to make the vehicles of the future even lighter.

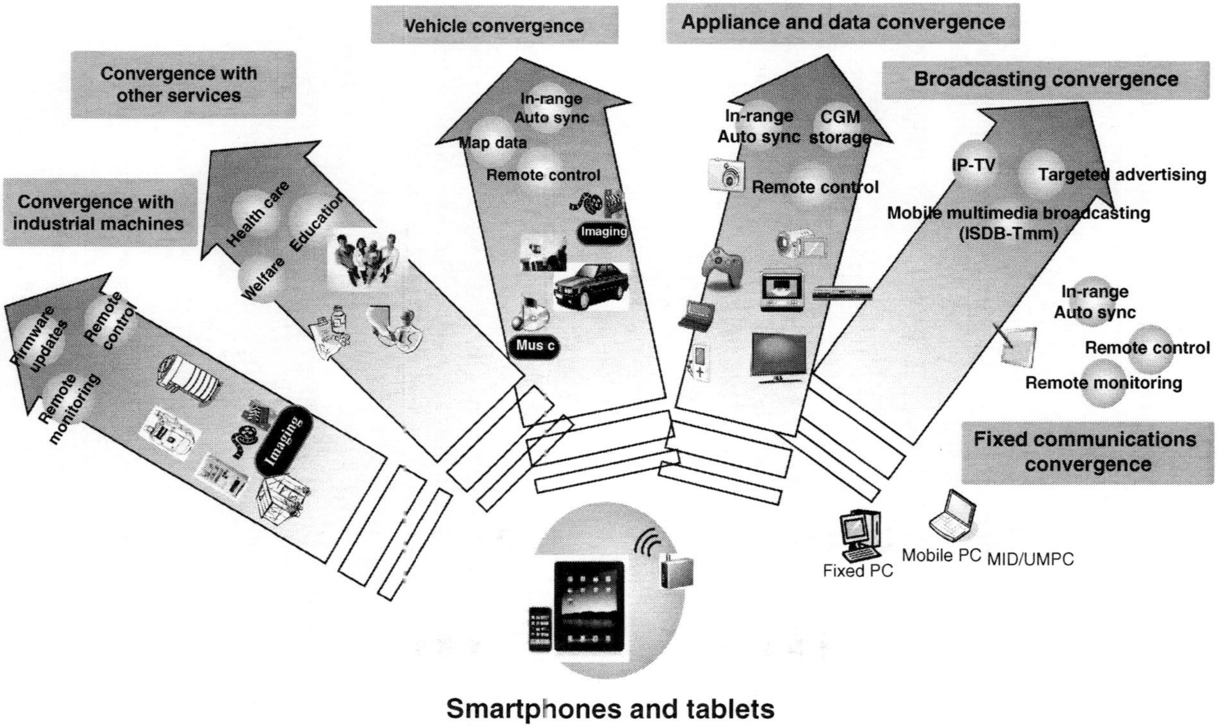

Figure 9.2 Smartphone convergence and innovation
Source: Based on NTT DOCOMO publications.

These companies must also respond to demands for vehicle computerization. It is as if vehicles are becoming a single computer that features not only mobile phone and e-mail functions, but also includes multimedia functions demanded by customers for access to content such as news articles, music, video, etc., and even in-vehicle telematics functions such as e-commerce.

For this reason in Japan, for instance, telecommunications carriers and automobile companies have embarked on joint ventures to develop ICT for cars through strategic alliances (e.g. Toyota with KDDI; Nissan with NTT DOCOMO), and have partnered with Apple in the US to provide in-vehicle music distribution functions with iPod, as well as a range of other IT and software vendors.

Partnerships have also been formed with major content providers who have begun providing wireless telematics services to vehicles (branded two-way vehicle data transmission software systems such as the Toyota G-Book, Nissan CARWINGS and Honda Premium Club). In this way, automobile makers and external partners have integrated the boundaries between organizations and are advancing the creation of new value chains (see Figure 9.3).

It is the integration of dissimilar knowledge transcending the boundaries between organizations in a variety of businesses and industries that has given birth to these new high-tech products and services offered with smartphones and automobiles, and has created new value chains as new strategic frameworks.

Accordingly, companies need to rethink the organizational capability needed to create new knowledge (to develop new products, services, business models, etc.) through dynamic integration and sharing across organizational boundaries between the knowledge possessed by people and groups to create the new value chains of the future. As an organizational capability, acquiring the ICT capability to use ICT across multiple organizational boundaries and dynamically integrate knowledge is the most important element of modern corporate competitiveness.

9.2 Strategic management through ICT capability

From the viewpoint of strategic management, the essence of acquiring ICT capability is encapsulated in the following to points. First is ICT-related product planning and development and the formation of new business models (e-businesses) for customer value creation through ICT. This also includes the creation of new business models through convergence, and is a factor that has been identified by many telecommunications carriers,

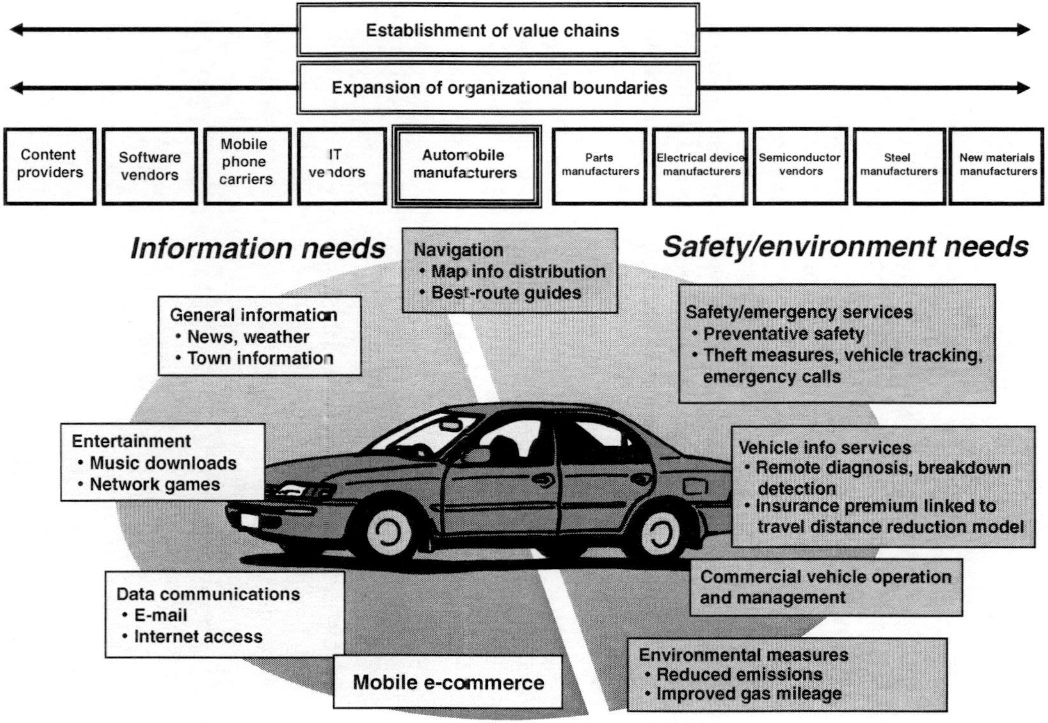

Figure 9.3 Automotive convergence and innovation
Source: Kodama (2007a).

ICT vendors and a range of leading corporations as being a crucial to remain competitive in providing new products and services to end users (both corporate and consumer).

Furthermore, the content industry (broadcasting, publishing, movies, music, games and software, etc.) is also expanding its range of new services through the implementation and use of ICT. This suggests a strengthening of quality and diversification of content services offered to the consumer market.

Second is an issue common to all industries—the idea of ongoing corporate transformation through the use of ICT to upgrade and improve existing businesses and even create new businesses (related to the first point). In other words, continually expanding existing business (exploitative activities) while simultaneously pioneering the businesses of the future (exploratory activities) is an important strategic objective for a company. This is the spiraling practice of the business domains (I–II–III–IV) examined and discussed in Chapters 5 and 8, and it is crucial that companies can demonstrate ICT capability and strategic innovation capability to respond to circumstances both inside and outside of themselves (see Figure 8.3 in Chapter 8).

For this reason, many corporations thoroughly understand the importance of ICT as a corporate strategic tool, and thus it is a major issue for corporations to figure out how to reach the objectives of corporate strategy through the development, deployment (or independent development) and use of ICT. In short, as well as the physical existence of ICT, the acquisition of ICT capability is indispensable to achieve corporate strategy.

As intangible corporate assets involving abilities to develop, implement and use ICT in the processes of formulating and implementing corporate strategy, this book has emphasized the importance of approaching ICT capability as a difficult-to-copy resource, and through a company's ICT capability, actions must be taken that pursue the two objectives of strategic management mentioned earlier.

Obviously, ICT virtual space networks enable information sharing in routine business across physically separate locations, or the formation of virtual and project management teams to solve new problems, or the linking of geographically dispersed personnel. The business activities of Cisco Systems and Buckman Laboratories using video and web conferencing systems mentioned in Section 8.9 in Chapter 8 are examples of these.

As described in Figure 8.5 in Chapter 8, the business processes that run as traffic in real and virtual spaces create synergies and enable the sharing of data, context and knowledge, and inspire new product development.

Organizational practitioners form knowledge communities (SCs, CoPs, networked CoPs) in real and virtual spaces as situations dynamically change and corporate strategic and organizational contexts interact.

In the product development process using ICT, high-tech corporations do not only pursue business activities in real space, but also routinely and thoroughly pursue business activities over broadband within and between companies, from product design and manufacture all the way through to sales and support.

Getting back to ICT development, the Toyota Motor Corporation is an example of a company that has developed and uses ICT support tools by digitalizing its accumulated manufacturing skills and know-how (JIT and TQM) and has developed the "Human-Integrated Assist System" or HIA (Sakai and Amasaka, 2005) to support its manufacturers and engineers, and support improvements and upgrades to its business processes.

Leading Japanese distribution company, 7-Eleven, is another company that has also developed ICT for its supply chains (the concept of the ICT system and basic specifications) and has collaborated with external ICT vendors to develop the necessary hardware and software.

Dell, a company that sells consumer PCs over the Internet, relies heavily on external partners for its component manufacture. Dell has to bring low-cost PCs to the market to meet individualized consumer needs, and thus must optimize parts procurement. Dell achieves the efficiencies of vertical disintegration[1] through outsourcing with the close-knit coordination activities of vertical integration. For Dell to efficiently assemble PCs as ordered by customers, parts need to be manufactured and delivered by external partners to Dell's assembly plants in a timely manner (there are five of these plants worldwide), and the company system also enables it to reduce its parts inventories.

Dell creates ICT knowledge communities that closely share information about the company's mass customization and corporate solution businesses, and also shares knowledge in real time with parts manufacturers to reduce coordination costs and maintain supply chain efficiency.

Notably, Dell forms tight-knit knowledge communities among its parts manufacturers and corporate customers to encourage information and knowledge sharing to gather information about customer needs in a timely fashion and raise the quality of the services it provides.

In general, close coordination is possible with vertical integration in manufacturing organizations to develop and manufacture parts or completed products. However, Dell, in conjunction with its strategic

ICT outsourcing partners, is able to reduce its governance costs as well as maintain quality in coordinating tasks by promoting the sharing of contexts and information between different companies.

Just like in the Dell case, companies deploy and use ICT to build vertical boundaries as optimized value chains by determining their organizational and corporate boundaries, and in the process of developing, implementing and using ICT, practitioners in companies raise the level of their organizational ICT capability through the interplay of strategic and organizational contexts as they engage in both routine and strategic activities.

Furthermore, in providing services to customers via ICT through media interactions such as SNS, new customer competences (Prahalad and Ramaswamy, 2000; Kodama, 2002b) can be taken in, and new businesses (products and services) can be established to create value for customers based on these.

Thus a factor that determines corporate competitiveness is the synergies of the physical ICT resources that companies develop, deploy and use to offer new products and services through their ICT capability—the intangible assets (e.g. Brynjolfsson, 2000) of practitioners built up through their skills in developing, implementing and using ICT.

As described previously, the process of developing, implementing and using ICT does not only raise the level of efficiency of business processes, but also increases creative knowledge and competences needed to develop new products and build new businesses through convergence, and in turn beneficially influence ICT capability—the intangible assets of both practitioners and organizations.

9.3 Future research issues

In the ICT, energy, automotive, electronics, semiconductor, biotechnology, pharmaceutical and materials science fields, the most advanced core technologies are dispersed in various companies and organizations around the world, and these core technologies are the source of innovation for new products and services. To come up with distinguished new products, global high-tech corporations face an increasing need to develop new products and services based on new technologies brought about through the convergence of dissimilar ones.

The reason for this is that there are already many cases in the market place where new and imaginative and previously unheard-of products and services have been produced through the fusion of different technological fields. And thus the necessity to develop business strategies that can respond to and compete with the convergence of differing technologies and services, develop products and services across dissimilar industries, and form new business models is becoming more and more pronounced.

Furthermore, the advances of ICT have shortened the time and space needed to carry out business processes in supply chains across a whole range of industries, accelerated decision-making and raised efficiency, and given birth to new e-business models that transcend and converge dissimilar industries.

These new e-businesses encourage the 3Cs across entire industries, and give rise to dynamic business ecosystems, which have been the starting point for the revolution in Internet and social game businesses such as those using iPod, iPhone and iPad. It is critical that companies continually acquire and develop ICT capability to build these sorts of business ecosystems.

As technologies and ICT continue their rapid advance and diversification, companies have to demonstrate the ICT capability needed to develop new technologies and root out new business models, and pursue innovation that offers new value to customers through the creation of ICT businesses that span different industries and merge different technologies. Not only is it necessary to integrate and converge specialized knowledge in different areas within a company but also important to fuse knowledge between companies.

However, to give birth to new products, services and business models through convergence by building ICT businesses across differing technologies and industries, exactly what strategic and organizational actions do companies need to take? And what do leadership and management have to do to achieve these things? These are the sorts of multifaceted issues that many global corporations are facing.

Although the details of strategic actions of individual industries and companies differ from one another, the key concepts of corporate action in recent years are collaboration and ICT capability, factors that are applied to (or created for) the convergence worldview.

In promoting these collaborative strategies, companies do not only need to integrate diverse knowledge across the different organizations and specializations within themselves, but also need to form networks with best partners around the world to integrate the best knowledge dispersed across the globe with their own, and acquire ICT capability.

However, there is almost no clarification offered by academic research into business transformation models involving micro strategic processes and organizational mechanisms needed to support collaboration and ICT capability, or innovation through convergence. How do corporations use ICT capability in collaborative strategies with customers and stakeholders to achieve innovation? How do business ecosystems achieve innovation? In this convergence environment, how should companies and industries set boundaries, and change them dynamically to achieve innovation as new business territories? What strategic and organizational actions do companies need to take to demonstrate ICT capability on dynamically changing corporate boundaries? What are the business transformation models that leaders and managers need to adopt in these circumstances? What is the relationship between ICT capability and leadership? These are just some of the practical issues challenging many of the global corporations of today.

More logical and empirical research is required from multiple business viewpoints that examine the dynamic processes of ICT capability, collaboration strategies, corporate boundaries, corporate alliances, strategy formulation, organizational structures, capabilities and cultures, and the leadership behind successful (or unsuccessful) innovation through convergence.

Appendix: Research Methodology

The author adopted a qualitative research methodology due to the need for rich data that could facilitate the generation of theoretical categories he could not derive satisfactorily from existing theory. In particular, due to the exploratory nature of this research and my interest in identifying the main people, events, activities and influences that affect the progress of ICT innovation, he selected the grounded theory-based study of data interpretation, which was blended with the case study design and with ethnographic approaches (Locke, 2001).

The research data came primarily from longitudinal study during a 17-year period (1995–2011) examining new knowledge creation process with respect to new products and services development at large and small-medium companies in competitive ICT and other high-tech fields. This research paradigm, which was based on in-depth qualitative study, has some similarity to ethnography (Atkinson and Hammersley, 1994) and other forms of research (Lalle, 2003) that derive their theoretical insights from naturally occurring data, including interviews or questionnaires (Marshall and Rossman, 1989). Especially, the author of this book himself serves as a project manager of new ICT product development in NTT and NTT DOCOMO, Japan's largest telecommunications companies. This experience provided the author with direct knowledge and detailed information with which the accuracy of the empirical analyses in this research was enhanced. Research data and insight are gained alongside or on the back of the intervention.

The data collected over the 17 years of the intervention have been derived from work with practitioners involved with a large number and variety of customers and outside partners as well as internal organization members. During these interventions, the expressed experiences, views, action-centered dilemmas, and actual actions of participants were recorded as research data in a variety of ways, including notes, internal and outside rich documents, etc. The theory that has emerged from this research has centered on the concepts of ICT capability collaborated with outside partners and customers.

The data analysis for the research consisted of three stages:

(1) Developing in-depth case history of a big and small project's activities from the raw data that the author could gain all the information
(2) Open coding and subsequent selective coding the in-depth case history for the characteristics and origin of ICT capability
(3) Analyzing the pattern of relationships among the conceptual categories

In the first stage of the data analysis, the author constructed chronological descriptions of the project's activities with respect to ICT capability, describing how it came about, when it happened, who was involved, and major outcomes. Through this work, he completed an in-depth case history of the project.

The second stage of analysis involved coding the in-depth case history with respect to its characteristics, origin and effects. This was a highly iterative procedure that involved moving between the in-depth case history, existing theory and the raw data (Glaser and Strauss, 1967). Data were subjected to continuous, cyclical, evolving interpretation and reinterpretation that allow patterns to emerge.

The grounded theory approach was adopted based upon the researchers' interpretation and description of phenomena based on the actors' subjective descriptions and interpretations of their experiences in a setting (Locke, 2001). This "interpretation of an interpretation" strives to provide contextual relevance (Silverman, 2000). From the in-depth case history, the author initially advanced first-order descriptions based on broad categories that were developed from the existing theory, and then refined these categories by tracing patterns and consistencies (Strauss, 1987). The analysis continued with this interplay between the data and the emerging patterns until the patterns were refined into conceptual categories (Eisenhardt, 1989). The third stage of data analysis was to examine the empirical in-depth case results across the selected categories and the theoretical literature, and to develop the logic of the conceptual framework and generate new theory.

Case studies are based on in-depth interviews with many senior managers of corporations, and on internal and external materials. From 1995 to 2003, the author worked as a project leader and manager in product development at NTT and NTT DOCOMO. During this period, he gathered data through informal dialogues with many partner companies.

Based on the data obtained from field studies, the author first produced in-depth cases concerning the companies. Next, based on this study, he performed analyses and observations from the viewpoint of ICT capability. Various scholars (Eisenhardt, 1989; Pettigrew, 1990; Yin, 1994) have discussed the validity of case studies. Case studies make it possible to explain the relevance and cause-and-effect relationships of a variety of observations through deep and detailed insights with consideration given to qualitative information and subjectivity resulting from the peculiarities of individual cases and the difficulties of general analyses. Case studies not only compensate for the weaknesses of generalities but are also indispensable in new, creative theorization.

Notes

Preface and Acknowledgments

1. See http://sankei.jp.msn.com/affairs/news/120404/crm12040408020002-n1.htm. This article (in Japanese) stresses the importance of having video communication tools always connected and always on. Creating a *Ba* with permanently connected videoconferencing facilities is already an important action that leading companies take to share knowledge. This book discusses this phenomenon.

1 ICT and Boundary Innovation

1. For more details, see Kodama (2011b, Chapter 1).
2. Strategic activities in companies that aim to create customer value and operate in speed economy in the era of global convergence must not lose sight of the importance of creating win–win relationships among customers, companies (their staff), and their partners and stockholders. In other words, for companies to create "customer value-creation businesses," they must place strategic importance on creating win–win relationships among all stakeholders. Therefore, as companies provide new value to their customers, companies must also place emphasis on the creation of competitive profit structures and business models that mutually benefit partner companies, by creating new markets through co-evolution management. The concepts and activities of co-evolution management in companies result in profits for shareholders, but more importantly achieve long-term profit through innovation, and serve as the wellspring for sustained business competitiveness.
3. However, since the details of the new governance models needed to create, maintain and develop business ecosystems will remain a major business issue into the future, the creation of knowledge communities to network knowledge will be important as business frameworks. The ecosystems that emerge from the formation of knowledge communities correspond to the co-evolution model based on dialectical concepts (e.g. Kodama, 2009a, 2009b). However, because there is scant research into specific business theories about the actual processes required to create this co-evolution model, refer to Kodama (2011b) for information about company-wide and intercompany business model theories.
4. Refer to the appendix for research methodologies.

2 The Advancement of ICT Tools and Knowledge, and Innovation Management

1. Based on interviews with Toray and published materials.
2. Based on interviews with Canon and published materials.
3. Based on interviews with NEC and published materials.

3 The Innovation and Market Expansion of Video Communications

1. Based on interviews and hearings with videoconference manufacturers (43 companies) and videoconference consultants (two persons).
2. However, even more important for manufacturers is to decide whether to use these modules or use independent development in order to create value. With black box-type modular development, companies have to embed their own unique technological know-how by integral architecture. For instance, the range of analog devices, precision components and TI DSP that Japanese manufacturers are good at producing, and Intel's MPUs also have value due to their modularity. The key to digital products, then, is deciding how many modules should be developed as black boxes (Kodama, 2007d).

4 Collaborative ICT Tools and Organizational Development

1. See, for example, Kodama (1999a, 1999b, 1999c).
2. A large volume of published IT-related content that focuses on the current Web 2.0 and cloud computing emphasizes that these prevalent technologies contribute to reducing corporate IT investment and boosting business efficiency (in practical terms, they are generally moving in the right direction). As for ICT tools that support practitioners' real-time decision-making and practical action in their daily business activities, little attention was paid to this area in the previous world of narrowband (phone, ISDN, ADSL, and 2G mobile phones). Due to the rapid development of broadband in recent years, however, including the expansion of fiber optics and high-speed mobile communications (such as 3/3.5G/3.9G mobile phones, smartphones and wireless LANs), a large number of companies have come to pay attention to the significance and effect of VCTs on collaboration. Japan is especially advanced in terms of fiber-optic infrastructure and commercialization of NGN (next-generation networks) where it is a global leader, and the country also has highly developed mobile phone businesses.
3. John Chambers, Chairman and CEO of global IT pioneer Cisco Systems, comments as follows:

   > Consider just one application: high-definition videoconferencing. With this, people as far away from each other as Singapore and Cincinnati can sit across the virtual table from one another. You hear the faraway voice as if it were in the same room. You see the other person's pupils dilate, forehead sweat, and fingers tap from thousands of miles away. This kind of instant, virtually in-person technology changes customer service models, family relationships, and even our environment. A sales rep meets via TelePresence (our brand of hi-def conferencing) with one customer in Japan at 9 a.m., another in Frankfurt at 10 a.m., and a third in New York at 1 p.m. ... Multiplied over the thousands of Cisco employees who fly each year, this can lead to significant carbon reduction. We aim to cut our carbon emissions by 10 percent this year by using TelePresence.
   >
   > Chambers (2007)

Moreover, Toshiyuki Shiga, COO of Nissan Motor Company Ltd, has also noted the following regarding video conferencing:

> Now the system is evolving, and you can talk with the feeling that you are in the same room. Since it conveys expressions and subtle body language as well as speech, rich communication becomes possible. It feels quite natural to undertake nuanced negotiation through videoconferencing.
>
> Shiga (2006)

Details of how this technology is used in Cisco Systems and other areas, including film-making and restaurants, can be viewed on *CBS News* at http://www.youtube.com/watch?gl=JP&hl=ja&v=YT56p263hOk

4. In the transition from the industrial to the information society, and then to today's "knowledge society," the elements most important to companies are high levels of expertise and skills embodied as "knowledge" and "wisdom." As one of the economic changes to society arising from ICT development, ICT enables not only more efficient flow of knowledge, but also integrates heterogeneous knowledge distributed throughout the world and is highly likely to create new knowledge (Kodama, 1999a, 1999b, 2002c). ICT both reduces the time and cost required to gather, accumulate, and transfer large quantities of information and knowledge, and enables the creation of new values through the formation of virtual knowledge networks.
5. The light of ICT is accompanied by a dark side: the problems of the digital divide, security, privacy infringement and illegal access. These negative aspects should all have solutions. High-quality broadband services give people more comfortable, convenient, safe and fulfilling lifestyles, and help companies to enhance business efficiency and customer services, and develop new markets.

5 Product Development and Collaborative ICT Tools

1. These surveys were conducted as academic research. As a condition of publishing this research, company names for interviews and surveys have been withheld.
2. All types of communication (e.g. telephone, e-mail, etc.) require certain manners and some degree of knowledge for them to be effective. These may include tone of voice or summarizing skills and so forth when talking on the telephone, or understanding netiquette, written words, how to use "cc" and "bcc," and how to quote properly, etc. when using e-mail. However, communications with video require different and new types of media literacy. For instance, field angle, background, clothing, facial expressions, gestures, camera position and so forth have an intrinsic relationship with the degree to which context and understanding are communicated. These are the elements that determine the quality of communication and the context when communicating with other people across a network.

   For example, physical interferences such as background noise where VCTs are in use, inappropriate gesturing by the presenter or bad camera positioning can give the other party a sense of discomfort. In other words, it is not that simple to create an atmosphere in which deep information sharing can be carried out and important decisions can be made. If business people do not have good quality media literacy, context sharing will not be possible. Therefore, to maximize the richness of VCTs, new and unfamiliar "media literacy capabilities" are required.

3. The second important skill that VCT users need to acquire is "video producer capabilities." Specifically, to make the most of diverse media and visual functions that VCTs offer, users need to be able to select the best types of media to express the details of the subject at hand, whether they be photographs, video footage, documented materials or other media. In addition to media literacy mentioned, this is another factor that determines quality of communication and context, because users need to be able to devise ways to put forth a range of video content in conjunction with other types of media when engaged in a product presentation, sales training or in the context of meetings, rather than just present explicit knowledge as information about products, documents or types of video.

   This implies that trial and error is required in the ways that VCTs are used to respond to changing circumstances. As well as that, tacit knowledge-like factors such as subtle and nuanced hand and body movements, nervousness and so forth also need to be effectively communicated to the other party. If users do not have a high level of these "video producer capabilities," they will not be able to sufficiently share context, and the level of information sharing could fall.
4. Transformational elements involve external and internal change, and affect business elements that build corporate systems, such as strategy, organization, culture, competence and leadership (see Raynor, 2006 for research regarding strategic uncertainty).
5. Campbell and Park (2005) argue that since reducing organizational and resource uncertainty is difficult, projects that are high risk in terms of organization and resources should be rejected after screening.
6. The likelihood of experiencing a certain amount of failure in the strategic selection domain rises with outstanding leaders and managers. This is also a working hypothesis from the author's own office experience.
7. This is due to the existence of the knowledge boundaries between the product planning divisions that supervise the creation of business concepts and ideas, the development divisions that realize them, and the production and manufacturing divisions (see Kodama, 2007a).
8. Numerous studies (e.g. Nonaka and Takeuchi, 1995) exist regarding the theoretical frameworks relating to the creation of knowledge such as new or breakthrough ideas. Analysis from various viewpoints will be the subject of future research topics: for example, the creative process for business concepts arising from the synthesis of market and technology paradigms.
9. The validity of the Figure 5.2 capability map (derived from previous research) was confirmed through interviews held with high-level management in 37 high-tech companies, including product development directors, research directors, product planning directors, etc. The results of these interviews were categorized and coded in order to be described by the capability map. Even though there were some slight differences depending on the company, in general their validity in the four domains in the capability map in Figure 5.2 have been verified through qualitative studies, in terms of resource allocation and passage of time in product development processes.

10. Carlile (2004, p. 566) said that instead of viewing the firm "as a bundle of resources" (Wernerfelt, 1984; Barney, 1991) it will be viewed "as a bundle of different types of boundaries" where knowledge must be shared and assessed".

6 Workplace and Collaborative ICT Tools

1. At this point in time, IT had already been made into a commodity, and it had been reported that in practice, IT itself was not a source of corporate competitiveness (Carr, 2003, 2004). On the other hand, from the position-based view and resourced-based view in strategy research in academia, IT itself does have that potential to raise the efficiency of operations, but because IT is easy to imitate, IT alone is not a source of competitiveness, is difficult to differentiate from other companies and has been identified by academics working in the field of strategic research as unable to provide sustained competitiveness (e.g. Porter, 1991, 2001; Barney, Wright and Ketchen Jr., 2001; Mata, Fuerst and Barney, 1995; Clemons and Row, 1991). However, in contrast to these insights into IT as something that cannot provide a corporation with competitiveness (Carr, 2003, 2004), more recent research has identified new implications.
2. See http://news-sv.aij.or.jp/t400/s_gyomu/fuoff/6Ibm.htm
3. See http://www.nopa.or.jp/prize/contents/prize/16/01.html
4. Op. cit. 2.
5. Op. cit. 2.
6. Based on records of CIAJ talks given by Mr. Yoshio Kita, Managing Director of IBM Japan, and interviews with him.
7. See http://www.sony.jp/pcs/products/PCS-XG80/

7 ICT Innovations in Health Care and Welfare

1. Android was not the first. There is also the Linux-based LiMo Platform for mobile phones, while Java is an example of an executable environment and framework that is model independent. Looking at the many detailed differences one by one, it could be thought that there is nothing particularly groundbreaking about Android. However, Android is the first platform to combine all of these aspects. The biggest feature of Android is the fact that it is based on the Linux kernel, and is therefore an open source platform optimized for mobile telephones that provides an application-executable environment and framework.
2. Refer to the following URL: http://techcrunch.com/2011/09/23/conceptboard-debuts-better-whiteboarding-for-google-hangouts/
3. Whether innovation is carried out by the vendor or the user, information required for innovation can be roughly classified as needs information and technology information. Information stickiness is defined by Hippel (1998, 2002) as equivalent to the costs related to transferring information required for innovation. In other words, the stickier the information required for innovation the more the cost to transfer it.

Information stickiness is influenced by two factors. Firstly, is the tacitness of the information itself, and the degree to which it can be converted into words or easily encoded for transferal. Highly tacit information costs a lot of money to transfer, and so is considered to be very sticky. The second factor that influences stickiness is the problem of the capabilities of the source and receiver of the information. If capabilities are low, then there is higher costs associated with transferring information accurately, which also makes the information stickier.

In answering the question of whether innovation will happen at the vendor or the user side, Hippel argues that innovation will take place where information is stickiest. For instance, needs information is required for innovation, and if the user has highly sticky needs information, then it will be expensive to transfer it to the vendor for product development. In this case, rather than transfer the highly sticky information, it is more desirable that users who have that information reflect their own demands in the product design themselves—a much cheaper approach. Hence, in cases like these, the user becomes the innovator.

Vendors have conventionally conducted market research through surveys and interviews to understand user needs. While it is understandable that this sort of market research is necessary to transfer information about the needs that exist in the marketplace as accurately as possible, there are actually difficulties with this approach that exist on principle, because needs information is generally highly tacit, and there will be a large cost associated with transferring it, there is an increased likelihood that in order to keep costs down, needs information might not be completely understood in the end.

These ideas suggests that it is more rational for the vendor to be released from the involved task of digging up and transferring user needs information due to the highly sticky nature of it. Instead, letting the user participate in product development and making it easy for users to achieve their desires themselves eliminates the need to transfer sticky needs information and enables response to a much wider diversity of user needs, with greater speed and at lower costs than traditional methods. It's in these sorts of scenarios that innovation should be carried out by the user.

The stickiness of needs and technology information also affects product architecture planning. Ideally, when information is highly sticky, well-informed users themselves can reflect needs information in the market without having to transfer it, whereas technology information should be reflected by expert vendors. For this reason, the spaces in product architectures usually developed entirely by vendors need to be appropriately modularized into areas that are controlled by the user and areas that are controlled by the vendor. By suitably modularizing product architecture, vendors and users can independently add innovations as required, because they do not need to concern themselves with each other's information.

4. As an example in the area of machine tools, Fanuc was released from the demands of machine tool makers and end users, which enabled the company to concentrate on innovating its core hardware and software technologies. Conversely, machine tool makers and end users were not swayed by the changes Fanuc made to its hardware and software, and were able to achieve unique functionality themselves (Shibata and Kodama, 2009).

5. Programming languages have also gradually evolved from simple procedural and structured programming languages into abstract data programming languages.
6. A lot of attention is paid to the time it takes to administer treatment in stroke cases. In one cause of stroke, cerebral infarction, blood vessels become blocked in the brain, and the time it takes to administer treatment is critical. If treatment can be administered within three hours, the thrombolytic agent rt-PA can be used.

   Also, in 2010, clearance was given for embolectomy devices like Merci Retriever that can remove blood clots causing cerebral infarction from blood vessels up to eight hours after occurrence. These devices have been used clinically in Europe and America since 2003, and their benefits have been reported in clinical research in recent years.

   Under the slogan "Time Lost is Brain Lost," the National Stroke Association in the US has been engaging in educational activities to raise awareness and speed up treatment in stroke cases to minimize the degree of resulting brain impairment. Unfortunately, however, the medical system in Japan does not adequately recognize the importance of time in these cases, and only has a few hospitals with stroke specialists on call 24 hours. The emergency medical system also has many other problems, including long waiting times between ambulance transportation and hospital admission.
7. Currently, the automotive industry is vigorously searching for new sources of power to replace internal combustion engines and reduce carbon risk. If electric vehicle motors are adopted to replace internal combustion engines, it is expected that modularization of automobiles will progress rapidly due to considerable decreases in complexity, and with less complexity design rules for modularization will be easier to issue.
8. This type of architecture innovation is the type of breakthrough innovation that brought about the transistor, which went on to win out over vacuum tube electronics. Many obstacles to architecture innovation are organizational problems rather than technical problems. When a particular product architecture stabilizes, organizational structures and business processes also adjust to fit the architecture, because once the methods of linking and joining together components that comprise a product are established, more efficiency can be achieved by dividing labor and sharing information within organizations to respond to the product architecture in this way. This means that as more efficiency is achieved, divisions of labor and information flows within organizations become more entrenched, which makes it more difficult for an organization to bring about innovation by transforming the product architecture.

   This problem is more prominent in American and Japanese companies. Generally, American corporations have a fair degree of specialization and segmentalization as well as a tendency to systemize and apply rules. As a result, labor divisional structures that are established to match a particular product architecture are difficult to change to respond to a new product architecture. On the other hand, whether for good or bad, labor divisions in Japanese corporations remain flexible, and are more easily adaptable to product architecture than American corporations (e.g. Kodama, 2011a).
9. Refer to the following URL: http://www.eweek.com/c/a/Mobile-and-Wireless/Polycom-Expands-Collaboration-to-iPad-Android-Tablets-744803/

8 ICT Capability and Knowledge Integration

1. See http://sankei.jp.msn.com/affairs/news/120404/crm12040408020002-n1.htm. This article stresses the importance of having video communication tools always connected and always on (in Japanese). Creating a *Ba* with permanently connected videoconferencing facilities is already an important action that leading companies take to share knowledge.
2. One reason that both journalists and social science researchers find it difficult to gather substantive and detailed data could be because VCTs are corporate strategy support tools. Very few academic papers or journalists specializing in this area have analyzed the relationships between VCTs and corporate management, including corporate and organizational innovation. Moreover, since the usage structures and methods of VCTs comprise a company's own expertise (intellectual property) and knowledge of tools used by other companies is limited to superficial case studies, details, specific methods and effects are difficult to grasp.

   For research on analyses of decision-making in group work using videoconferencing, see, for example, Gowan and Downs (1994); for case examples in business, see Kodama (1999c); for applications in distance learning, see, for example, Kodama (2001b); for development of regional dissemination of information, see, for example, Kodama (2001c); for application in the education, medical care and welfare sectors, see, for example, Kodama (2002b).
3. Much of the existing research does not ascertain the formulation and implementation of ever-changing ICT strategies in a dynamic, competitive environment on a real-time axis, nor does it analyze ICT capability. In other words, the existing research lacks a dynamic analysis.
4. The author calls a company's organizational capability to use both radical and incremental innovation "strategic innovation capability" (refer to Kodama, 2011a).
5. Deep integration and coordination of awareness is often carried out in top and middle management teams in leading Japanese corporations (refer to Kodama, 2007a).
6. For example, refer to Owen-Smith and Powell (2004) and Lin and Kulatilaka (2006).
7. This is the average shortest distance between any arbitrary nodes on a network.
8. The number of clusters describes the number of clumps of nodes on a network.
9. A "creek" describes groups of nodes on a network that are directly connected to each other.
10. A "hub" has a great number of links to other parts of the network but an extremely small number of nodes.

9 Implications and Conclusion: Convergence and ICT Capability

1. Vertically integrated business activities that were effective at the dawning of the PC, computer, appliance and electronic manufacturing era (including

the more recent digital appliance field) suffered disintegration with changing technological and market circumstances (technological changes such as standardization of technical interfaces and modularization, and the advancement of ICT tools).

These circumstantial changes brought remarkably lower transaction costs between companies and the market, which enabled final product makers to more efficiently outsource component manufacturing, which in time caused the final product makers vertical boundaries to change (e.g. Christensen, Raynor and Verlinden, 2001).

In recent years, many more major companies that sell branded products now specialize in product R&D and sales, and outsource manufacturing to electronic manufacturing services (EMS), rather than use their own global manufacturing facilities. This has resulted in vertically integrated business activities to become modularized and segmentalized, which has accelerated the pace of vertical disintegration and disaggregation (e.g. Lichtenberg, 1992), and has thus given birth to PC and semiconductor industries with horizontally integrated value chains (Kodama, 2007a).

References

Albert, R. and Barabasi, A. (2000) "Topology of evolving networks: Local events and universality," *Physical Review Letters*, 85(24), 5234–5237.

Allen, J. T. (1970) "Communication networks in research and development laboratories," *R&D Management*, 1(1), 14–21.

Allen, J. and Henn, W. (2006) *The Organization and Architecture of Innovation: Managing the Flow of Technology* (Oxon: Routledge).

Alvesson, M. (1995) *Management of Knowledge-Intensive Companies* (New York: De Gruyter).

Amabile, T. and Khaire, M. (2008) "Creativity and the role of the leader," *Harvard Business Review*, October, 100–109.

Amburgey, T., William, T. and Barnett, P. (1993) "Resetting the clock: The dynamics of organizational change and failure," *Administrative Science Quarterly*, 38(1), 51–73.

Atkinson, P. and Hammersley, M. (1994) "Ethnography and participant observation," in N. K. Denzin and Y. S. Lincoln (eds) *Handbook of Qualitative Research*, pp. 105–117 (Thousand Oaks, CA: Sage Publications).

Barabasi, A. (2002) *Linked: The New Science of Networks* (Cambridge, MA: Perseus Books Group).

Bartlett, C. and Ghoshal, S. (2000) *Transnational Management* (Boston, MA: McGraw-Hill).

Barley, S. R. (1986) "Technology as an occasion for structuring: Evidence from observations of CT scanners and the social order of radiology departments," *Administrative Science Quarterly*, 31(1), 78–108.

Barney, J. (1991) "Firm resources and sustained competitive advantage," *Journal of Management*, 17(3), 99–120.

Barney, J., Wright, M. and Ketchen Jr., D. (2001) "The resource-based view of the firm: Ten years after 1991," *Journal of Management*, 27(3), 625–641.

Bechky, M. (2003) "Making organizational theory work: Institutions, occupations, and negotiated orders," *Organization Science*, 22(5), 1157–1167.

Benner, M. and Tushman, M. (2003) "Exploitation, exploration, and process management: The productivity dilemma revisited," *Academy of Management Review*, 28(2), 238–256.

Bharadwai, A. S. (2000) "A resource-based perspective on information technology capability and firm performance: An empirical investigation," *MIS Quarterly*, 24(1), 169–196.

Boudreau, M. and Robey, D. (2005) "Enacting integrated information technology: A human agency perspective," *Organization Science*, 16(1), 3–18.

Brown, S. J. and Duguid, P. (1991) "Organizational learning and communities-of-practice," *Organization Science*, 2(3), 40–57.

Brown, S. J. and Duguid, P. (2000) "Balancing act: Capturing knowledge without killing it," *Harvard Business Review*, 78(3), 73–80.

Brown, S. J. and Duguid, P. (2001) "Knowledge and organization: A social–practice perspective," *Organization Science*, 12(6), 198–213.

Brown, S. L. and Eisenhardt, M. K. (1997) "The art of continuous change: Linking complexity theory and time-paced evolution in relentlessly shifting organizations," *Administrative Science Quarterly*, 42(1), 1–34.

Brown, S. L. and Eisenhardt, K. M. (1998) *Competing on the Edge* (Boston, MA: Harvard Business School).

Brynjolfsson, E. (2000) *Understanding the Digital Economy: Data, Tools, and Research* (Boston, MA: MIT Press).

Brynjolfsson, E. and Hitt, L. (1995) "Information technology as a factor of production: The role of differences among firms," *Economics of Innovation and New Technology*, 3(3–4), 183–200.

Brynjolfsson, E. and Hitt, L. (1996) "Paradox Lost? Firm-level evidence of high returns to information systems spending," *Management Science*, 42(4), 541–558.

Brynjolfsson, E. and Hitt, L. (1998) "Beyond the productivity paradox," *Communications of the ACM*, 41(8), 49–56.

Buckman, R. (2003) *Building a Knowledge-Driven Organization* (New York: McGraw Hill).

Buhler, P. A. and Vidal, J. M. (2005) "Towards adaptive workflow enactment using multiagent systems," *Information Technology and Management*, 6(1), 61–87.

Campbell, A. and Park, R. (2005) *The Growth Gamble* (London: Nicholas Brealey Publishing).

Carlile, P. (2002) "A pragmatic view of knowledge and boundaries: Boundary objects in new product development," *Organization Science*, 13(4), 442–455.

Carlile, P. (2004) "Transferring, translating, and transforming: An integrative framework for managing knowledge across boundaries," *Organization Science*, 15(5), 555–568.

Carlson, J. R. and Zumd, R. W. (1999) "Channel expansion theory and the experiential nature of media richness perceptions." *Academy of Management Review*, 42(2), 153–170.

Carr, N. G. (2003) "IT doesn't matter," *Harvard Business Review*, May, 41–49.

Carr, N. G. (2004) *Does IT Matter?* (Boston, MA: Harvard Business School Press).

Chakravarthy, B. (1997) "A new strategy framework for coping with turbulence," *Sloan Management Review*, 38(2), 69–82.

Chambers, J. (2007) "Why the technology revolution will go on and on," *Forbes*, May 7, 162–164.

Chesbrough, H. (2003) *Open Innovation* (Boston, MA: Harvard Business School Press).

Child, J. and McGrath, R. (2001) "Organizations unfettered: Organizational form in an information-intensive economy," *Academy Management Journal*, 44(6), 1135–1148.

Child, J. and Rodrigues, S. B. (2003) "Corporate governance and new organizational forms: Issues of double and multiple agency," *Journal of Management and Governance*, 7(4), 337–360.

Christensen, C. M. (1997) *The Innovator's Dilemma: When New Technologies Cause Great Firms to Fail* (Boston, MA: Harvard Business School Press).

Christensen, C. M. and Raynor, M. (2003) *The Innovator's Solution* (Boston, MA: Harvard Business School Press).

Christensen, M., Raynor, M. and Verlinden, M. (2001) "Skate to where the money will be," *Harvard Business Review*, 79(10), 72–83.

Clark, K. B. and Fujimoto, T. (1991) *Product Development Performance* (Boston, MA: Harvard Business School Press).
Clemons, M. K. (1991a) "Corporate strategies for information technology: A resource-based approach," *Computer*, 24(11), 23–32.
Clemons, M. K. (1991b) "Evaluation of strategic investments in information technology," *Communications of the ACM*, 34(1), 22–36.
Clemons, M. K. and Row, M. C. (1991) "Sustaining IT advantage: The role of structural differences," *MIS Quarterly*, 15(3), 275–292.
Cooper, R. G. (1988) "The new product process: A decision guide for management," *Journal of Marketing Management*, 3(3), 238–258.
Cooper, R. G. (1990) "Stage-gate systems: A new tool for managing new products," *Business Horizons*, 33(3), 44–54.
Cramton, C. (2001) "The mutual knowledge problem and its consequences for dispersed collaboration," *Organization Science*, 12(3), 346–371.
Daft, R. L. and Lengel, R. H. (1984) "Information richness: A new approach to managerial behavior and organizational design," in B. M. Staw and L. L. Cumming (eds) *Research in Organizational Behavior*, pp. 191–233 (Greenwich, CT: JAI Press).
Davenport, T. H. (1993) *Process Innovations: Reengineering Work through Information Technology* (Boston, MA: Harvard Business School Press).
Davenport, T. H. and Prusak, L. (2000) *Working Knowledge: How Organizations Manage What They Know* (Boston, MA: Harvard Business School Press).
Davidow, W. H. and Malone, M. S. (1992) *The Virtual Corporation: Structuring and Revitalizing the Corporation for the 21st Century* (New York: HarperCollins Publishers).
DeFillippi, R. J. (2002) "Information technology and organizational models for project collaboration in the new economy," *Human Resource Planning*, 25(4), 7–18.
DeFillippi, R. J. and Arthur, M. (1998) "Paradox in project-based enterprise: The case of filmmaking," *California Management Review*, 40(2), 125–139.
DeSanctice, G. and Poole, P. (1994) "Capturing the complexity in advanced technology use: Adaptive structuration theory," *Organization Science*, 5(2), 121–147.
DeSanctis, S. and Jackson, H. (1994) "Coordination of information technology management: Team-based structures and computer-based communication systems," *Journal of Management Information Systems*, 10(4), 85–110.
Dewar, R. and Dutton, E. (1986) "The adoption of radical and incremental innovations: An empirical analysis," *Management Science*, 32(11), 1422–1453.
Dougherty, D. (1992) "Interpretive barriers to successful product innovation in large firms," *Organization Science*, 3(2), 179–202.
Duarte, D. and Tennant Snyder, N. (2000) *Mastering Virtual Teams: Strategies, Tools, and Techniques that Succeed* (San Francisco, CA: Jossey-Bass Publishing).
Eisenhardt, K. (1989) "Building theories from case study research," *Academy of Management Review*, 14(4), 532–550.
Eisenhardt, K. and Martine, J. (2000) "Dynamic capabilities: What are they?" *Strategic Management Journal*, 21(10–11), 1105–1121.
Eisenhardt, K. and Sull, D. (2001) "Strategy as simple rules," *Harvard Business Review*, 79, 106–116.
Emirbayer, M. and Mische, A. (1998) "What is agency?" *American Journal of Sociology*, 103(4), 962–1023.

Fiala, P. (2005) "Information sharing in supply chains," *Omega*, 33(5), 419–424.
Fine, H. (1998) *Clock speed: Winning Industry Control in the Age of Temporary Advantage*, Perseus Books.
Floyd, W. and Wooldridge, B. (1999) "Knowledge creation and social networks in corporate entrepreneurship: The renewal of organizational capability," *Entrepreneurship Theory and Practice*, 23(3), 123–142.
Forsgren, M. (1997) "The advantage paradox of the multinational corporation: Nordic contribution to international business research," in I. Bjorkman and M. Forsgren (eds) *The Nature of the International Firm*, pp. 69–83 (Copenhagen: Handelshojskolens forlag).
Fuchs, C. (2007) "Towards a dynamic theory of virtual communities," *International Journal of Knowledge and Learning*, 3(4–5), 372–403.
Fuller, S. (2001) *Knowledge Management Foundations* (London: Butterworth-Heinemann).
Gann, D. and Salter, A. (1998) "Learning and innovation management in project-based, service-enhanced firms," *International Journal of Innovation Management*, 2(4), 431–454.
Galbraith, J. R. (1973) *Designing Complex Organizations*, Reading, MA: Addison-Wesley.
Gemser, G. and Leenders, M. (2011) "Managing cross-functional cooperation for new product development success," *Long Range Planning*, 44(1), 26–41.
Giddens, A. (1979) *Central Problems in Social Theory: Action, Structure and Contradiction in Social Analysis* (Berkeley, CA: University of California Press).
Giddens, A. (1984) *The Constitution of Society* (Berkeley, CA: University of California Press).
Glaser, B. and Strauss, A. (1967) *The Discovery of Grounded Theory: Strategies for Qualitative Research* (Chicago: Chicago University Press).
Gomes, J., Weerd-Nederhof, P., Pearson, A. and Cunha, M. (2003) "Is more always better? An exploration of the differential effects of functional integration on performance in new product development," *Technovation*, 23(2), 185–191.
Gowan, J. and Downs, J. (1994) "Video conferencing human-machine interface: A field study," *Information and Management*, 27(6), 341–356.
Griffin, A. and Hauser, J. R. (1996) "Integrating R&D and marketing: A review and analysis of the literature," *Journal of Product Innovation Management*, 13(3), 191–215.
Grinyer, P. and McKiernan, P. (1994), "Triggering major and sustained changes in stagnating companies," in H. Daems and H. Thomas (eds) *Strategic Groups, Strategic Moves and Performance*, pp. 173–195 (New York: Pergamon).
Gunasekaran, A. and Ngai, E. (2004) "Information systems in supply chain integration and management," *European Journal of Operational Research*, 159(2), 269–295
Gupta, A. K., Raj, S. P. and Wilemon, D. (1986) "A model for studying R&D marketing interface in the product innovation process," *Journal of Marketing*, 50(2), 7–17.
Hagel, J. and Singer, M. (1999) "Unbundling the corporation," *Harvard Business Review*, 77(2), March–April, 133–141.

Hagel III, J. and Brown, J. S. (2005) "Productive friction," *Harvard Business Review*, 83(2), 139–145.

Hammer, M. and Champy, J. (1993) *Reengineering the Corporation: A Manifesto for Business Revolution* (New York: HarperBusiness).

Hargadon, A. (2003) *How Breakthroughs Happen: The Surprising Truth about How Companies Innovate* (Boston, MA: Harvard Business School Press).

Henderson, R. and Clark, K. (1990) "Architectural innovation: The reconfiguration of existing product technologies and the failure of established firms," *Administrative Science Quarterly*, 35(1), 9–30.

Henrie, M. and Sousa-Poza, A. (2005) "Project management: A cultural literature review," *Project Management Journal*, 36(2), 5–14.

Hinds, P. and Kiesler, S. (1995) "Communication across boundaries: Work, structure, and use of communication technologies in a large organization," *Organization Science*, 6(4), 373–393.

Hippel, E. (1998) "Economics of product development by users : The impact of 'sticky' local information," *Management Science*, 44(5), 629–644.

Hippel, E. (2002) "Horizontal innovation networks – by and for users," *MIT Sloan School of Management Working Paper*, 4, 366-02.

Hobday, M. (2000) "The project-based organisation: An ideal form for managing complex products and systems?" *Research Policy*, 29(7–8), 871–893.

Huber, G. (1991) "Organizational learning: The contributing processes and the literature," *Organization Science*, 2(1), 88–115.

James, H. (2010) The American Scene, Createspace, US.

Jantsch, E. (1980) *The Self-Organizing Universe* (Oxford: Pergamon Press).

Jarvaenpaa, S. and Leidner, D. (1999) "Communications and trust in global virtual teams," *Organization Science*, 10(6), 791–815.

Jelinek, M. and Schoonhoven, B. (1990) *The Innovation Marathon: Lessons from High Technology Firms* (Oxford: Basil Blackwell Inc.).

Johansson, F. (2004) *The Medici Effect* (Boston, MA: Harvard Business School Press).

Jones, M. (1999) "Information systems and the double mangle: Steering a course between the Scylla of embedded structure and the Charybdis of strong symmetry," in T. J. Larsen, L. Levine, J. I. DeGross (eds) *Information Systems: Current Issues and Future Changes*, pp. 287–302 (Laxenburg, Austria: IFIP).

Kahn, K. B. (1996) "Interdepartmental integration: A definition with implications for product development performance," *Journal of Product Innovation Management*, 13(2), 137–151.

Kanter, R. M. (2001) *Evolve! Succeeding in the Digital Culture of Tomorrow* (Boston, MA: Harvard Business School Press).

Kaplan, S., Murray, F. and Henderson, R. (2003) "Discontinuities and senior management: Assessing the role of recognition in pharmaceutical firm response to biotechnology," *Industrial and Corporate Change*, 12(4), 203–233.

Katz, R. and Allen, T. (1982) "Investigating the Not Invented Here (NIH) syndrome: A look at the performance, tenure, and communication patterns of 50 R&D project groups," *R&D Management*, 12(1), 7–12.

Khurana, A. and Rosenthal, S. R. (1998) "Towards holistic "front ends" in new product development," *Journal of Product Innovation Management*, 15(1), 57–74.

King, A. and Tucci, L. (2002) "Incumbent entry into new market niches: The role of experience and managerial choice in the creation of dynamic capabilities," *Management Science*, 48(2), 171–187.

Kodama, M. (1999a) "Community management support through community-based information network," *Information Management & Computer Security*, 7(3), 140–150.

Kodama, M. (1999b) "Strategic business applications and new virtual knowledge-based businesses through community-based information networks," *Information Management & Computer Security*, 7(4), 186–199.

Kodama, M. (1999c) "Customer value creation through community-based information networks," *International Journal of Information Management*, 19(6), 495–508.

Kodama, M. (1999d) "Strategic innovation at large companies through strategic community management—an NTT multimedia revolution case study," *European Journal of Innovation Management*, 2(3), 495–508, 95–108.

Kodama, M. (2000) "Business innovation through customer-value creation: Case study of a virtual education business in Japan," *Journal of Management Development*, 19(1), 49–70.

Kodama, M. (2001a) "Creating new business through strategic community management," *International Journal of Human Resource Management*, 11(6), 1062–1084.

Kodama, M. (2001b) "Distance learning using video terminals—an empirical study," *International Journal of Information Management*, 21(3), 227–243.

Kodama, M. (2001c) "New regional community creation, medical and educational applications through video-based information networks," *Systems Research and Behavioral Science*, 18(3), 225–240.

Kodama, M. (2002a) "Transforming an old economy company through strategic communities," *Long Range Planning*, 35(4), 349–365.

Kodama, M. (2002b) "Strategic partnership with innovative customers: A Japanese case study," *Information Systems Management*, 19(2), 31–52.

Kodama, M. (2002c) The promotion of strategic community management utilizing video-based information networks," *Business Process Management Journal*, 8(5), 462–489.

Kodama, M. (2003a) "Strategic community-based theory of the firms: Case study of NTT DoCoMo," *The Journal of High Technology Management Research*, 14(2), 307–330.

Kodama, M. (2003b) "Strategic innovation in traditional big business," *Organization Studies*, 24(2), 235–268.

Kodama, M. (2004) "Strategic community-based theory of firms: Case study of dialectical management at NTT DoCoMo," *Systems Research and Behavioral Science*, 21(6), 603–634.

Kodama, M. (2005) "Knowledge creation through networked strategic communities: Case studies on new product development in Japanese companies," *Long Range Planning*, 38(1), 27–49.

Kodama, M. (2006) "Strategic community: Foundation of knowledge creation," *Research-Technology Management*, 49(5), 49–58.

Kodama, M. (2007a) *The Strategic Community-based Firm* (Basingstoke: Palgrave Macmillan).

Kodama, M. (2007b) *Knowledge Innovation: Strategic Management as Practice* (Cheltenham: Edward Elgar Publishing.

Kodama, M. (2007c) *Project-based Organization in the Knowledge-based Society* (London: Imperial College Press).

Kodama, M. (2007d) "Innovation through boundary managing: Case of Matsushita Electric Reforms," *Technovation*, 27(1–2) 15–29.

Kodama, M. (2007e) "Innovation and knowledge creation through leadership-based strategic community: Case study on high-tech company in Japan," Technovation, 27(3), 115–132.

Kodama, M. (2009a) *Innovation Networks in Knowledge-Based Firms: Developing ICT-based Integrative Competences* (Cheltenham: Edward Elgar Publishing).

Kodama, M. (2009b) "Boundaries innovation and knowledge integration in the Japanese firm," *Long Range Planning*, 42(4), 463–494.

Kodama, M. (2011a) *Knowledge Integration Dynamics: Developing Strategic Innovation Capability* (Singapore: World Scientific Publishing).

Kodama, M. (2011b) *Interactive Business Communities: Accelerating Corporate Innovation through Boundary Networks* (Farnham, Surrey: Gower Publishing).

Kogut, B. and Zander, U. (1992) "Knowledge of the firm, combinative capabilities and the replication of technology," *Organization Science*, 5(2), 383–397.

Kydd, C. T. and Ferry, D. L. (1994), "Managing use of video conferencing," *Information and Management*, 27(6), 369–375.

Lalle, B. (2003) "The management science researcher between theory and practice," *Organization Studies*, 24(7), 1097–1114.

Lampel, J. and Bhalla, A. (2007) "Let's get natural: The discourse of community and the problem of transferring practices in knowledge management," *Management Decision*, 45(7), 1069–1082.

Lave, J. and Wenger, E. (1991) *Situated Learning, Legitimate Peripheral Participation* (New York: Cambridge University Press).

Lawrence, P. and Lorsch, J. (1967) *Organization and Environments: Managing Differentiation and Integration* (Cambridge, MA: Harvard Business School Press).

Leifer, R., McDermott, M., O'Connor, C., Peters, S., Rice, M. and Veryzer, W. (2000) *Radical Innovation: How Mature Companies can Outsmart Upstarts* (Boston, MA: Harvard Business School Press).

Leonard-Barton, D. (1992) "Core capabilities and core rigidities: A paradox in managing new product development," *Strategic Management Journal*, 13(S1), 111–125.

Leonard-Barton, D. (1995) *Wellsprings of Knowledge: Building and Sustaining the Sources of Innovation* (Boston, MA: Harvard Business School Press).

Lichtenberg, F. (1992) *R&D Investment and International Productivity Differences* (Boston: National Bureau of Economic Research Inc.).

Lin, L. and Kulatilaka, N. (2006) "Network effects and technology licensing with fixed fee, royalty, and hybrid contracts," *Journal of Management Information Systems*, 23(2), 91–118.

Lindkvist, L. (2004) "Governing project-based firms: Promoting market-like processes within hierarchies," *Journal of Management and Governance*, 8(1), 3–25.

Lipnack, J. and Stamps, J. (1997) *Virtual Teams People Working Across Boundaries with Technology* (New York: John Wiley & Sons).

Locke, K. (2001) *Grounded Theory in Management Research* (Thousand Oaks, CA: Sage).

Lundin, R. A. and Midler, C. (1998) *Projects as Arenas for Renewal and Learning Processes* (London: Kluwer Academic).

Maekawa, M. (2009) *Managing "Ba" for Changing the World* (in Japanese) (Tokyo: Jitsugyo-Nihonsya).

Malone, T. and Crowston, K. (1994) "The interdisciplinary study of coordination," *ACM Computer Surveys*, 26, March, 87–119.

March, J. (1991) "Exploration and exploitation in organizational learning," *Organization Science*, 2(1), 71–87.

Markides, C. (1997) "Strategic innovation," *Sloan Management Review*, 38(2), 9–23.
Markides, C. (1999) *All the Right Moves: A Guide to Crafting Breakthrough Strategy* (Boston: Harvard Business School Press).
Marshall, C. and Rossman, G. (1989) *Designing Qualitative Research* (London: Sage).
Mata, F. J., Fuerst, W. L. and Barney, J. B. (1995) "Information technology and sustained competitive advantage: A resource-based analysis." *MIS Quarterly*, 19(4), 487–505.
Miura, S. (2012) "Managing convergence through ICT," *Nihon Keizai Shimbun*, April 18, 20.
Morone, G. (1993) *Winning in High-Tech Markets* (Boston, MA: Harvard Business School Press).
Nakamura, K. (2005) "Management innovation through IT (in Japanese)," *Diamond Harvard Business Review*, September, 51–52.
Nakamura, S. (2001) *Breakthrough Innovation* (in Japanese) (Tokyo: Ohmu Inc.).
Nelson, R. and Winter, S. (1982) *An Evolutionary Theory of Economic Change* (Boston: Belknap Press).
Newman, M. E. J. (2004) "Fast algorithm for detecting community structure in networks," *Physical Review E*, 69(6), 1–5.
Nisbett, R. (2003) *The Geography of Thought* (New York: The Free Press).
Nohria, N. (1997) "What is the optimum amount of organizational slack? A study of the relationship between slack and innovation in multinational firms," *European Management Journal*, 15(6), 603–611.
Nohria, N. and Ghoshal, S. (1997) *The Differentiated Network: Organizing Multinational Corporations for Value Creation* (San Francisco, CA: Jossey-Bass).
Nonaka, I. and Takeuchi, H. (1995) *The Knowledge-Creating Company* (New York: Oxford University Press).
Nonaka, I. and Konno, N. (1998) "The concept of 'Ba': Building a foundation for knowledge creation," *California Management Review*, 40, 40–54.
Nonaka, I., Toyama, R. and Konno, N. (2000) "'Ba' and leadership: A unified model of dynamic knowledge creation," *Long Range Planning*, 33(1), 5–34.
Ocker, R., Fjemestad, J., R. Hiltz and Johnson, K. (1998) "Effects of four models of group communication on the outcomes of software requirements determination," *Journal of Management Information Systems*, 15(1), 99–118.
Odenwald, S. (1996) *Global Solutions for Teams, Moving from Collision to Collaboration* (Burr Ridge, IL: Irwin Professional Publishing).
Orlikowski, W. J. (1992) "The duality of technology: Rethinking the concept of technology in organizations," *Organization Science*, 3(3), 398–427.
Orlikowski, W. J. (1996) "Improvising organizational transformation over time: A situated change perspective," *Information Systems Research*, 7(2), 63–92.
Orlikowski, W. J. (2000) "Using technology and constituting structures: A practice lens for studying technology in organizations," *Organization Science*, 11(4), 404–428.
Orlikowski, W. J. and Barley, S. R. (2001) "Technology and institutions: What can research on information technology and research on organizations learn from each other?" *MIS Quarterly*, 25(2), 145–165.
Orlikowski, W. J. and Robey, D. (1991) "Information technology and the structuring of organizations," *Information Systems Research*, 2(2), 143–169.
Orr, J. (1996) *Talking about Machines: An Ethnography of a Modern Job* (Ithaca, NY: ILP Press).

Owen-Smith, J. and Powell, W. (2004) "Knowledge networks as channels and conduits: The effects of spillovers in the Boston biotechnology community," *Organization Science*, 15(1), 5–22.

O'Connor, C. and Rice, P. (2001) "Opportunity recognition and breakthrough innovation in large established firms," *California Management Review*, 43(2), 95–116.

O'Connor, G. (2006) "Open, radical innovation: Toward an integrated model in large established firms," in H. Chesbrough, W. Vanhaverbeke and J. West (eds) *Open Innovation: Researching a New Paradigm*, pp. 62–81 (New York: Oxford University Press).

O'Connor, G. (2008) "Major innovation as a dynamic capability: A systems approach," *Journal of Product Innovation Management*, 25(4), 313–330.

O'Connor, G. and DeMartino, R. (2006) "Organizing for radical innovation: An exploratory study of the structural aspects of RI management systems in large established firms," *Journal of Product Innovation Management*, 23(6), 475–497.

O'Connor, G., Leifer, R., Paulson, P. and Peters, P. (2008) *Grabbing Lightning: Building a Capability for Breakthrough Innovation* (US: Jossey-Bass).

O'Hara-Devereaux, M. and Johansen, R. (1994) *GlobalWork: Bridging Distance, Culture and Time* (San Francisco, CA: Jossey-Bass Publishing).

O'Reilley III, C. and Tushman, M. (2004) "The ambidextrous organization," *Harvard Business Review*, 82, April, 74–82.

Pan, S. and Leidmer, L. (2003) "Bridging communities of practice with information technology in pursuit of global knowledge sharing," *The Journal of Strategic Information Systems*, 12(1), 71–88.

Peirce, S. (1898) *Reasoning and the Logic of Things*, in K. L. Ketner (ed.) The Cambridge Conferences Lectures of 1898 (Cambridge, MA: Harvard University Press).

Peltokorpi, V., Nonaka, I. and Kodama, M. (2007) "NTT DoCoMo's launch of I-Mode in the Japanese mobile phone market: A knowledge creation perspective," *Journal of Management Studies*, 44(1), 50–72.

Pettigrew, A. M. (1990) "Longitudinal field research on change: Theory and practice," *Organization Science*, 1(1), 267–292.

Pine, B. (1993) "Making mass customization happen: Strategies for the new competitive realities," *Strategy & Leadership*, 21(5), 23–24.

Pisano, G. (1994) "The governance of innovation: Vertical integration and collaborative arrangements in the biotechnology industry," *Research Policy*, 20(3), 237–249.

Polanyi, M. (1966) *The Tacit Dimension* (New York: Doubleday & Co. Inc.).

Porter, M. (1980) *Competitive Strategy: Techniques for Analyzing Industries and Competitors* (New York: Free Press).

Porter, M. E. (1991) "Toward a dynamic theory of strategy," *Strategic Management Journal*, 12(1), 95–117.

Porter, M. E. (2001) "Strategy and the Internet," *Harvard Business Review*, March, 63–78.

Powell, T. C. and Dent-Micallef, A. (1997) "Information technology as competitive advantage: The role of human, business, and technology resources," *Strategic Management Journal*, 18(5), 375–405.

Prahalad, C. K. and Ramaswamy, V. (2000) "Co-opting customer competence," *Harvard Business Review*, 78(1), 79–87.

Raynor, M. (2006) *The Strategy Paradox: Why Committing to Success Leads to Failure* (New York: Currency).

Robey, D., Boudreau, M-C. and Rose, G. M. (2000) "Information technology and organizational learning: A review and assessment of research," *Accounting, Management and Information Technologies*, 10(2), 125–155.

Robey, D. and Sahay, S. (1996) "Transforming work through information technology: A comparative case study of geographic information systems in county government," *Information Systems Research*, 7(1), 93–110.

Rosenberg, N. (1982) *Inside the Black Box: Technology and Economics* (Cambridge: Cambridge University Press).

Ross, J. W., Beath, C. M. and Goodfue, D. L. (1996) "Building long-term competitiveness through IT assets," *Sloan Management Review*, 38(1), 31–45.

Sakai, H. and Amasaka, K. (2005) "'V-MICS', advanced TPS For strategic production administration: Innovative maintenance combining DB and CG," *Journal of Advanced Manufacturing Systems*, 4(1), 5–20.

Sakkab, Y. (2002) "Connect & Develop Complements Research & Develop at P&G," *Research-Technology Management*, 45(2), 38–45(8).

Sanchez, R. (1996) "Strategic product creations: Managing new interactions of technology, markets, and organizations," *European Management Journal*, 14(2), 121–138.

Shah, P. (2000) "Network destruction: The structural implications of downsizing," *Academy of Management Journal*, 43(1), 101–112.

Shannon, C. and Weaver, W. (1949) *The Mathematical Theory of Communications* (Urbana: University of Illinois Press).

Shibata, T. and Kodama, M. (2009) "Cultural mythology and global leadership in Japan," in E. Kessler and D. Wong-Mingji (eds) *Cultural Mythology and Global Leadership*, pp. 343–358 (Cheltenham: Edward Elgar Publishing).

Shiga, T. (2006) "Negotiation through videoconferencing (in Japanese)" *Nihon keizai Shinbun*, 16, January, 4.

Silvermann, D. (2000) *Doing Qualitative Research* (Thousand Oaks, CA: Sage).

Skyrrme, D. J. (2001) *Capitalizing on Knowledge: From E-Business to K-Business* (London: Butterworth-Heinemann).

Song, X. M., Montoya-Weiss, M. M. and Schmidt, J. B. (1997) "Antecedents and consequences of cross-functional cooperation: A comparison of R&D, manufacturing, and marketing perspectives," *Journal of Product Innovation Management*, 14(1), 35–47.

Spender, C. (1990) *Industry Recipes: An Enquiry into the Nature and Sources of Managerial Judgment* (Oxford: Basil Blackwell).

Star, S. L. (1989) "The structure of ill-structured solutions: Boundary objects and heterogeneous distributed problem solving," in M. Huhns and I. L. Gasser (eds) *Readings in Distributed Artificial Intelligence*, pp. 37–54 (Menlo Park, CA: Morgan Kaufman).

Strauss, A. (1987) *Qualitative Analysis for Social Scientists* (New York: Cambridge University Press).

Suchman, L. (1987) *Plans and Situated Actions* (Cambridge: Cambridge University Press).

Taifi, N. and Passiante, G. (2012) "Speeding up NPSD through strategic community creation: Case of automaker after-sales services partners," *The Service Industries Journal*, forthcoming.

Tanaka, K. (2011) "Technological integration among different," *Nihon Keizai Shimbun*, June 1, 29.

Teece, D., Pisano, G. and Shuen, A. (1997) "Dynamic capabilities and strategic management," *Strategic Management Journal*, 18(7), 509–533.

Thatcher, M. and Pingry, D. (2004). "An economic model of product quality and IT value', *Information Systems Research*, 15(3), 268–286.

The New York Times (1999) "Japan bets on a wired world to win back its global niche," August 30.

Tippens, M. J. and Sohi, R. S. (2003) "IT competency and firm performance: Is organizational learning a missing link?" *Strategic Management Journal*, 24(8), 745–761.

Tushman, M. (1979) "Work characteristics and subunit communication structure: A contingency analysis," *Administrative Science Quarterly*, 24(1), 82–98.

Tushman, M. and Romanelli, R. (1985) "Organizational evolution: A metamorphosis model of convergence and reorientation," *Research in Organizational Behavior*, 7(2), 171–222.

Tushman, M. L. and Anderson, P. (1986) "Technological discontinuities and organizational environments," *Administrative Science Quarterly*, 31(3), 439–465.

Vanhaverbeke, W. and Peeters, N. (2005) "Embracing innovation as strategy: The role of new business development in corporate renewal," *Creativity and Innovation Management*, 14(3), 246–257.

Venkatraman, N. (1991) "IT-induced business reconfiguration," in M. S. Scott Morton (eds) *The Corporation of the 1990s: Information Technology and Organizational Transformation*, pp. 15–32 (Oxford: Oxford University Press).

Venkatraman, N. (1994) "IT-enabled business transformation: From automation to business scope redefinition," *Sloan Management Review*, 34(2), 73–87.

Venkatraman, N. (1997) "Beyond outsourcing: Managing IT resources as a value center," *Sloan Management Review*, 38(3), 51–64.

Walsham, G. (1997) "Actor-network theory and IS research: Current status and future prospects," *Proceedings of the IFIP TC8 WG 8.2 international conference on Information systems and qualitative research*, pp. 466–480 (New York: Chapman & Hall, Ltd).

Watts, J. (2003) *Six Degrees: The Science of a Connected Age* (New York: W. W. Norton and Company).

Watts, J. and Strogatz, S. (1998) "Collective dynamics of 'small-world' networks," *Nature*, 393(4), 440–442.

Weick, K. E. (1979) *The Social Psychology of Organizing*. Second edition (Reading, MA: Addison-Wesley).

Weill, P. and Broadbent, M. (1998) *Leveraging the New Infrastructure: How Market Leaders Capitalize on Information Technology* (Boston, MA: Harvard Business School Press).

Weill, P. and Ross, J. W. (2004) *IT Governance: How Top Performers Manage IT Decision Rights for Superior Results* (Boston, MA: Harvard Business School Press).

Wenger, E. C. (1998) *Community of Practice: Learning, Meaning and Identity* (Cambridge: Cambridge University Press).

Wenger, E., McDermott, R. and Snyder, W. M. (2002) *Cultivating Communities of Practice* (Boston, MA: Harvard Business School Press).

Wenger, E. C. (2000) "Communities of practice: The organizational frontier," *Harvard Business Review*, 78(1), 139–45.

Wernerfelt, B. (1984) "A resource-based view of the firm," *Strategic Management Journal*, 5(2), 171–180.

Windeler, A. and Sydow, J. (2001) "Project networks and changing industry practices: Collaborative content production in the German television industry," *Organization Studies*, 22(6), 1035–1060.

Winter, S. (2000) "The satisficing principle in capability learning," *Strategic Management Journal*, 21(10–11), 981–996.

Winter, S. (2003) "Understanding dynamic capabilities," *Strategic Management Journal*, 24(10), 991–995.

Wiseman, C. (1988) *Strategic Information Systems* (New York: Richard D. Irwin).

Worren, N., Moore, K. and Cardona, P. (2002) "Modularity, strategic flexibility, and firm performance: A study of the home appliance industry," *Strategic Management Journal*, 23(12), 1123–1140.

Yin, R. K. (1994) *Case study Research: Design and Methods*, 2nd ed. (London: Sage).

Zigurs, I. (2003) "Leadership in virtual teams: Oxymoron or opportunity?" *Organizational Dynamics*, 31(4), 339–351.

Zollo, M. and Winter, G. (2002) "Deliberate learning and the evolution of dynamic capabilities," *Organization Science*, 13(3), 339–351.

Name Index

Subject Index